Orion *steams through the*
(Skyfotos Ltd).

PASSENGER SHIPS OF THE ORIENT LINE

To Freda, Caroline and Louise, without whose help this book could not have been written

PASSENGER SHIPS OF THE ORIENT LINE

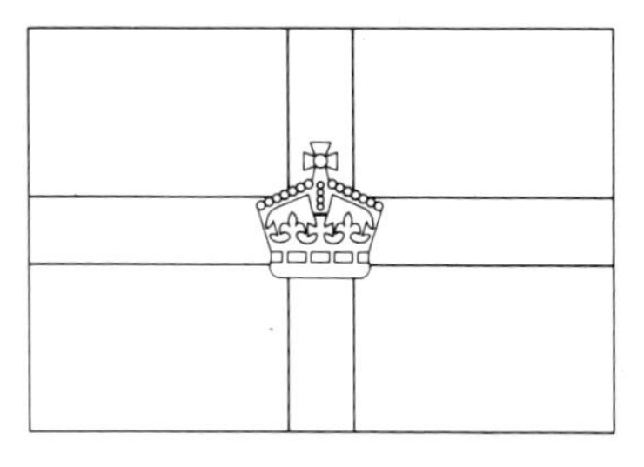

NEIL McCART

Patrick Stephens
Wellingborough, Northamptonshire

First published 1987

British Library Cataloguing in Publication Data

McCart, Neil
Passenger Ships of the Orient Line.
1. Orient Line 2. Ships—Great Britain
I. Title
623.8'243 VM385.07

ISBN 0-85059-891-5

Patrick Stephens Limited is part of the
Thorsons Publishing Group

Printed in Great Britain by
R.J. Acford Limited, Chichester, Sussex

1 3 5 7 9 10 8 6 4 2

Contents

ORONSAY
LONDON

Introduction

In the 82 years from its formation in 1878 to 1960 when it was merged with the P&O, the Orient Steam Navigation Company, or the Orient Line as it was more commonly known, gained a reputation for providing ships of comfort and quality which were second to none. From small beginnings with four chartered ships, the company became a byword for travellers to and from Australia. Indeed, the use of the company's ship *Ophir* as a royal yacht in 1901 broke with the convention that P&O was the 'only' way to travel.

This book looks at the history of this famous shipping line through the stories of the 31 passenger ships owned by the company. It describes their triumphs, such as the launch of the *Orion*, the liner for the future, and their tragedies, including the terrible events off the isolated island of Islay in Scotland, only a few weeks before the end of the First World War: the *Otranto*, one of the five 1909 sisters, was packed full of US troops when she was involved in a collision which almost cut her in two. She was wrecked with the loss of over 400 lives.

As far as possible, major events have been told in the words of eye-witnesses, who were very often crew members or passengers, and sometimes in great danger. One such passenger, who was but 13 years old at the time, vividly recalls the sinking of *Orcades* (2) in October 1942 some 300 miles south-west of Cape Town, and a similar memory stays with a US citizen who was on board *Oriana* in 1970 when there was a near disastrous fire in her boiler room. I have tried to cover the war histories of these vessels in as much detail as possible, for these were the years when they carried the largest number and the widest variety of passengers. Hundreds of thousands of Allied troops were conveyed worldwide on board Orient Line ships, either to battlefronts or back to their homes when the long-awaited peace finally came.

I make no apologies for devoting such a long chapter to the *Oriana*. Although she was always overshadowed by P&O's *Canberra* and in later years thought of as purely a P&O ship, *Oriana* was a 'superliner' in the early 1960s. Launched by HRH Princess Alexandra, *Oriana* was, at the time, thought to herald a new Elizabethan age, and for 25 years she proudly displayed the Red Ensign all around the globe, with her unusual profile making her instantly recognizable wherever she was in the world.

Many of the vessels featured in the book have received little attention from biographers in the past. I hope my book will compensate for this, and that the reader will be taken back to the years when the ships of the Orient Steam Navigation Company sailed proudly and elegantly across the sea lanes of the world.

Left Oronsay *in King George V drydock, Southampton, after her familiar 'Welsh Hat' steampipe was fitted* (Southampton City Museums).

ORIENT LINE CRUISES

NORWAY

13 DAYS from 20 GUINEAS.

APPLY :- 5 FENCHURCH AVENUE LONDON E.C.3

A Short History of the Orient Line

Although the origins of the Orient Line go back to 1797 when the London shipbroking firm of James Thompson & Co was founded, this book is concerned with the ships owned by the Orient Steam Navigation Company. It is a title which conjures up visions of the grand illusion which was the British Empire and, indeed, the company's ships with such glorious names as *Ormuz, Ophir, Orient, Orsova* and *Omrah* were built to serve one of the main lifelines of the Empire, between London and Australia.

By 1869 the firm of James Thompson & Co had become Anderson, Anderson & Co on the retirement of the last of the Thompson family to be involved, and the new company prospered thereafter. In early 1874 they were looking to run a steamship service to Australia, and in order to test the market they chartered a small 1,000-ton vessel, the SS *Easby,* from another London firm, Frederick Green & Co, whose main trading interests were in India. The *Easby* sailed for Port Phillip via the Cape and seven months later was followed by an iron screw barque of 3,000 tons, the *St Osyth*. The voyages were a success and it was at this point that fate took a hand when a fleet of vessels which were suitable for the route became available.

Between 1869 and 1873 the Pacific Steam Navigation Company (PSNCo), whose main interest was the Liverpool–Valparaiso route, had built 22 steamers to cater for a boom in their South American trade. When this did not materialize and there was insufficient business to support a weekly service, they were forced to lay-up eleven of their ships in Birkenhead in 1874 and 1875. So in early 1877 Anderson, Anderson & Co, in conjunction with Frederick Green & Co, entered into negotiations with the PSNCo for the charter of four of their newer ships which were lying idle. As a result the *Lusitania, Chimborazo, Cuzco* and *Garonne* were hired with a guarantee of earnings and an option to purchase them if the venture was successful. The first three sailed during 1877 and the voyages were indeed profitable, so the two partner firms exercised their option to acquire the vessels and to this end, on February 12 1878, they registered the Orient Steam Navigation Company with capital of £44,642.

From the start the new company was known as the Orient Line and, as they were in competition with P&O, the emphasis was on quality and imagination, and on making their ships superior. Initially the service to Australia sailed via Cape Town on the outward passage amd via Suez homeward bound. Although P&O ships served the Australian ports, they had no direct service and consequently, despite the lack of a mail subsidy, the profits for the Orient ships were good. Solid though they were, however, the ex-PSNCo vessels were not purpose-built, and so in November 1879 the *Orient*, which had been built for the company, entered service. At the time she

Left *Orient Line cruise poster, 1925* (P&O).

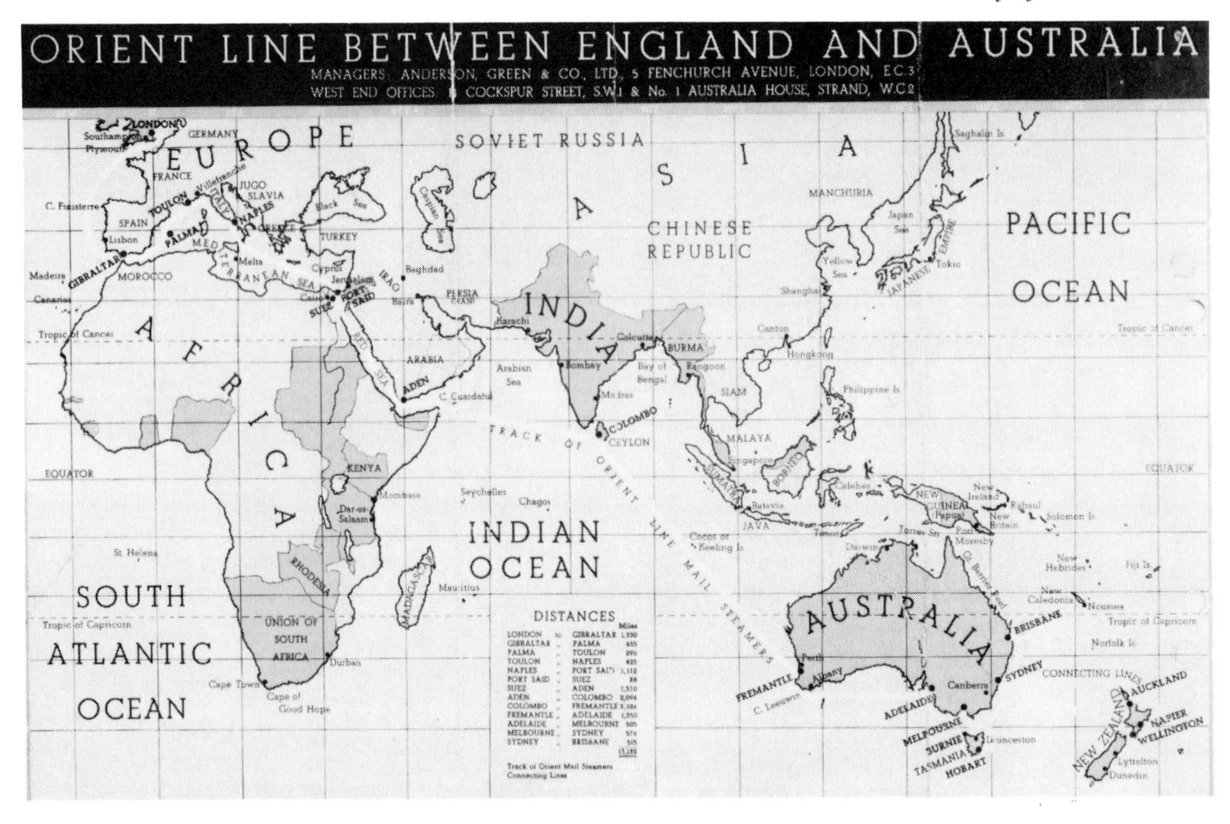

Above *Map showing the Orient Line route between England and Australia after the First World War* (P&O).

Left *Orient Line cruise poster, 1925* (P&O).

Far left *Orient Line cruise poster, 1913* (P&O).

Opposite Top left and right *Orient Line cruise posters of the 1920s* (P&O).

Right *Orient Line cruise poster of the 1930s* (P&O).

Far right *Orient Line advertising poster of the 1950s* (P&O).

NORWAY
ORIENT LINE
CRUISES

ORIENT
LINE
CRUISES
CRUISE FILMS SHOWING HERE TO-DAY

ORIENT LINE
cruise cruise cruise
NORWAY

TO AUSTRALIA

was the largest ship in the world apart from the *Great Eastern*.

However, this introduction coincided with P&O starting direct fortnightly sailings to Australia via Suez, and the Orient Line shareholders, Anderson, Anderson & Co, Frederick Green & Co and the PSNCo decided to match this competition by putting four PSNCo ships on to the service to run in conjunction with the Orient ships. In 1881 alternate sailings were routed via Suez on outward voyages but, in 1883, when part of the New South Wales mail contract was secured, the Cape route was abandoned in favour of the Suez Canal. In order not to clash with P&O over coal supplies at Aden, the Orient Line secured a lease on the island of Diego Garcia, thus by-passing the former port.

In 1888 both the Orient Line and P&O were awarded a joint Australian mail contract with a shared responsibility for coaling and with all the ships sailing by way of Colombo. It was the end of the Diego Garcia station and the start of co-operation between the two companies. In 1901 the link between the Orient Line and the PSNCo was strengthened, and the company marketed their voyages under the title 'Orient-Pacific Line'. However, this harmony did not last, as in 1906 the Royal Mail Steam Packet Company acquired the PSNCo and the new partners wanted a bigger say in the operation. The Orient Line was persuaded to adopt buff funnels to match those of the RMSP, and the service now became 'Orient Royal Mail Line'. The relationship between the new partners was not good and in mid-1907 the Royal Mail Line gave notice that they were withdrawing from the partnership when their contract expired in 1909. There is no doubt that the Royal Mail Line thought that the Orient Line would be unable to survive alone, and they bid alongside both the Orient and P&O for the mail contract. Things did not work out as they had imagined, for the contract went once again to Orient and P&O, and the Orient Line directors were able to raise money from their own resources to finance the six 12,000-ton vessels of 1909. These splendid ships put even the celebrated 'M' class of the P&O in the shade.

By the end of the First World War the Orient Line had lost four ships totalling 45,200 gross tons—almost half their 1914 fleet—and they purchased three surrendered German ships to augment their service. However, in 1919 an even more important event took place when P&O acquired 51 per cent of the Orient Steam Navigation Company's shares, and from that time on the two companies developed alongside each other, although the Orient Line kept its own proud and separate identity.

During the 1920s five 20,000-ton ships were built for them and, although profits fell during the world depression of 1931, the company rode out the hard times well. In September 1935 the magnificent liner *Orion* was delivered, and with her corn-coloured hull and clean silhouette she was a landmark in British maritime history. However, war broke out again and between 1939 and 1945 half the Orient Line's fleet was lost. In August 1939 the company owned eight ships of 161,858 gross tons, four of which were sunk by enemy action, two by U-boats, one by enemy surface craft and one by aircraft.

When the war ended the company's surviving vessels were retained on government service, and the first post-war sailing for the Orient Line mail service took place when *Orion* left London on February 25 1947. During the 1950s three vessels were built to replace war losses, but only three years after the last of these entered service the first steps were taken to absorb the Orient Line fleet into that of the P&O Company.

In May 1960 the P&O-Orient Lines (Passenger Services) Ltd was formed to operate the ships of both companies, and the remaining 49 per cent Orient shareholding was bought up by P&O. Later that year the biggest, fastest and the last Orient Line ship *Oriana* entered service. By 1964 the Orient Line livery of corn-coloured hulls had disappeared and the ships were given P&O white livery. In 1966 the Orient was dropped from the company title and the remaining ships, *Orcades, Oronsay, Orsova* and *Oriana*, became part of the P&O fleet.

A Voyage East with the Orient Line in 1912

It is interesting to follow a typical Orient Line voyage between London and Brisbane in the years before the Great War of 1914–18 tore Europe and the old order apart. These days, when Australia is just over 24 hours' flying time away, it is easy to underestimate the enormous adventure the Edwardian passenger was undertaking, particularly the third-class passengers who would never be able to return to their country of origin.

For most people the great adventure started at London's St Pancras Station, where they boarded the special 'boat trains' to Tilbury. One or two of these trains would be reserved for the first and second class passengers, with the 700 or so third class passengers travelling separately. Down at the docks there would be a hive of feverish activity as the ship's crew prepared to go to sea. Coaling ship would have taken place the previous day, and by the time the passengers arrived the task of cleaning her down would have been completed. Early on sailing day officials from the company and the Board of Trade would go aboard to inspect all the accommodation, paying particular attention to that occupied by steerage passengers. By the time the inspections were completed, the first 'boat trains' would be arriving at the dockside.

In the days before the construction of the passenger landing stage at Tilbury the ship would sail either direct from the dockside or, more often, from an anchorage in the river. When it was the former, passengers could walk straight on board, but more often they were ferried out to the vessel in tenders. As formalities were completed, the ship's stewards lined up at the top of the gangways prepared for each class, in readiness to receive their charges and guide them to their cabins. For the third class passengers, the final formality before they embarked was a medical inspection by the Board of Trade. This was much resented by the passengers but, although it was degrading, it was necessary. So, as each one of the 700 men, women and children filed by, the medical officers scrutinized them, and in any cases of doubt the suspect had to go to one side for a thorough medical examination. Many steerage passengers were from Ireland, in search of higher wages and a better life. An hour before sailing time the bells would ring, all the visitors would stream ashore, and if the ship was leaving from the dockside there would be many moving farewells as the great liner was slowly moved through the locks into the Thames.

Soon, where the river widens, the ship passed Southend and the Nore lightship, then as darkness fell she would pass between Ramsgate and the Goodwin Sands. During the night she would steam down the Channel past a string of twinkling lights indicating the towns of the south coast. Off Portland the Channel pilot would be dropped, and by dawn the following day the ship would be in Plymouth. During this brief call a tender would bring on mail and take off the last letters home. For the majority of passengers this stop was the last link with their homeland, for

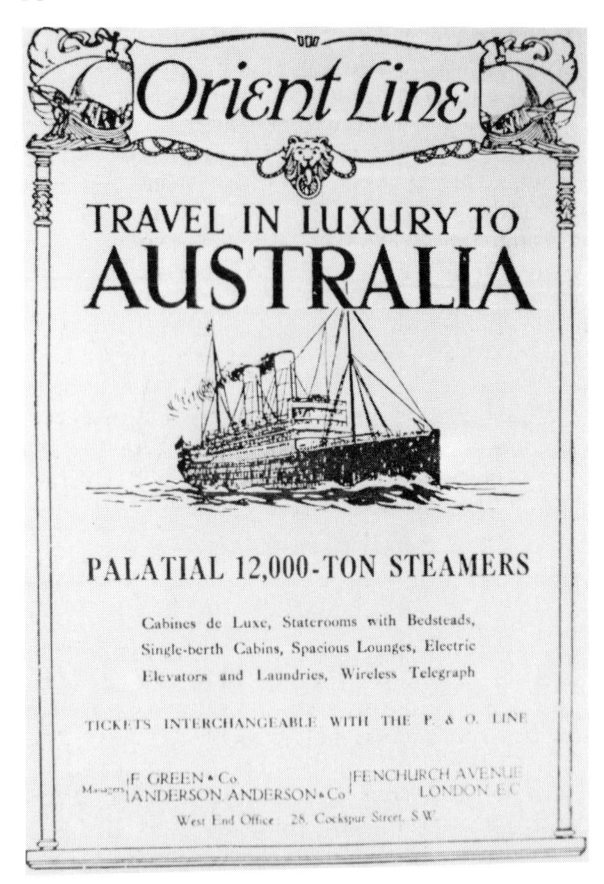

the ship would then set course for Ushant on the north-west corner of France, and many of the passengers would be full of trepidation at the prospect of the 365-mile crossing of the Bay of Biscay which lay before them.

Three days out from Plymouth the ship steamed into Gibraltar Bay, where she would be surrounded by bum-boats whose owners were eager to sell their wares of tobacco, Spanish lace and fruit, and as this was the first visit to a foreign port for most of the passengers, business was always brisk. After only a few hours' stay the ship would be under way again, and after rounding Europa Point she was in the Mediterranean and setting course for Cape Sicie.

On her arrival off the Cape she would enter the land-locked waters of the great harbour and naval base of Toulon. At one time the Orient Line ships used to call at Marseilles, but the frequent delays in embarking and disembarking during bad weather caused them to adopt Toulon as the Continental port. During this stay the overland passengers would be embarked together with the overland mails, and then they sailed for Naples. The approach to Naples would usually be made in the early morning, and when the ship had anchored inside the breakwater she would be surrounded by bum-boats again. Passengers going

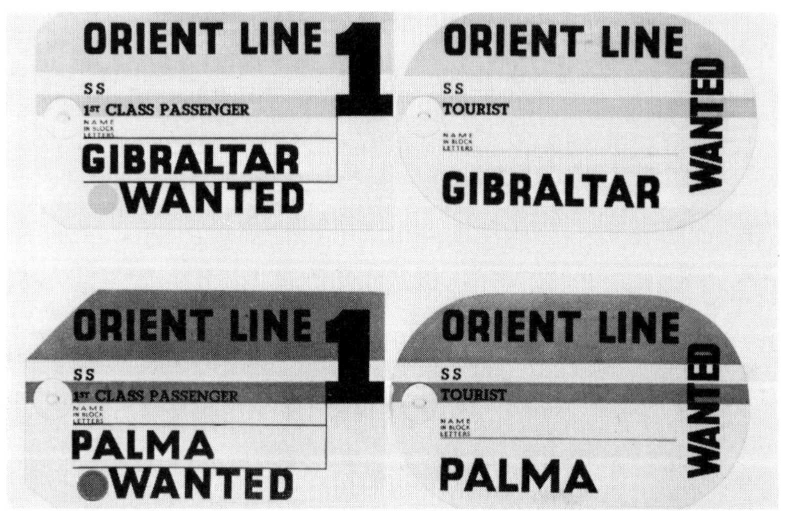

Above left *Orient Line advertisement* (A.M. Aitken).

Left *Orient Line baggage labels* (P&O).

Right *Accident! Boat away!* (Orient Line).

Far right *Coaling ship, Port Said* (Orient Line).

ashore would be landed by tender at the Immacolatella Nuova Quay.

Steaming out of the harbour the ship sailed past the beautiful towns of Castellamare and Sorrento, and between the mainland and the fairy island of Capri. A few hours out they would pass by Stromboli and through the Straits of Messina, between Messina and Reggio. She then steamed north to Taranto where she would anchor off the harbour and stay just long enough to embark the mail. Then, in the early hours of the following morning, the final link with the continent of Europe was broken, as the ship set course for Port Said. The coast of Egypt is usually approached before one realizes it, the first indication of land being the lighthouse at Damietta looming out of the mist. As they approached the breakwater at Port Said—in those days dominated by the statue of Ferdinand de Lesseps—preparations would have been completed on board and ashore for coaling ship. Just as soon as the ship was moored, big square barges loaded with coal and teeming with local labourers were towed alongside. Down came the coaling ports, and long planks were heaved up. Then as soon as all was ready the labourers swarmed up with baskets of coal in an endless procession, not stopping until the bunkers were full.

As soon as coaling was completed the ship would then begin its transit of the canal, and in those days all traffic was conducted by the Suez Canal Company. One pilot would take the ship to Ismaila where another took over for the remainder of the transit. For the majority of passengers this would be their first experience of Africa, and as the ship steamed slowly south they would pass the small native sailing craft, and see hundreds of Arabs employed repairing the banks. Occasionally they would pass a patrol of soldiers of the renowned Egyptian Camel Corps, as well as huge steam dredgers. The Suez Canal was certainly then, as it is today, a place of many contrasts. Outward bound, little time was lost at Suez, and as soon as the pilot was away the ship set course into the Gulf of Suez past the island of Shadwan and into the Red Sea. During the passage down the Red Sea, if the ship found itself in a following wind with a speed equal to that of the vessel, it appeared to those on board to be in a dead calm. In those days before air-conditioning the atmosphere below deck was stifling, particularly for the steerage passengers, many of whom would sleep in any available space on the upper deck. It must have been something of a relief to round the island of Perim

Left *Ladies' tug-of-war* (Orient Line).

Right *End of the voyage, Bulimba Wharf, Brisbane* (Orient Line).

and pass Aden, after which the fresher breezes of the Indian Ocean made conditions much more bearable.

By now the passengers in all three classes would have organized themselves, and the 'sports committees' would be laying on various tournaments to pass the long days at sea. In the first class there would be deck quoits teams, tug-of-war, jockey racing and, for the ladies, the egg and spoon race. In the tourist class they had pillow fighting on a spar and potato racing, while, in the steerage, boxing tournaments were arranged for the fit young men emigrating to Australia. Looking at the photographs of these events, one cannot help but feel sympathy for the competitors who seem to be weighed down with clothing regardless of the temperature.

The only speck of land which would be sighted on the voyage to Colombo was the coral atoll of Minicoy, rich with palm groves, and whose lighthouse could be seen sending its flashing signal round the horizon in the dark of the night. Colombo was the first port of call east of Suez, and just outside the harbour the pilot would come aboard. Once inside the breakwater our Orient liner would be made fast to a buoy, and the ship would be surrounded by small boys diving for coins thrown by passengers. Then, as tenders took the passengers ashore for their excursions to Mount Lavinia and Kandy, the serious business of coaling began again. Barges of coal came alongside, only this time they had a series of platforms on which stood swarms of coolies who passed the bags of coal up to the coaling ports from hand to hand. Once again, work continued without a break until the bunkers were full. With her bunkers and water tanks replenished and her passengers on board again, our Orient liner would cast off her moorings, thread her way through the shipping and round the breakwater. She would steam along the coast and past the old Dutch settlement of Point de Galle. At Dondra Head the ship would set course for Australia, and in this equatorial region the weather is often unsettled with heavy rainstorms sweeping the ocean. On the second day out our ship would 'cross the line' and, in accordance with tradition, Father Neptune would visit, a canvas pool being rigged up for the ceremonies.

A little further south, passengers may have glimpsed the Cocos Islands in the far distance, but more often than not these were just out of sight. The landfall at Australia was not inspiring, the first land to be sighted being Rottnest Island. Soon after this the ship would be boarded by the pilot. She would then anchor in the roads for a medical inspection, before steaming into the harbour and mooring at the long wharf in Fremantle. It was here that the first of the immigrants would leave the ship, and a few new faces would be seen on board, for in those days there were no rail communications between Western Australia and the eastern half of the country.

Twelve hours after leaving Fremantle the most westerly corner of Australia, Cape Leeuwin, was reached and the ship would then steam along the inhospitable southern coast to the Great Australian Bight. Here the great rollers swing in from the Antarctic Ocean, and very often this section of the voyage was most uncomfortable; the travellers would be relieved when the ship went alongside the wharf in the outer harbour at Adelaide. Here many passengers who were in a hurry to reach the eastern Australian states would disembark and continue their journey by train, and so it was with a much reduced passenger list that our Orient liner would leave Adelaide bound for Melbourne. After leaving the outer harbour the ship would turn sharply into Investigator Strait and through Backstairs Passage, the narrow channel that separates the mainland from Kangaroo Island. The run to Melbourne was for the most part made within sight of land, and once Cape Otway was rounded the ship would set course for Port Phillip Bay, the small inland sea off Melbourne. On the run into the bay passengers would gain some charming views of nicely wooded scenery, and of the seaside resort of Sorrento. At the mouth of the bay the pilot would be embarked before the ship proceeded to Port Melbourne Railway Pier where she was made fast. It is said that any passenger who travelled in the Edwardian era would remember the Melbourne stop for the rough wooden beams of the Railway Pier and the need to dodge the busy shunting engines, before boarding a train or tram for the journey into the city. Normally the steamer would remain overnight before leaving for Sydney.

The arrival off Port Jackson Heads marked the entrance to Sydney Harbour, and for most of the passengers the end of the journey. If the day was fine the run up to the berth would be a

memorable one for most passengers; as the ship swung through the channel, they would pass bay after bay lined with picturesque beaches. When the ship reached Macquarie Point, with the aid of tugs she would back into the Orient Wharf at Circular Quay. Once the mail and cargo had been landed our Orient liner would set sail once more on the last leg of the outward voyage, this time with only a few remaining passengers, bound for Brisbane. Now the coastline scenery is more interesting than that of the south coast, and on her arrival off Cape Moreton she would take the pilot on board. She would then round the northern tip of Moreton Island and steam south through the Moreton Channel. With a full tide she would pass the Pile Light and enter Brisbane River to dock alongside the Bulimba Wharf within the city of Brisbane itself. Her outward voyage was now at an end and the last passengers would disembark here. Transport was laid on for the emigrants who were brought out by the Queensland government, and they would be conveyed to receiving homes, before going on to the occupations that awaited them. For them a great adventure lay ahead, but for the Orient steamer and her crew at Bulimba Wharf, there was simply the routine hard work of preparing the vessel for the long voyage home.

Garonne 1878

The honour of being the first ship registered under the ownership of the Orient Steam Navigation Company fell to the *Garonne*, although she was actually built for the Pacific Steam Navigation Company in 1871. Her story begins on April 22 1871 when Mr William Ewing, the foreman shipwright with Messrs Napier & Sons, the Glasgow shipbuilders, launched the *Garonne*. He had been employed by Napier's for 30 years and had in fact launched every vessel built by that firm from HMS *Black Prince*, an armour-clad frigate, onwards.

Garonne was the first of four very similar sisters to be launched, all of them of around 3,800 gross tons and all destined for the PSNCo's Liverpool to Valparaiso service. She was a barque-rigged vessel, with square yards in the fore and main; she had clipper bows with a figurehead and clipper stern, and also a single funnel and one flush deck. She was named after the great French river which rises in the Pyrenees and enters the Gironde estuary below Bordeaux. *Garonne* had accommodation for about 60 first, 100 second and 320 third class passengers. The first class passenger spaces were aft and the accommodation was very similar in layout to that which would have been found in sailing packets. One table ran along the entire length of the large dining saloon, from which branched little alleyways with berthed cabins for one, two or three passengers. On the upper deck were a drawing room, smoking room and a writing room. The second class saloon and cabins were on the same deck but further forward and the third class accommodation was on the lower deck.

Garonne made her maiden voyage from Liverpool to South America on June 29 1871, calling at south Chilean ports. In 1872 a mail subsidy of £10,000 was granted to PSNCo to run a weekly service to South America, and the company entered into a large shipbuilding programme. However, by 1874 it was becoming clear that they had over-reached themselves as the growth in both passengers and cargo did not come up to expectations. The company introduced several economy measures, but these were not enough and in 1875 11 of their ships were laid up in Birkenhead Docks, among them the *Garonne*.

In February 1877 Anderson, Anderson & Co in conjunction with Frederick Green & Co offered to charter four of the vessels for a passage each to Australia, with an option to purchase the ships if the voyages were successful. As it happened, *Garonne* was not ready for her charter voyage in 1877 and was thus in England when the Orient Steam Navigation Co was set up in February 1878. They purchased *Garonne* for £71,570 and she therefore became the first ship registered by the new company. The first sailing, in the month after the new company was formed, was taken by the *Garonne* and she left London, flying the Orient Line houseflag, on March 5 1878. She was commanded by Captain de Steiger and she had a good complement of passengers on board; 69

Above *The first ship owned by the Orient Steam Navigation Company* (P&O).

Below Garonne *in the Thames* (P&O).

plus 6 servants in the first class, 78 plus 1 servant in the second class and 220 third class passengers. She called at Plymouth on March 8, three days after she had left South-West India Docks in London, and on March 30 she anchored in Table Bay, showing the Orient flag for the first time at the Cape. She arrived at Adelaide on April 21 1878, after a passage of 47 days.

The return voyage was made via Suez, and for a few hours in June 1878 she was grounded off Ras Hafun in Somalia. Fortunately she was refloated with no damage and was able to proceed on her way. *Garonne* left London on her second Orient Line voyage on July 29 1878, commanded by Captain W. F. Owen. Again the outward journey took her via Cape Town, and she arrived safely in Adelaide 47 days later. On March 19 1879, while on her third round voyage to Australia, *Garonne* went aground once again, this time on the Topley Shoal off Adelaide. It was two days before she was refloated, but luckily again she had not sustained any damage and was able to complete her voyage. Exactly one year later, on March 19 1880, *Garonne* left Sydney with the members of the Australian cricket team among her passengers. They were coming to England to play the first test matches between the two sides. No definite fixtures had been arranged and some English 'gentlemen' were not prepared to play against Australian professionals. There had in fact been riots when England played in Sydney the year before. Whatever the rivalries on the field, the Australian test side had a magnificent passage on board the *Garonne*, before coming ashore by tender at Gravesend on May 4 1880.

On June 13 1881 *Garonne* was sent to Birkenhead where new boilers were installed by J. Laird & Co at a cost of some £12,000. Later that year she left London for Sydney carrying lifting equipment which was to be used for raising the new Orient liner *Austral*, which had sunk while coaling in Sydney Harbour. On May 2 1888, when *Garonne* was outward bound for Australia, and in the Red Sea in a position 18°N, 40°E, she was in collision with another steamer, the SS *Lucinda*. *Garonne* jettisoned some 300 tons of coal and disembarked her third class passengers onto another vessel, the SS *Lady Armstrong*, which then accompanied *Garonne* to Aden. Once there it was decided that *Garonne* could continue her voyage and the third class passengers were re-embarked. At the end of the ensuing lawsuit it was agreed that *Garonne* did what was right and *Lucinda* everything that was wrong. The case went to appeal but the judgement was confirmed.

On her return from Australia in November 1888, the *Garonne* had been scheduled for a cruise to Mediterranean ports. However, the idea was abandoned because of low bookings. Whatever the reason for the lack of interest in November 1888, five months later the situation was very different. The Orient Line had organized a month's cruise, leaving London on April 6 1889 and calling at Lisbon, Gibraltar, Algiers, Malta, Palermo, Cagliari, Malaga, Cadiz and Plymouth before returning to London on May 6 1889. The publicity brochure for the 'pleasure cruise' ran as follows: 'The *Garonne* has hitherto been employed in the company's mail service between England and Australia, and from her great size, and excellent sea-going qualities, presents an unrivalled opportunity for making the pleasure excursion above described. She is fitted with electric light, hot and cold baths, etc. The cuisine will be one of the highest class, and wines, beers and spirits of the best quality can be purchased on board at moderate prices. In port the routine of meals, etc, will be carried on as if at sea, and passengers can live on board and pass to and from the shore at reasonable hours. Boat services between the ship and shore and vice versa will be provided free of expense. Arrangements will be made by the company's agents at the several ports of call, with a view to assisting passengers to make advantageous use of their time on shore.' Fares for the cruise were between £50 and £70 per person, and the length of time spent in port ranged from 6 hours in Cagliari, to 58 hours in Malaga.

The vessel was commanded by Captain W. E. White RNR, and among the passengers was a

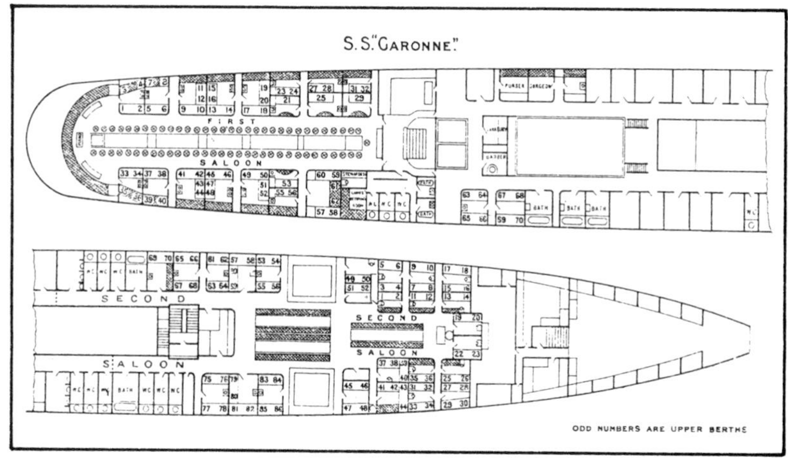

First and second saloon accommodation, Garonne (Orient Line).

small theatrical group chaperoned by Mr W. S. Gilbert, who with Arthur Sullivan had recently added *The Yeomen of the Guard* to his list of successes. One passenger described his fellow travellers thus: 'They included all sorts and conditions of men—city-men from London, industrialists from the Midlands, and a small group of hunting men. Only a few had persuaded their wives to accompany them on this new adventure.' He goes on to describe the first few days of the voyage. 'My cabin, being right forward, got the full force of the half-gale we encountered in the Bay of Biscay, as we battered our way, under sail and steam and light from lack of cargo, to Lisbon, our first port of call.'

However, things obviously got better. 'It was a leisurely cruise. We steamed an easy 12 knots, and were never rushed and hurried at the successive ports we visited.' After spending a few days ashore in Spain, our intrepid traveller 'rejoined the *Garonne* at Cadiz, but had no time to do more than drive hurriedly through this well laid out and attractive city. The sunshine we had enjoyed in Spain followed us through "The Bay" and until we disembarked from the *Garonne*, grateful to officers and crew for all they had done for our comfort and enjoyment. This sentiment was voiced by Mr W. S. Gilbert when he proposed the Captain's health at our last dinner. So ended the first yachting cruise.' The cruise had indeed been a success, so much so that later in the year *Garonne* made another 'pleasure cruise', this time to the fjords.

Garonne continued in the Orient Line service for another eight years, and by November 1897 she had made 25 mail voyages and 41 cruises. She had in fact concentrated on this sphere of activity after her last mail sailing in 1889. By 1897 she was well and truly outdated and the Orient Line added four purpose-built vessels to their fleet; *Orient* 1879, *Austral* 1882, *Ormuz* 1887 and the *Ophir* of 1891. *Garonne* was no longer required and in November 1897 she was sold to John Porter of Liverpool for £9,500, and almost at once she was resold to F. Waterhouse of Seattle USA. Under the US flag she carried miners and prospectors to the Klondike gold rush and also served the US government as a troopship during the Spanish-American War. She was finally sold to Italian shipbreakers at Genoa in 1905 after a career of 34 years.

Technical data
Gross tonnage: 3,876
Net tonnage: 2,468
Length overall: 382 ft, 1 in (116.46 m)
Breadth: 41 ft, 5 in (12.62 m)
Depth: 35 ft, 8 in (10.87 m)
Main engines: Single screw, two-cylinder compound engine, 550 nhp, 13 knots
Boilers: Coal-fired, steam pressure 65 psi
Passengers: First class 60, Second class 100, Third class 320

Lusitania 1878

Like *Garonne,* the *Lusitania* was constructed for the Pacific Steam Navigation Co as part of their 1871 expansion programme. She was built at Birkenhead by Laird Brothers at a cost of £91,852 and was a barque-rigged vessel very similar in size and profile to *Garonne.* She was launched in June 1871 and by the end of September that year she was ready to sail on her maiden voyage to Valparaiso.

Lusitania had a gross tonnage of 3,877 and she was a single-screw ship powered by two-cylinder compound engines which developed 550 nhp and gave her a service speed of 13 knots. She carried 85 first, 100 second and 270 third class passengers. First saloon passengers were accommodated aft on the main deck, with a few cabins forward of the dining saloon and the majority aft of it. Second saloon passengers were berthed forward on the same deck with most of the cabins in alleyways ranged along either side of the dining saloon. On the upper deck aft was the first class deck saloon or lounge with the first class smoking room forward of this. Right forward on the upper deck was the second class smoking room, while the emigrants in the third class were down below on the lower deck. The name *Lusitania* was taken from the ancient name of a Spanish province, equating approximately to the modern country of Portugal.

Lusitania made her maiden voyage from Liverpool to the South American ports on September 29 1871. She reached Valparaiso as scheduled without any incidents, but only a few hours after leaving the port for the voyage home she shed three of her four propeller blades. There was no dock at Valparaiso which was able to take her and it was not possible to beach her either. In the event a large wooden caisson was built around her stern and the water pumped out, which enabled a new propeller to be fitted. After this drama *Lusitania* settled down to a regular service for her owners, although by 1874 she was laid up in Liverpool along with ten other PSNCo vessels. Messrs Anderson, Anderson & Co had been watching these developments and in conjunction with Messrs F. Green & Co they came to an agreement for starting a steamship service to Australia in competition with the giant P&O Company.

In late 1877 they were able to charter four of the PSNCo vessels which were lying idle in Liverpool, and in December of that year *Lusitania* made her first voyage to Australia on charter to the Orient Line. She left the South West India Dock on June 26 1877 and called at Plymouth three days later. She sailed via the Cape but without calling at Table Bay, and made the voyage from Plymouth to Port Phillip (Melbourne) in just over 38 days. From there she steamed on to Sydney and for her return to London she sailed via the Suez Canal taking 41 days in all. In London the Orient Steam Navigation Co had been registered on February 12 1878 and they exercized their option to purchase the chartered PSNCo vessels when they returned from Australia. Thus in May 1878, after

Above Lusitania *in the Thames* (P&O).

Below Lusitania, *looking very spick and span* (National Maritime Museum).

her second charter voyage, *Lusitania* was bought outright by the Orient Line.

She made her first voyage under the Orient Line houseflag on June 28 1878, commanded by Captain Hemson. She sailed as before via the Cape, but this time she did call in at Cape Town, and the voyage to Adelaide was made in 47 days. The PSNCo had built their steamers with unusually large coal bunkers and so *Lusitania* was easily able to cope with the long distances between ports. It was early November 1878 before she returned to London, and she left once again on her third voyage to Australia on November 26. She arrived in Adelaide on January 15 1879 after a journey of 50 days.

In July 1882 a British military expedition was despatched to Alexandria to overcome the rebellion against the Egyptian government by Arabi Pasha, the Egyptian War Minister. On July 24 1882 *Lusitania* was hired by the government as a troop transport for two months, at the rate of 22s 6d per ton per month. In September 1882 she was re-engaged by the government, although by now the campaign was all but over as Sir Garnet Wolseley had defeated the rebels at the battle of Tel-El-Kebir. By September 13 1882 British troops had occupied Cairo and in December that year Arabi Pasha was imprisoned in Ceylon. By the end of January 1883 all the large-scale troop movements were over and on February 16 *Lusitania* was discharged from government service.

Lusitania had been back in Orient Line service for just over a year when she was chartered to the Admiralty as an armed merchant cruiser. It was brought about by events on the Russian-Afghanistan border and the Russian army's seizure of the border town of Panjdeh. The British authorities in India feared a Russian invasion of Afghanistan and the Indian Army was mobilized. The Russian Press was crying out for their army to advance to Herat in Afghanistan, and in the House of Commons the Prime Minister, William Gladstone, requested £6½ million credit for war purchases. War fever was in the air and there is no doubt that the two countries were on the brink of hostilities.

Among the preparations the government took for the conflict, if it came, was the hiring of *Lusitania* to the Admiralty. She was chartered for six months at 22s 6d a ton per month (or £3,000 a month if the crew were dispensed with). *Lusitania* was in Australian waters when she was hired, and she remained there for the duration of her naval service. By the autumn of 1885 the Panjdeh incident had blown over. It had been a strange confrontation with Britain, Germany, Austria-Hungary and Italy on the one side and Russia, with France, on the other. If the Russians had ever considered sparking off a great European conflict, then they had swiftly discarded the idea. The great conflict in fact occurred in 1914, when only the line-up of the protagonists differed from the situation 29 years before.

When *Lusitania* was re-delivered to the Orient Line, the government paid £5,000 to the company for the replacement of fittings, and on February 6 1886 she was sent to J. Richardson & Sons for a major refit. She had new boilers installed along with triple-expansion engines, at a cost of £17,372, and she was back in London on May 1 1886. Eleven days later she sailed once more for Australia, commanded by Captain Ruthven, and for the next six years she plied the route to the antipodes. On February 4 1892 negotiations were concluded between the Orient Line and the PSNCo for *Lusitania* to be chartered back to her original owners for 12 months, and on February 27 1892 she sailed for Liverpool to serve with them again. It was April 16 1893 before *Lusitania* was returned to the Orient Line, and she went back to the Australian route for four years, making her final sailing to Sydney in December 1897. For her remaining few years with the Orient Line she cruised to the Mediterranean and to Scandinavia. It was while she was on a cruise to the northern capitals in August 1899 that she collided with a breakwater at Copenhagen. By now her service with the Orient Line was coming to an end and on February 27 1900, six months after her accident, she was sold to Elder Dempster for £15,000 to run on their Beaver Line service to Canada.

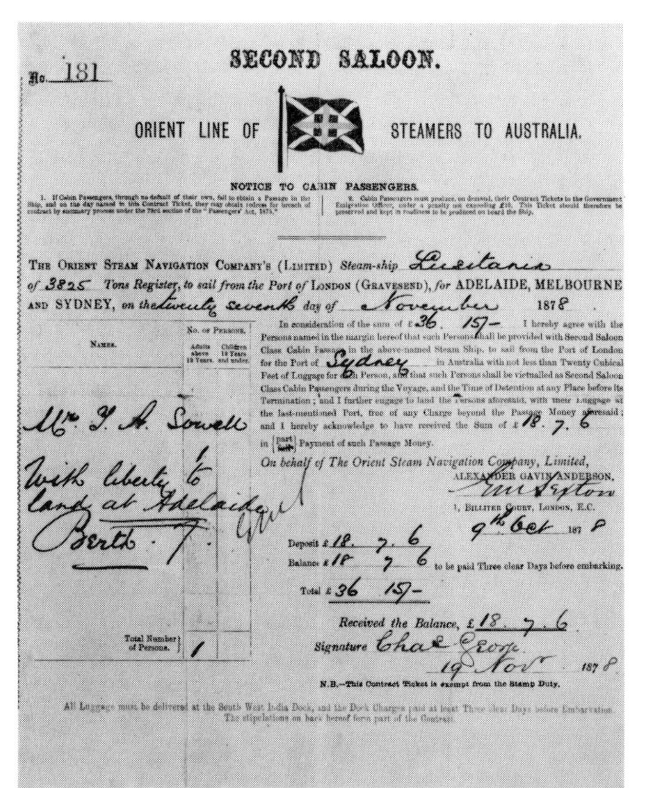

No. 181

SECOND SALOON.

ORIENT LINE OF STEAMERS TO AUSTRALIA.

NOTICE TO CABIN PASSENGERS.

1. If Cabin Passengers, through no default of their own, fail to obtain a Passage in the Ship, and on the day named in this Contract Ticket, they may obtain redress for breach of contract by summary process under the 73rd section of the "Passengers' Act, 1855."

2. Cabin Passengers must produce, on demand, their Contract Tickets to the Government Emigration Officer, under a penalty not exceeding £10. This Ticket should therefore be preserved and kept in readiness to be produced on board the Ship.

THE ORIENT STEAM NAVIGATION COMPANY'S (LIMITED) *Steam-ship* Lusitania *of* 3825 *Tons Register, to sail from the Port of* LONDON (GRAVESEND), *for* ADELAIDE, MELBOURNE AND SYDNEY, *on the* twenty seventh *day of* November 1878.

NAMES.	No. of Persons. Adults above 12 Years.	Children 12 Years and under.
Mr. J. A. Sowell		
With liberty to land at Adelaide		
Berth 7.		
Total Number of Persons.	1	

In consideration of the sum of £36. 15/- I hereby agree with the Persons named in the margin hereof that such Persons shall be provided with Second Saloon Class Cabin Passage in the above-named Steam Ship, to sail from the Port of London for the Port of Sydney in Australia with not less than Twenty Cubical Feet of Luggage for each Person, and that such Persons shall be victualled as Second Saloon Class Cabin Passengers during the Voyage, and the Time of Detention at any Place before its Termination; and I further engage to land the Persons aforesaid, with their Luggage at the last-mentioned Port, free of any Charge beyond the Passage Money aforesaid; and I hereby acknowledge to have received the Sum of £18. 7. 6 in part Payment of such Passage Money.

On behalf of The Orient Steam Navigation Company, Limited,
ALEXANDER GAVIN ANDERSON,
1, BILLITER COURT, LONDON, E.C.
9th Oct 1878

Deposit £18. 7. 6
Balance £18 7 6 to be paid Three clear Days before embarking.
Total £36 15/-

Received the Balance, £18. 7. 6
Signature Chas George
19 Nov 1878

N.B.—This Contract Ticket is exempt from the Stamp Duty.

All Luggage must be delivered at the South West India Dock, and the Dock Charges paid at least Three clear Days before Embarkation. The stipulations on back hereof form part of the Contract.

Above *Second class passage ticket,* Lusitania, c *1878* (P&O).

Above right *Orient Line advertisement for* Lusitania*'s West Indies cruise, January 1895* (P&O).

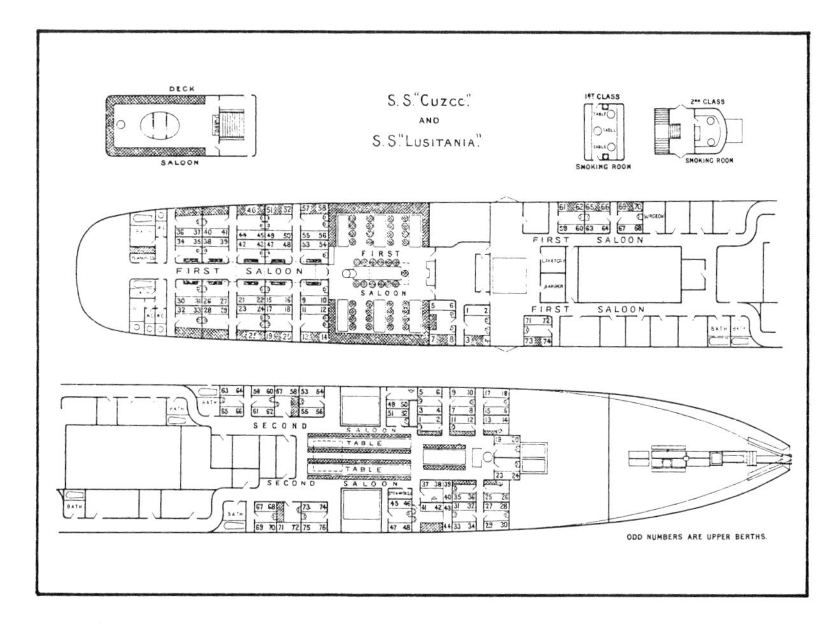

Right *First and second saloon accommodation,* Cuzco *and* Lusitania (Orient Line).

Lusitania's last year of service was spent between Liverpool, Rimouski, Quebec and Montreal, for the most part carrying emigrants to Canada. She normally took ten to 12 days crossing the Atlantic—a slow crossing even in those days. She left Liverpool for the last time on Tuesday June 18 1901 with about 500 passengers on board. The crossing was uneventful, but on the evening of Thursday June 27 she ran aground on a reef at Seals Cove, 12 miles north of Cape Race on the Avalon Peninsula, Newfoundland. With her after holds full of water and with a swell breaking over her, it was clear that there was little hope of getting her clear. All the passengers and crew were taken off safely into the steamer *Glencoe,* and they were landed at St John's at 11 pm that day. Her officers and captain remained near to the ship until the full extent of the damage could be assessed, but within a few hours she had taken on a heavy list and she was declared a total loss. Her career had spanned 30 years and had just taken her into the 20th century.

Technical data
Gross tonnage: 3,877
Net tonnage: 2,494
Length overall: 379 ft, 10 in (115.79 m)
Breadth: 41 ft, 4 in (12.89 m)
Depth: 35 ft, 3 in (10.72 m)
Main engines: Single screw, two-cylinder compound engine, 550 nhp, 13 knots
Boilers: Coal-fired, steam pressure 65 psi
Passengers: First class 85, Second class 100, Third class 270

Cuzco and *Chimborazo* 1878

These two ships were the near sisters of *Garonne* and *Lusitania,* and like them had originally been built for the Pacific Steam Navigation Co. They were both constructed at Glasgow by John Elder & Co, with *Chimborazo* being the first to be launched on June 21 1871 followed by *Cuzco* on October 18 of the same year. The names of both ships betrayed the origins of their owners and the route for which they were intended. Chimborazo is a volcano in the South American state of Ecuador, and rising as it does to a height of 20,000 ft is one of the highest mountains in the New World. Cuzco was the ancient capital of Peru, and continues to be one of the country's chief cities. Both vessels contained almost identical accommodation to that of their two sisters already described, and they carried a similar number of passengers. Together the two ships had cost the PSNCo some £182,000 to build.

Chimborazo left Liverpool on October 13 1871 for her maiden voyage to Valparaiso; in those days a journey of some 57 days calling at nine ports. *Cuzco* made her maiden sailing on January 13 1872. However, the boom in trade with South America did not last, and just over two years after *Cuzco* entered service the two ships were laid up in Liverpool.

In late 1877 the Orient Line chartered both of the vessels, along with *Garonne* and *Lusitania,* for their proposed monthly service to Australia. *Chimborazo* was the second of the four chartered vessels to leave London for Australia, when she sailed from South West India Dock on August 12 1877, followed soon afterwards by *Cuzco* on August 23. *Chimborazo* actually made two voyages on charter to the Orient Line, and she left London at the start of the second voyage on January 21 1878, just three weeks before the formation of the Orient Steam Navigation Company. It was during this passage on March 15 1878 that she went aground for a time at Jervis Bay and the repairs, which were carried out at Sydney, took several weeks.

In March 1878 *Cuzco* was purchased outright by the new company for £78,150 and at 9.30 am on April 19 1878 she left Gravesend Reach on her first voyage to Sydney under Orient Line ownership. She left Plymouth at 6 pm the following day and arrived at Cape Town at 12.30 am on May 11. She left that port three days later and, just when it seemed that she would be making a record run, misfortune struck. At 7 am on May 28 1878, when she was in a position 41°14′S, 107°43′E, her propeller shaft broke and she was forced to continue the voyage under canvas. She reached Adelaide on June 10, arriving at Portland, Victoria on June 14 where she remained for three days before eventually arriving in Port Phillip, Melbourne at 5.45 pm on June 18 1878, where repair work was carried out.

Chimborazo was purchased from the PSNCo for £72,270 in August 1878 on her return to London, and she sailed on her first voyage under the Orient Line flag on September 27 that year,

Above Cuzco (P&O).

Below Cuzco *off Gravesend* (National Maritime Museum).

commanded by Captain Murdock. She made better time on this voyage, arriving in Adelaide after just 46 days.

On February 8 1880 *Chimborazo* left Plymouth, after her routine call, for Australia. However, the voyage started disastrously when she struck extremely heavy weather the next day in the Bay of Biscay. The howling winds and huge waves caused serious damage, with hatches and skylights being washed away and other deck fittings suffering under the battering from the elements. Worse, however, was the loss of one passenger and three crew members who were washed overboard and drowned. So serious was the havoc caused that *Chimborazo* turned back to Plymouth where she arrived late on February 10. She was delayed for a week in the port while repairs were carried out, most of the replacement parts and fittings being sent from the *Cuzco* and *Garonne* to make good the damage.

In August 1887 the Orient Line decided to have new engines and boilers installed in *Cuzco,* and the contract for the work was won by Fairfields of Glasgow who submitted a tender for £30,000, with an additional £7,600 for deck refurbishments. *Cuzco* left London on August 17 1887 and she remained out of service for the rest of the year. By late January 1888 the work was completed and on her trials the new triple-expansion engines gave her a speed of 15.31 knots.

On her second sailing from London to Sydney following the refit, *Cuzco* was steaming through the Bay of Biscay on a perfectly calm summer's day, when she was struck by what was described at the time as 'an extremely severe tidal wave'. It was a sunny day and, as most of the passengers were relaxing on deck, the result was that over 60 people were injured. The second class dining saloon was turned into a temporary hospital and those with the worst injuries were laid out on the tables until such time as the ship's surgeon, assisted by two passengers who were doctors, could attend to them. Some of the injured were admitted to hospital at Gibraltar and some at Marseilles, but unfortunately four crew members died. One lady passenger was very severely injured, but she refused to leave the ship, and on arrival at Sydney she had to be disembarked on a stretcher. Also as a result of the incident, five names were added to the passenger lists as there were five premature births on board.

The first class drawing room, Cuzco (P&O).

Happily, this extremely unfortunate voyage proved to be exceptional for, with her new engines, *Cuzco* soon became a very fast and popular ship, especially in Australia where the arrival of the mail ship was eagerly awaited. An extract from the *Melbourne Argus* of April 1890 describes a typical voyage of the time: The RMS *Cuzco* of the Orient Line arrived at 5 o'clock yesterday morning from London, with passengers and cargo. The *Cuzco* was cleared and after receiving speedy pratique, was taken alongside the railway pier, Williamstown. *Cuzco* left London on February 28, and after embarking passengers and receiving mails, took her departure from Plymouth at 6.30 pm on the 1st ult. Thence strong N and NE winds, with a high sea, prevailed across the Bay of Biscay and along the Peninsular coast, until arrival at Gibraltar at

6.20 am on the 5th ult. Thence to Algiers, which now appears to be a regular port of call with the steamships of the Orient Line, the *Cuzco* had fine weather. Leaving Algiers at 1.20 pm on the 7th ult the *Cuzco* had again fine weather to Naples, where she awaited the arrival of mails and passengers overland from 6.30 pm on the 9th ult until 4.15 am on the 10th.

'After leaving for Port Said a fresh gale, with continuous rain, was encountered until noon next day when the weather moderated. It again became threatening, however, and from midnight of the 11th ult until noon of the 12th the steamer had to contend with a hard gale and a high sea. Variable winds and weather prevailed afterwards until anchoring at Port Said at 7.30 pm on the 13th ult. After taking in coal, the Canal was entered at 2.45 am on the 14th ult and Suez was reached at 8.10 pm. The passage of the Red Sea was commenced at 9.10 pm, same date, and a fine weather passage without any distressing heat was accomplished to Aden, which was passed at 8.55 pm on the 18th ult. The weather across the Arabian Sea was equally pleasant, and Colombo was reached at 11 am on the 25th ult. After coaling and taking in cargo, the *Cuzco* left at 5.30 pm and commenced the long stretch of direct steaming for Albany. Strong trades with a very lively sea were encountered across the Indian Ocean, and King George's Sound was reached on the 5th inst. The voyage was resumed the same day, and moderate weather prevailed across the Great Australian Bight. Adelaide was reached on the night of the 8th inst, and after landing mails, passengers and cargo, a departure was taken for Melbourne at 1 pm on the 9th inst. From Adelaide the *Cuzco* had a smooth journey and fair skies, Port Phillip Heads were entered at 2.40 am yesterday. There was one case of measles during the passage, and a stowaway who was at work got injured internally. Duncan M'Laren, a steerage passenger, died on the 10th ult. His wife was a passenger on board. After discharge of cargo the *Cuzco* will proceed to Sydney as per advertisement.'

In January 1891 the *Chimborazo* ran aground on Mariner Reef, Troubridge Shoal, in the Gulf of Adelaide. Happily there was little damage and she was able to continue her voyage home to London. On her return she spent the spring and summer cruising in the Mediterranean and the Norwegian fjords. On July 10 1891 she ran aground once again, this time on Torghatten Island during a cruise round Norway. She was quickly refloated and suffered only slight damage to her underwater hull. *Chimborazo* now had only three years' service left with the Orient Line and this was spent cruising. On October 9 1894 she was sold to F. J. Pitcher of Liverpool and renamed *Cleopatra*. In 1895 she passed to the ownership of the Ocean Cruising and Highland Yachting Company and two years later, in 1897, she was broken up at Preston in Lancashire.

For *Cuzco* there were still a few years of service with the Orient Line left, and on May 12 1902 she was chartered to her former owners, the PSNCo, for one round voyage to Australia. It was her last passage to that continent for on her return she was used solely for cruising. As a survivor of the days when merchant vessels were making the transition from sail to steam, she was the last of the Orient Line's four steamers which had inaugurated their service to Australia. But by now she was completely outdated and on January 20 1905 she was sold to the Italian shipbreakers, Luigi Pittaluga, of Genoa. One of the last people to see her was Mr Fred Jervis, an Australian on his way to the UK as a boy, who recalls seeing *Cuzco* in the Genoese scrapyard, 'looking derelict and forlorn'.

Technical data

Gross tonnage: 3,898 (*Cuzco*), 3,847 (*Chimborazo*)
Net tonnage: 2,439 (*Cuzco*), 2,443 (*Chimborazo*)
Length overall: 384 ft 2 in (117.09 m) (*Cuzco*), 384 ft (117.04 m) (*Chimborazo*)
Breadth: 41 ft 5 in (12.62 m) (*Cuzco*), 41 ft 4 in (12.59 m) (*Chimborzao*)
Depth: 35 ft 5 in (10.76 m)
Main engines: Single screw, two-cylinder compound engine, 550 nhp, 13 knots
Boilers: Coal-fired, steam pressure 65 psi
Passengers: First class 70, Second class 92, Third class 228 (*Cuzco*); First class 72, Second class 92, Third class 265 (*Chimborazo*)

Above Chimborazo *off Tilbury* (P&O).

Below *Embarkation day on board* Chimborazo *off Tilbury* (National Maritime Museum).

Orient 1879

In 1878 the managers of the Orient Line placed the order for the first purpose-built passenger ship for the Australian mail, and when she entered service she was considered to be the finest vessel in the Australian trade. The order went to the Glasgow shipbuilding firm of John Elder & Co, and she was launched on Thursday June 6 1879 by Lady Gertrude Boyle, the daughter of the Earl of Glasgow. The new vessel was named *Orient* after a very successful clipper ship of 1856, owned by James Thompson & Co, the firm which later became Anderson, Anderson & Co, the managers of the Orient Line. In fact the old clipper *Orient* was sold only in 1879, the year the steamship of the same name entered service.

The launching ceremony was quite an event on the Clyde as the *Orient* was the largest vessel, in terms of gross tonnage, to have been built there. She had cost £148,344 to build. Messrs Elder & Co opened their yards to the public for them to witness the occasion, and the ground on both sides of the river was crowded with spectators. After the launch a number of dignitaries were entertained to lunch in the company's model room at Fairfield. The chairman of John Elders, Mr William Pearce, spoke of the *Orient* providing a service between London and Melbourne in 36 days, an improvement of two days on any other ship sailing the same route. Mr James George Anderson, in his reply on behalf of the Orient Line, said that 'the *Orient* and her engines rep-present the very greatest advancement in naval architecture and engineering'. The function ended with the toast, 'Success to the ship *Orient*'.

The *Orient* was a single-screw ship powered by a 5,400 ihp compound engine, the steam at 74 psi being provided by four double-ended boilers. She had a gross tonnage of 5,386 and her passenger capacity was 220 first, 130 second and 300 steerage class. If need be, the second class accommodation could be increased to 300 at the expense of the same number of steerage berths. She had two funnels and was rigged as a four-masted barque, the two forward masts carrying yards and being square rigged. She was built, as was usual, to Admiralty specifications for con-version to an armed merchant cruiser and fittings were provided for two six-pounder guns, with neat teak carriages brass-mounted, fitted and secured complete. *Orient* was also the first steamer built to carry refrigerated cargo and she had space for 1,130 tons, 460 tons of which were stowed in number two hold on the orlop deck. She could also carry 3,248 tons of non-refrigerated cargo. The first class cabins were situated on the main deck forward and aft of the dining saloon, and they were fitted for two, three or four passengers. A number of the lower berths in the largest cabins extended to form double beds. The dining saloon ran the whole width of the ship and seated 100 passengers at one sitting.

Above right *First class music room, SS* Orient (Orient Line).

Right *First class writing room SS* Orient (Orient Line).

In the centre of the room was a skylight which went up through two decks to provide natural daylight and ventilation. The first class drawing room was on the upper deck and was oval in shape and built around the saloon skylight. Both the first class sitting room and smoking room were situated on the hurricane deck, which was the next deck up. The second class passengers were accommodated aft on the main deck. Their cabins, again for two, three or four passengers, were on both sides of the vessel with the dining saloon in the centre. The two refectory-type tables ran from forward to aft with bench seats. The drawing room for this class was right aft and was built around the elliptical stern. Third class passengers were accommodated in open berths on the lower deck, and the single women were provided with a large self-contained deck-house fitted with berths and washrooms, which was situated aft on the upper deck.

The new ship ran her trials on the Clyde in September 1879, and she achieved a speed of 15.75 knots over the measured mile. Her passage between the Clyde and London was quite an event with a large number of guests and members of the press being invited on board. The resultant publicity was impressive, *The Times* devoting two full columns to the voyage. The publicity continued after she had tied up alongside the South West India Dock, for she was handed over to a group of London hospitals as a show ship for four days. She was crowded with visitors, and *The Times* stated that the docks were as busy as the streets of London had been for the visit of the Shah of Persia some weeks before. In all, the events raised some £800 for the hospital charities.

On November 1 1879 *Orient* sailed from London to Sydney via Cape Town. She was commanded by Captain Robert Studdart and the voyage of 11,584 miles was completed in 38 days 14½ hours. One of her main features was her large coal capacity, and on this round voyage she burned some 7,516 tons, having started in London with 2,800 tons. It was the difficulty of providing coaling bases on the route to Australia which had enabled sailing ships to maintain a hold of the trade to the antipodes long after they had been ousted from the Atlantic, but now that the new ships had such large coal capacities, the clippers were soon to be eclipsed. At this time Orient Line ships made the outward voyage to Sydney via Cape Town, returning by way of the Suez Canal and the Mediterranean. It was on the homeward part of *Orient*'s second voyage, just a day out from Gibraltar, on July 22 1880, that a gunshot was heard in the first class staterooms. Several stewards rushed to the scene, and it transpired that a passengers had been in the habit of keeping a loaded revolver with him. He claimed that it had fired accidentally, but as the bullet had only narrowly missed a lady in the next cabin, the captain confiscated the firearm and removed the man's sleeping quarters to the spar deck, much to the relief of the other passengers.

Left *An early view of* Orient *in the Suez Canal* (Southampton City Museums).

It is interesting to see the scale of fares during this first year of the *Orient*'s service between London and Australia. For men travelling alone an 'open berth' in steerage cost 14 guineas, while a closed 'four-berth' third class cabin was slightly more expensive at 18 guineas per berth. For a 'two-berth' cabin in the same class the fare was 20 guineas per berth. Of course, the latter two categories were largely reserved for families and married couples respectively. For second class passengers fares were between 35 and 45 guineas and first class fares started at 50 guineas.

In 1875 the British government purchased a major shareholding in the Suez Canal Company, and from then until 1956 the Canal was to play a key role in the country's communications with the East, and in her foreign policy. In 1882 Egypt was ruled by the Khedive Ismail who was sympathetic to both Britain and France, but in the summer of that year a revolt broke out within the country against his regime. Under the guise of protecting his government, Britain invaded Egypt, Alexandria was bombarded, warships entered the Canal and British troops occupied

Port Said, Ismaila and Suez. The *Orient*'s large coal capacity was now turned to the government's advantage, when they chartered her in July 1882 as a troop transport. The company were paid the rate of 27s 6d per ton a day for the vessel. She embarked troops of a Guards Regiment in London, together with some of the principal army officers for the campaign, including HRH The Duke of Connaught. *Orient* made several trips between London and Alexandria, and the campaign ended with the British putting down the rebellion on September 13 1882, the date which marks the beginning of the British occupation of Egypt which was to last for 74 years. The *Orient* was returned to her owners, but the usefulness of the vessel was not lost on government authorities and 18 years later she was to be taken up again on government service.

On November 29 1883 the *Orient* left Gravesend for Australia with 700 passengers, which was the largest number ever to have been carried to that continent on a single voyage, and this led to some publicity in the press. By now both the outward and homeward sections of the voyage were made via the Suez Canal, which was reached 12 days after leaving London. One passenger died in the stifling heat of the Red Sea, but conditions on board improved when the breezes of the Indian Ocean blew through the ship. The major coaling stop for Orient ships was now the island of Diego Garcia and the *Orient* called there on December 28 1883 for that purpose. She arrived in Adelaide on January 11 1884, with the number of passengers remaining the same as it had been when she left London, a baby boy having been born during the voyage. Later that year the vessel was taken into dock and the gas lamps on board were replaced by electric lights, which were a great improvement.

For the next 14 years the *Orient* ran between England and Australia, but technical advances were catching up with her, and on her return to London at the end of 1897 it was decided to modernize her. On December 19 of that year she went up to the Tyne where the Wallsend Slipway Company carried out the work. The passenger accommodation was modernized and her compound machinery was replaced with 7,000 ihp triple-expansion engines, which increased her speed to 16½ knots. The major alterations were carried out above decks, with a forecastle deck being constructed forward, and a turtle deck aft. The four masts, the two forward of which were square rigged, were replaced by two pole masts, and the two funnels were replaced by a single, very tall funnel. The work cost the Orient Line £39,325, and on June 4 1898 the modernized *Orient* returned to London to take up the mail service once more—but in just over a year she was to be sailing as a troopship again.

In South Africa at this time trouble was brewing between the British in the Cape Colony and Natal, and the Afrikaner republics of the Orange Free State and the Transvaal. The discovery of huge deposits of gold in the Transvaal had made the British determined to annex the territory, and the gold boom was financed largely by British capital and workers from the Cape Colony, the 'Uitlanders'. These workers were deliberately denied civil rights as they might well have voted a union with the Cape Colony. The problem had come to a head with the question of the franchise for the British 'Uitlanders' in the Transvaal and, despite a meeting between the Governor of the Cape Colony, Sir Alfred Milner, and President Paul Kruger of the Transvaal, the two sides were inexorably drawn towards war. In Britain the public had been prepared for a war to 'free the Uitlanders', and by early October 1899 there were almost 20,000 Imperial troops in the Cape and Natal. On October 7 that year the *Orient* was taken up by the government as a troop transport. She was chartered at a daily rate of 22s 6d per ton, with an allowance of £500 for the replacement of fittings. She was the first steamer to carry frozen meat to the troops, and on her second trooping voyage the Orient Line contracted for victualling the troops at a rate of 1s per head per day, thus saving the government a large amount of work buying stores, etc. She had been fitted out as transport number 24, to

Above Orient *after her refit in 1898 with a single tall funnel and turtle-back stern* (P&O).

Below *Wounded British soldiers being embarked on to the* Orient *for the voyage home during the South African War* (South African Defence Force).

carry 3,000 men and 400 horses, and in the early days she ran between Southampton and Cape Town. She would make the voyage in ten days, usually calling at Plymouth and St Vincent, a route she had plied in the early months of her career before the Orient Line began using the Suez Canal. She also made voyages between Cape Town and Australian and New Zealand ports carrying troops to the Transvaal War.

Altogether *Orient* was in government service for three years, one month and three days, and during that time she transported 374 officers and 9,000 men to the front. She also made the occasional passage carrying prisoners to St Helena, and wounded soldiers back home. This very unnecessary war finally ended with the Treaty of Vereeniging on May 31 1902, but *Orient* was kept on government charter for a further five months, mainly repatriating Australian and New Zealand troops from South Africa. She was finally returned to the Orient Line on November 10 1902, a year after Queen Victoria's death, and at a time when the world was changing rapidly.

The *Orient* ran on the Orient Line mail service between London and Australia for three years before being chartered to the Royal Mail Company for a round voyage to Australia in October 1906. In 1909 the Orient Line were taking delivery of five new liners, and the *Orient* was now 30 years old—a very good age considering the technical advances that had been made—and it was obvious that her career was nearing its end. The *Orient* left Tilbury on her final voyage on July 23 1909, and she arrived in Brisbane on September 9 that year. She left the port of Fremantle, and Australia, for the last time on September 30 1909 and arrived back in Tilbury Dock a month later on October 31. During her long service she had steamed between three and four million miles, but now the 'old lady' was laid up pending a decision on her disposal. A year later, on November 1 1910, she was sold to Luigi Pittaluga of Genoa for scrap at a price of £12,500, although this did not include her refrigeration machinery and donkey boilers, which had been removed and sold separately. The old ship was renamed *Oric* for the delivery voyage, and she left London under tow for Italy and oblivion.

Technical data
Gross tonnage: 5,386
Net tonnage: 3,231
Length overall: 460 ft (140.20 m)
Breadth: 46 ft 4 in (14.11 m)
Depth: 35 ft 1 in (10.69 m)
Main engines: single screw, three-cylinder compound engine, 5,400 ihp, 15 knots; 1898, triple-expansion engines, 7,000 ihp, 16½ knots
Boilers: Coal-fired, steam pressure 74 psi
Passengers: First class 220, Second class 130, Steerage class 300

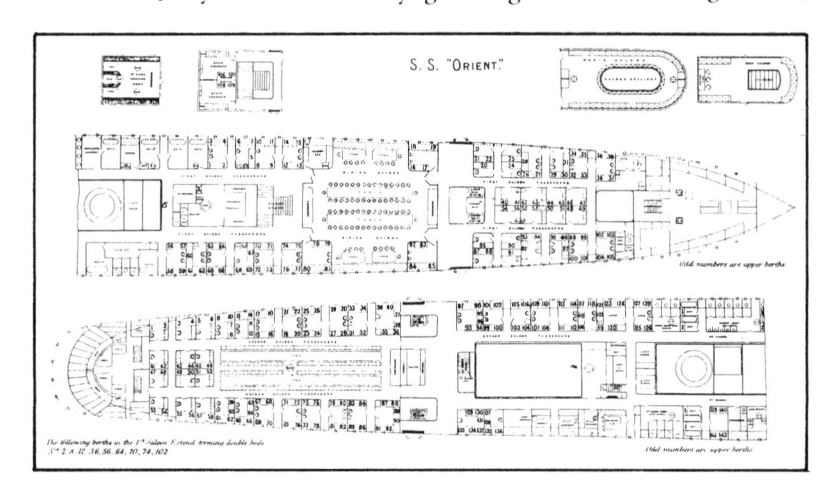

Deck plans for first and second class passengers, SS Orient (P&O).

Austral 1882

The second ship to be built for the Orient Line was the 5,524 gross ton *Austral,* and in her day she was a magnificent ship constructed wholly of mild steel. She was built by John Elder and Company of Glasgow, and was an improved version of the *Orient* which had entered service in 1879. *Austral* was launched on Christmas Eve 1881, after an unsuccessful attempt two days previously. The hard frost on December 22 had frozen the tallow used on the launching ways and she had moved only five feet. Her name was, of course, a reference to the southern hemisphere, and she was a good-looking ship, being rigged as a four-masted schooner with a straight stem, elliptical stern and two upright funnels.

Austral ran her trials on the Clyde on Friday April 26 1882, achieving a speed of 17.3 knots, and at 5 pm the following day she left Cumbrae Head for the Thames, passing the Margate Sand Buoy after a run of 42 hours and 10 minutes. She sailed up the river to the Albert Dock on Monday May 1 1882, after being held up by fog off Sheerness. She had averaged a speed of 16.10 knots for the voyage. A few days later she was opened to the public and thousands of Londoners flocked to see the new ship, which had been described in *The Times* as a 'floating palace'.

The *Austral* was undoubtedly the last word in 'steam and sail power' in 1882. She was a single-screw ship powered by a triple-expansion engine and the steam, at 95 psi, was provided by four double-ended boilers. The ashes from the coal-fired boilers were removed by steam friction hoists and forced through the side of the ship below the waterline, thus overcoming what had been a problem in passenger steamers. In addition to this the vessel had four masts, the fore and main being square-rigged, the mizen and jigger mast having fore and aft sails only. The total area of the sail was about 29,000 sq ft, which was enough, with a moderate breeze, to impel the *Austral* through the water at a speed of 6 knots. It was soon to prove invaluable.

The passenger accommodation catered for 120 first, 130 second and 300 steerage class passengers, distributed on the main, upper and lower decks. In addition to this the promenade deck was for the use of first class passengers. Their drawing room was on the upper deck, as were the first class staterooms. The former was a beautiful room finished in white enamel and gold, with settees arranged around the forward end and sides, and tables and chairs in the centre. The carpets were Indian and very luxurious, as were the curtains which were finished in silk and gold thread. Passing aft to the head of the main staircase, one came to the first class smoking room, which could be entered on either side. It was a comfortable room lit and ventilated from above, and all round the sides the walls were finished in solid oak and mahogany with ebony mouldings. The seating was of the bench type and there was a lift on the port side which communicated with the bar beneath. Also on the upper deck was the second class smoking room and the galleys for preparing food for all the pas-

Above Austral *in the Thames* (National Maritime Museum).

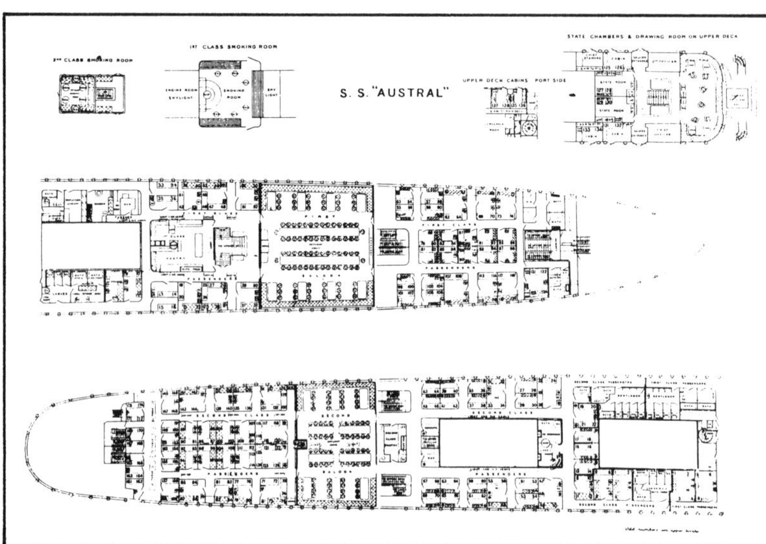

Left *Deck plans of SS* Austral (Orient Line).

sengers and crew. The main staircase led down to the main deck, where the first class cabins were situated forward, and amidships, aft of the foyer, was the first class dining saloon. It was about 40 ft square and arranged to seat 120 passengers. The ends of the room were formed from walnut panels holding richly carved and coloured coats of arms of the great countries of the world, and also the arms of the Orient Line with the company motto *Par non leonina societas.* The sides of the saloon were furnished with padded bench seats and cane seating, above which were painted glass sliding panels. The room was lit by 'Swan' electric lights and a magnificently finished dome skylight, which also assisted with ventilation. The second class dining saloon was further aft on the main deck, as were the second class cabins.

On the lower deck aft of the engine room was the third class or steerage accommodation, which was very basic. Single male passengers had 'open berths' on the side of the ship, while the ladies, families and married couples had small two-, three- or four-berth cabins. There were tables, seats and washbasins and, as the deck was completely enclosed, the whole area was well ventilated by means of large cowls.

One feature which was common to the whole ship, and in those days considered a luxury, were the 'Swan's incandescent lamps', which lit the entire vessel. The design of the *Austral* was undertaken by the company's naval architect, Mr J. W. Shepherd. She was also built in accordance with Admiralty requirements for ships which, in case of war, could be converted for use as armed cruisers.

The *Austral* sailed from London on her maiden voyage to Sydney at 10.40 am on Friday May 19 1882 commanded by Captain John Murdoch, and the next day she arrived in Plymouth where she embarked a further 50 passengers and 16 sacks of mail. She left the port after two hours with 402 passengers on board. The voyage passed without incident and she called at St Vincent and Cape Town for coal. Although the Orient Line had acquired the Indian Ocean island of Diego Garcia as a coaling station, *Austral* did not call there.

After returning to London by the same route she left the Albert Dock on her second voyage to Australia on September 7 1882. She had on board about 500 passengers and 900 tons of general cargo. She called again at St Vincent and Cape Town for coal, and this time things did not go so well. The first problem arose at the Cape, where there was a smallpox epidemic, and she was delayed for some time. When she finally sailed, she was only a day or so out to sea when machinery problems developed which put her engines out of order for 18 hours. Fortunately, she was able to continue the voyage under canvas at 7 knots, and she eventually reached Melbourne where some of her passengers and cargo were discharged. From there she steamed on to Sydney, where she arrived on November 3 1882, and was berthed alongside Circular Quay. On the following day, which was a Saturday, the remainder of the passengers, together with their luggage, were discharged. Captain Murdoch was under instructions, which had been given to him in London, to coal the vessel through the bunker ports in the side of the ship and not over the deck. Therefore he ordered that the ports be opened and the chief engineer empty the water ballast tanks. Nothing further was done that day, but on Sunday November 5 a collier, the *Woonoona,* was secured to the starboard side of *Austral,* her port side being alongside Circular Quay. Soon after midnight the collier began to discharge her coal through the starboard ports of the *Austral* and this continued until between 5 am and 6 am on Monday November 6, by which time some 220 tons of coal had been loaded into her bunkers. When Captain Murdoch came on deck to supervise the unloading of his vessel's remaining cargo he noticed that the ship had a list to starboard, and he immediately ordered coaling to be stopped, the bunkers to be trimmed and a remaining ballast tank on the starboard side to be emptied. During that day the remaining cargo was discharged and 181 tons of fresh water were taken on.

Captain Murdoch was worried about the starboard list the vessel had taken on that morning, and he arranged for the *Austral* to be moved to the company's moorings across from Circular Quay in Neutral Bay, so that she could be coaled on both sides at the same time. Accordingly, on the morning of Tuesday November 7 she was moved to Neutral Bay, and there the remainder of the ballast tanks were pumped out, an operation which was completed at 8 am the next day. Coaling was then continued with some urgency as the next day (Thursday November 9) was the Prince of Wales' birthday, and no work would be done after 8 am. By the time work did stop on the Thursday morning, 1,621 tons of coal had been taken on board and trimmed. At this time the ship appeared to have a very slight list to port. Nothing more was done until the morning of Friday November 10, when *Austral*'s engineers took a 10-ton portion of the propeller shaft ashore for repairs. This occupied them until midday and there was no work done that afternoon. At 10.45 pm that night the collier *Woonoona* was secured on the starboard side and coaling began once again on that side of the ship. At 11.30 pm the captain returned from shore and turned in, but was unable to sleep because of the noise and he got up at 1.30 am on what was now Saturday November 11. He watched for about five minutes before retiring to bed and he remembered nothing more until he was woken up a couple of hours later.

In the meantime, according to the foreman coal trimmer, at 2 am the after bunkers on the starboard side were full and they continued to coal the forward bunkers. At 3 am he noticed that the *Austral* had a slight list to starboard, but not sufficient to cause any apprehension on his part. Unfortunately, the after coaling ports had been left wide open, and although the forward ports were three feet above the water, the after ports were only a few inches from it. By filling the starboard ports aft, the list was to starboard and she was down slightly by the stern. At about 3.45 am that morning the crew of the *Woonoona* suddenly found the *Austral* was coming down on top of them, and the alarm was quickly raised. The officers and crew of the *Austral* escaped either onto the *Woonoona,* or onto a lighter which was secured to port. The coaling ports in the after section on the starboard side had by now been submerged and the torrent of water which poured in flooded the whole ship rapidly. In about 20 minutes from the first alarm, *Austral* sank on an even keel in about 40 ft of water. When the crew were mustered it was found that the purser, the refrigerating engineer and three lascars had not managed to escape and had drowned. All that remained above water of the *Austral* were her masts and funnels.

Divers were immediately sent down to the wreck to recover the bodies of those lost and to salvage fittings and valuables from the saloon. It transpired that the purser had been roused by the noise and had rushed on deck, but once up there he had decided to go below to dress and collect some belongings. He was obviously overwhelmed by the rush of water for his body was found still sitting in his chair, floating against the ceiling of his cabin. Over the next few months *Austral* was a holiday attraction as excursion steamers left Circular Quay every few minutes to view the wreck. Work to raise her was begun and pumps were despatched to the scene. A cofferdam was constructed on the upper deck and around the ship, and on Tuesday, February 27 1883 pumping started, watched by crowds of people who had congregated on Fort Macquarie and Kirribilli Point, where good views could be obtained. Two days later, at noon on March 1, the *Austral* rose to the surface. She was then towed about 400 yds from where she had sunk in Neutral Bay and grounded. The cofferdam was removed and the ship refloated and taken to Fitzroy Dock, Cockatoo Island, to be prepared for the voyage back home to England. The salvage operation had cost £50,000. Later a court of inquiry held that *Austral*'s master and chief officer were to blame for the accident, because they did not supervise the coaling operation.

Austral finally left Sydney under her own steam and in ballast on June 9 1883, but five days later she put into Auckland in New Zealand with engine trouble. After a two-day delay she sailed once again via Cape Horn, and she arrived in the Clyde on August 3 1883. After several days in the Queens Dock she was taken into Salterscroft

Above *With only her masts and funnels showing, the* Austral *lies in about 40 ft of water in Sydney Harbour, November 1882* (P&O).

Right *An excellent painting of* Austral *at sea* (Orient Line).

Graving Dock where she was given a complete overhaul. When the work was finished in the spring of 1884 her funnels had been lengthened by 16 ft, the extra sections being of smaller diameter than the original funnels, which gave her an odd appearance. The yards had also been removed from the fore and main masts. For the first five months after her return to service she was chartered to the Anchor Line to sail alongside their *City of Rome* on the Glasgow to New York run. She was very successful on this route, making seven return voyages, and only once did she exceed eight days to complete one leg of the voyage; in fact, at one time she held the record for the fastest Atlantic crossing. On September 14 1884, while *Austral* was on charter to the Anchor Line, a small steamer, the SS *Cassia,* ran into her off Greenock, but caused very little damage.

On October 27 1884 she returned to London from New York and went back to the Orient Line service, making her first sailing to Australia on November 11 that year, this time by way of the Suez Canal and not Cape Town. Only now, two and a half years after she had been handed over to the Orient Line, was the *Austral* able to settle in to the Australian mail service. On June 8 1886 some colonial and Indian VIPs were entertained on board at Tilbury, and in 1898 she was delayed in Sydney for two weeks with a damaged propeller. The first break in her career for 15 years came on February 9 1900, when she was chartered by the government for service as a troop transport for the South African war. However, after only two months this came to an end and she was handed back to the company on April 26 1900.

Although she returned to the Australian service for the Orient Line, it was obvious that her career would not last much longer. She was by now very outdated and was retained for only three more years, until the end of the war in South Africa, when other company ships were released by the government. On May 8 1903 she was sold to Messrs Gasladi of Genoa in Italy for £13,250, to be broken up. *Austral* had been a ship with many innovations, such as electric lights throughout, and she was the first Orient liner to have bathrooms, but she will always be remembered as the ship which sank at her moorings on a perfectly calm night, 94 years ago in Sydney Harbour.

Technical data

Gross tonnage: 5,524
Net tonnage: 3,214
Length overall: 456 ft (138.99 m)
Breadth: 48 ft 3 in (14.71 m)
Depth: 33 ft 10 in (10.33 m)
Main engines: Single screw, three-cylinder compound engine, 7,114 ihp, 17 knots
Boilers: Coal-fired, steam pressure 95 psi
Passengers: First class 120, Second class 130, Steerage class 300

Ormuz 1887

The third ship to be built for the Orient Line was the 6,031 gross ton *Ormuz*. She was constructed at Govan on the Clyde by the Fairfield Shipbuilding and Engineering Company of Glasgow, and she was the second Orient vessel to be built of mild steel. She was completed as a four-masted barque, with the two forward masts carrying full yards. She was a single-screw ship, powered by triple-expansion engines, the first to be fitted in an Orient liner, and had two funnels. In all she had an appearance very similar to that of the *Austral,* which had entered service some five years previously.

The *Ormuz* was launched on Wednesday September 29 1886, and she was the largest vessel to take to the water on the Clyde that year. She was named after the island in the Straits of Hormuz in the Persian Gulf, once, of course, the great emporium of eastern trade in the Middle Ages. Unfortunately, when the *Ormuz* was completed, just over three months after the launch, a large number of Clyde shipworkers were put out of work, a phenomenon not confined to the latter half of the 20th century on that famous river. In the first week of January 1887 the *Ormuz* ran a series of progressive trials on the Clyde and on one run over the measured mile she attained a speed of 18 knots, actually averaging 17.57 knots while developing 8,924 ihp. She arrived in Tilbury Docks on Tuesday January 11 1887, only nine months after the contract for her construction had been signed by the builders and owners. In fact, it was suggested at the time that such a quick completion of the work would inevitably lead to trouble, and that the new ship would never be a success.

The *Ormuz* had five decks, with the passenger accommodation on four of them. The promenade deck was 240 ft long and, for those who liked their exercise, ten times round the deck equalled one mile. Amidships on this deck was the first class lounge, which was in fact described as a deck saloon. It was a magnificent room furnished with writing tables, comfortable seating and a library. The walls were adorned with original paintings, amongst which were 'The Lower Thames, Woolwich' by C. W. Wyllie, 'The Upper Thames, Windsor' by John O'Conner, and 'Falmouth' by R. Napier Hemy. Well aft on the same deck was the first class smoking room, fitted with cane furniture and a bar. Below the promenade deck was the upper deck which was reached by the grand staircase. At the forward end was the first class coffee room, which was the name given to the dining saloon. It differed in many respects from saloons in previous ships, mainly because it was fitted with both large and small tables so that passengers could arrange themselves into parties for their own convenience. All the furniture was of solid mahogany, the walls being panelled with inlay in rosewood and satinwood, exhibiting the arms of the principal colonies. There was also a beautiful carving in wood of the Imperial arms. A kind of buffet screened a staircase at the forward end, and it was decorated with a carving of the

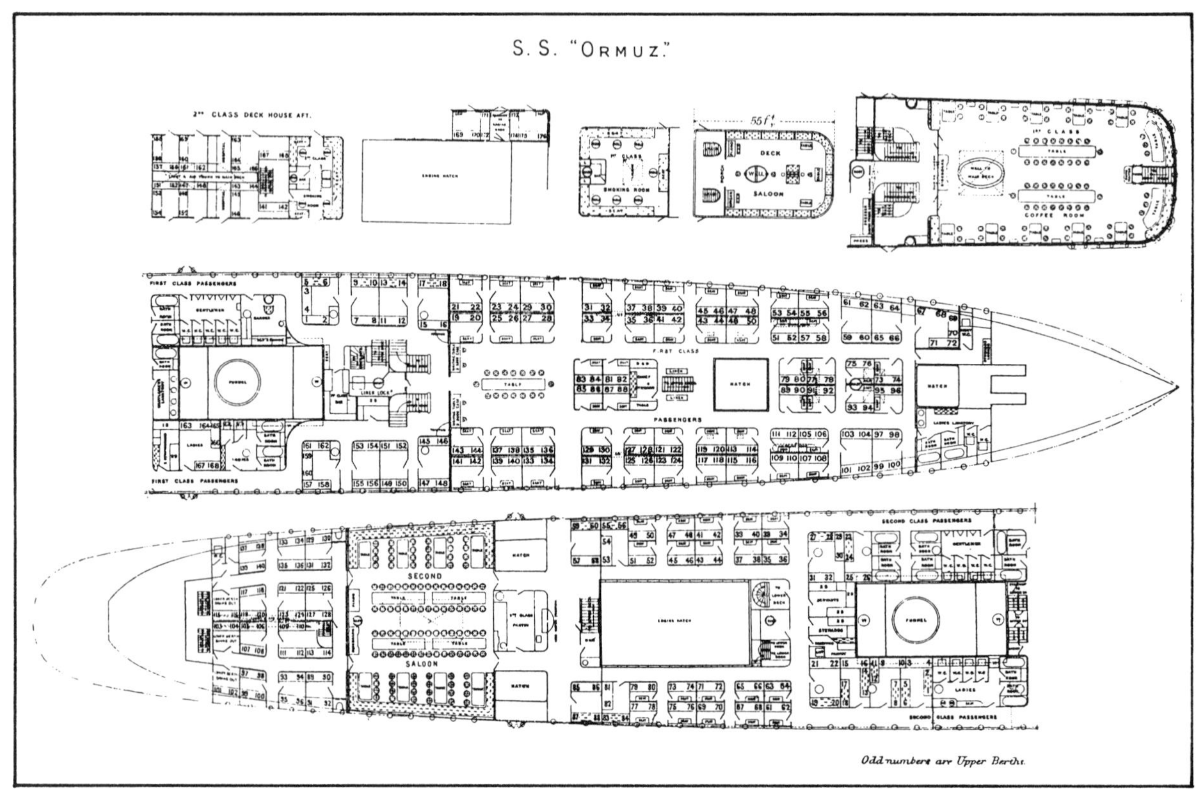
S. S. "ORMUZ."
2nd CLASS DECK HOUSE AFT.
ENGINE HATCH
1st CLASS
SMOKING ROOM
55 ft
DECK
SALOON
WELL
1st CLASS
TABLE
COFFEE ROOM
FIRST CLASS PASSENGERS
FIRST CLASS
PASSENGERS
FUNNEL
HATCH
TABLE
LADIES
SECOND
SALOON
ENGINE HATCH
SECOND CLASS PASSENGERS
GENTLEMEN
Odd numbers are Upper Berths.

Left Ormuz *off Tilbury, with the tender* Thames *lying alongside* (P&O).

Below left *Deck plans of* Ormuz (Orient Line).

Right *The promenade deck,* Ormuz (Orient Line).

royal arms. The whole saloon was well lit by large, square windows round the sides and by a small skylight at the forward end, and a large, splendidly finished well aft, both of which assisted with ventilation. At the after end of the grand staircase were the galley and pantry, which added to the comfort of the passengers by enabling the food to be served quickly and, therefore, hot.

Descending once again by the main staircase, the passengers found themselves on the main deck where all the first class cabins were situated. All of these were fitted with electric service bells and electric lights, which were unusual features at that time. Bathrooms were numerous, and the hot water, not being heated by steam jets blown directly into it, was cleaner and did not have the odour of steam about it. Most of the first class cabins were built for either one or two passengers, with a few set aside for up to six berths. The second class accommodation was aft on the same decks, the cabins and dining saloon being on the main deck and a smoking room on the upper deck. The standards of the second class in general were superior to those of the first class in earlier ships. The third class were accommodated aft on the lower deck, the whole space being fitted with cabins for two, four or six persons. Further forward on that deck were open berths for single men and women, with long tables and seats.

The whole of the steerage was self-contained, 'the object being both to insure the comfort of the steerage passengers, and also to avoid any annoyance to the travellers in the first and second saloons'! In the engine room the ship was fitted with 9,000 ihp triple-expansion engines, which drove a single screw and gave the vessel a service speed of 17½ knots. Steam was provided by six coal-fired double-ended boilers. each being 18 ft long and 15 ft in diameter and having six furnaces of corrugated steel, giving a working pressure of 150 psi. She was also placed on the Admiralty list for service as an auxiliary cruiser in time of war.

As the *Ormuz* lay in Tilbury Docks waiting to depart on her maiden voyage, she was the subject of great interest, and on Wednesday January 26 1887 a large number of guests were entertained on board by the managers of the line. Among these guests were the artists whose work adorned the public rooms, and Mr J. J. Stevenson who was

The first class dining saloon on Ormuz *in all its Victorian splendour* (Orient Line).

responsible for the general decoration of the vessel. Also present was Sir Saul Samuel, Agent General for New South Wales in Australia. As he pointed out in his speech, it was exactly 100 years to the day since the English effected their first settlement in Australia.

Ormuz left London on February 3 1887 for her maiden voyage to Melbourne and Sydney via Suez. She was commanded by Captain Hewison, and despite bad weather she delivered the mails to Sydney in 27 days, which was a record and by a good margin. She had also proved her critics wrong, and probably her main problem was her heavy coal consumption, which was not at all unusual in the 1880s. On her third outward voyage to Australia she reached Albany 12 hours after the P&O liner which had sailed from London a week earlier, and Adelaide 30 hours before it. These were the days when the two companies were fierce competitors, and the giant P&O Company did not have it all its own way. In the spring of 1889 the Orient Line claimed that *Ormuz* had beaten the record established by P&O's *Britannia* in the previous year. This was disputed by P&O, and in fact it was difficult to decide either way as the Orient vessels had 182 miles further to travel, for they called at Naples, whereas P&O's ships put in to Brindisi. However, during the voyage in question, *Ormuz* made daily runs of between 361 and 402 miles, and there is

The second class dining saloon, Ormuz. *It appears rather more confined than that of the first class* (Orient Line).

no doubt that she recovered an appreciable proportion of her handicap.

On her return to London in July 1889 the *Ormuz* took part in a special mini-cruise to a Naval Review at Spithead. She embarked passengers, who had all paid 10 guineas each, at Tilbury on Friday August 2 and sailed for the Solent that afternoon. She arrived there early the following morning and anchored off Ryde Sands for the review which took place in the afternoon. *Ormuz* put to sea at the end of the ceremony and took her passengers on a cruise down-Channel as far as the Channel Islands, before returning to Tilbury on the morning of Tuesday August 6 1889. It was more than four weeks later, on September 13, that she left once again for Australia, with fares for the voyage ranging from £17 to £70.

For the next ten years *Ormuz* ran without incident to Australia. On a homeward voyage in August 1900 she became the first Orient Line ship to call at Fremantle, returning to London in the September. She sailed from Tilbury on another round passage on October 12 1900, and arrived in Sydney one month later. She left the port homeward bound once again in December, and soon afterwards, at 2.30 pm on December 12, while entering Melbourne and inside Port Phillip Heads, *Ormuz* was in a serious collision with a cargo vessel, SS *Ismaila. Ormuz* suffered serious

A postcard view of Ormuz *in the early years of the twentieth century* (Orient Line).

damage to her stem, and the smaller vessel was holed in the starboard side down to the waterline. Both ships were able to make the port under their own power but it was clear that there was no question of them continuing their voyages. On board *Ormuz* all passengers were disembarked and her cargo was unloaded before she was taken into dock, where she was to remain for over eight weeks. It was late February 1901 before the repairs were completed and *Ormuz* was able to resume her homeward passage. She did not arrive in London until 5 pm on Saturday March 30 that year, and she made her next sailing to Australia 13 days later on April 12.

In 1906 she was the first Orient ship to adopt buff-coloured, rather than black, funnels, a move insisted on by the company's partners in the Australian run, the Royal Mail Steam Packet Company. Also in that year she was involved in an incident which resulted in the other vessel running aground. *Ormuz* left London for Brisbane on Friday April 20 1906 and arrived in Port Said on May 3. The previous day the Anchor liner *Assyria* had arrived in the port, bound from the Clyde to Calcutta. Late on Thursday May 3 both ships entered the Suez Canal in convoy, with *Ormuz* directly behind *Assyria*. They proceeded into the Great Bitter Lake and, in order to enter the canal at the south end of the lake, *Assyria* reduced speed and switched on her searchlight. The master of *Ormuz* decided to take the opportunity to overhaul *Assyria* and had her steered alongside the starboard side of the latter ship and then across her bows. *Assyria* went full astern and hard to port to avoid a collision, then hit a navigation light and went firmly aground in the Bitter Lake. *Ormuz* sailed on and left Suez at 7 am on Friday May 4 for Australia, where she arrived safely later that month. *Assyria* was refloated the following day and she too was able to resume her voyage. However, at a court of inquiry, Mr Justice Bucknill held *Ormuz* solely to blame for the incident and awarded the Anchor Line judgement and costs.

Almost 12 months later, on Wednesday 27 March 1907 *Ormuz* was again involved in a collision, this time in Gibraltar, with the pre-Dreadnought battleship, HMS *Africa*. Fortunately, only very minor damage was suffered by both vessels, and *Ormuz* was able to continue her voyage, arriving in Marseilles the following day. Four years later, although *Ormuz* was only 24 years old, she was already outdated. The five 1909 steamers had entered service, and with the *Orama* about to be handed over to the company, *Ormuz* was no longer needed. She left Tilbury for her last Orient voyage on August 18 1911 bound for Brisbane, where she arrived in early October that year. Later that month she left Australia for the last time and arrived back in London on Sunday November 26 1911.

For five months she was laid up in Tilbury, and then on April 9 1912 she was sold for £19,200 to the French Compagnie de Navigation Sud-Atlantique. They were a new company who were taking over the services to South America which had been operated by Messageries Maritimes, and they were buying rather elderly, but sound ships with which to start the new service. *Ormuz* was renamed *Divona* and her accommodation was altered to carry 108 first, 89 second, 54 intermediate and 330 third class passengers. Her funnels were lengthened and her gross tonnage increased to 6,812. She entered service between France and the River Plate in September 1912, and she continued until the outbreak of war, when she was taken up by the French government as a hospital ship. She survived the war and was handed back to her owners after the Armistice. Without doubt her career would have been well and truly over, had not her owners lost one of their new ships, the *Gallia*, in October 1916, so the *Divona* was put into service once again on the Bordeaux–River Plate service. However, this was short-lived, for with the completion of the company's *Massilia* in October 1920, the *Divona* was withdrawn and laid up. In 1922 she was finally sold to the French shipbreakers, Messrs Leferre-Despeaux. She was 35 years old and had certainly defied those who had predicted that she would be nothing but trouble for her owners.

Technical data

Gross tonnage: 6,031
Net tonnage: 3,225
Length overall: 482 ft (146.91 m)
Breadth: 52 ft 1 in (15.88 m)
Depth: 19 ft 1 in (5.82 m)
Main engines: Single screw, triple-expansion engine, 9,000 ihp, 17½ knots
Boilers: Coal-fired, steam pressure 150 psi
Passengers: First class 166, Second class 170, Steerage class 120

Ophir 1891

This famous little liner, known primarily for her service as a royal yacht during 1901, was the first twin-screw vessel on the Australian mail service. She embodied a complete breakaway from traditional design, with her two widely spaced funnels, heavily raked masts, her upright stem and clean elliptical stern, which all gave her a handsome appearance.

The *Ophir* was ordered in December 1889 and she was built at Govan by Robert Napier & Sons Ltd. Mr J. J. Stevenson was engaged to design and superintend the decoration of the public rooms for a fee of 400 guineas. *Ophir* was launched on April 11 1891 and was sponsored by Miss Green, the daughter of one of the managers. The new vessel was named after a goldfield district near Bathurst in New South Wales, Australia, although there are five other places called Ophir in countries as far apart as the USA and Malaya. She must have presented a splendid sight as she lay in the Clyde fitting out, alongside Napier's yard where she could be seen from the Govan Ferry.

Ophir's gross tonnage was 6,814 and her overall length some 482 ft. She had accommodation for 230 first class, 142 second and 520 steerage passengers. The first class public rooms were on the upper, promenade and main decks. The dining saloon, which was sumptuously decorated, was on the upper deck amidships, where it was considered that any movement at sea would be at a minimum. The distinguishing feature of the saloon was the arch-shaped dome with a beautiful stained-glass inner roof through which daylight entered and lit up the whole room. Round the sides of the dome were 11 large circular ports fitted with coloured glass and surrounded with carved gilt frames representing fruit and flowers, while in niches in between were carved female figures holding gilt chains from which electric lights were suspended over the middle of the room. There was a balcony overlooking the saloon, set apart for the ship's band. Also on the upper deck were 18 de luxe cabins, all fitted with electric lights and bells for cabin service. At the forward end of the promenade deck was the drawing room, a richly decorated apartment covering an area of 1,200 sq ft. The walls were lined with inlaid marquetry panels and landscapes in oil by Mr Napier Hemy. Access to this room was from the promenade deck or by the grand staircase. Also on the same deck was the smoking room, which was furnished with polished oak and carved panels by Gambi of Florence, the seats and sofas being covered with embossed leather. The room was full of snug corners, in each of which were small baize-covered tables surrounded by chairs and settees. As one contemporary magazine described it, 'The whole being suggestive of all that is required for the purpose of a quiet rubber of whist'.

Down below in the engine room *Ophir* was fitted with two independent sets of inverted, direct-acting, triple-expansion condensing engines, which developed 13,000 ihp. Steam was supplied by five double-ended cylindrical boilers,

Above *SS* Ophir, *a complete breakaway from traditional design, with two widely spaced funnels and heavily raked masts* (P&O).

Right *The architect's drawing of* Ophir*'s first class dining saloon* (P&O).

Royal Naval Review at Spithead,

To be held on 26th June, 1897,

IN HONOUR OF THE DIAMOND JUBILEE OF HER MAJESTY THE QUEEN.

GREAT CONCENTRATION OF BRITISH AND FOREIGN SHIPS OF WAR.

Grand and Imposing Spectacle.

Inspection of the Fleet by THE QUEEN or THE PRINCE OF WALES

The Orient Steam Navigation Company, Limited,

WILL DESPATCH THEIR TWIN-SCREW STEAMSHIP

"OPHIR," 6910 Tons Register, 10,000 H.P.,

From TILBURY for SPITHEAD on the 25th JUNE.

ITINERARY

PLACE.	MILES.	ARRIVAL.	TIME IN PORT.	DEPARTURE.
LONDON (TILBURY)	—	... .	...	Fri., 25th June, 4 p.m.
SPITHEAD	180	Sat., 26th June, 6 a.m.	80 hours.	Sun., 27th ,, noon.
HAVRE	90	Sun., 27th ,, 7 p.m.	24 ,,	Mon., 28th ,, 7 p.m.
LONDON (TILBURY)	175	Tues, 29th ,, 9 a.m.		

Passengers will join the "OPHIR" at Tilbury by a Special Train leaving St. Pancras Station at 2.10 p.m. on 25th June, for Tilbury, and the Ship will sail at 4 p.m.

Saturday will be occupied with the Review.

On Sunday the "OPHIR" will, subject to the discretion of the Commander, steam round the Fleet, and then proceed to sea by way of The Needles to Havre, where it will be open to the Passengers to spend Monday on shore. Trouville and Deauville, fashionable watering places on the Normandy Coast, are within one hour's run by Steamboat from Havre. The Ship is timed to be back at Tilbury on Tuesday Morning, the 29th June.

A Steam Tender will be in attendance on the Ship while at Spithead, and also at Havre.

FARES—12 and 15 Guineas each, according to position of berth. The exclusive use of a two-berth Cabin by one Passenger can be secured for a fare and a half. This includes meals and sleeping berth while on board, also Rail both ways between St. Pancras and Tilbury. Wines, Liquors, Mineral Waters, &c., can be purchased on board.

Managers:—F. GREEN & Co., ANDERSON, ANDERSON & Co., *Head Offices:*— FENCHURCH AVENUE, LONDON.

For Passage apply to the latter Firm, at 5, FENCHURCH AVENUE, E.C.,

Or to the WEST-END BRANCH OFFICE, 16, COCKSPUR STREET, S.W.

Orient Line press advertisement for a cruise by Ophir *to Spithead for the Royal Naval Review, 1897* (P&O).

each having six furnaces and a steam pressure of 160 psi. She had a service speed of 18 knots, and during her trials she attained almost 18¾ knots. She was designed for speed, had little cargo space, and her coal consumption of 125 tons a day rendered her expensive to run.

Ophir ran her trials in the Clyde off Skelmorlie for two days from October 22 1891, and then made a 48-hour voyage round to Tilbury. She was handed over to the Orient Line on October 30 that year, and she sailed on her maiden voyage to Australia seven days later. Her twin screws immediately proved themselves when she was able to continue her voyage despite engine trouble in the Bay of Biscay. However, a slight shadow was cast over her first year in service, when the managers of the line were involved in a lawsuit with the builders over her speed, coal consumption and lifting capacity. The builders agreed that, although in some respects she did not strictly comply with the contract, she was in fact more suitable for the trade. The litigation began on December 21 1891 and finally ended on July 26 1892 when the Orient Line were awarded judgement. *Ophir*'s first few years of service were uneventful, although she reduced the passage time between London and Albany by four days. She also became well known for her cruises to the Norwegian fjords.

In 1900 the *Ophir* became a household name throughout the world when it was announced that she was to be chartered to the Admiralty for use as a royal yacht, for the forthcoming tour of the Empire by Their Royal Highnesses the Duke and Duchess of Cornwall and York (later to be King George V and Queen Mary). She left London for a voyage to Brisbane on September 14 1900, and by the middle of November she had started her homeward journey, arriving in Tilbury at 9.30 am on December 22 1900, just in time for Christmas. By this time the interior designs had been settled and she was immediately taken on charter by the Admiralty, initially for six months at £6,915 per month (net), the government paying for everything. Work began at once under the supervision of Captain F. J. Pitt RN, of the Transport Department in the Admiralty, although the planning and execution of all alterations, including the provision of equipment such as plate, glass and linen, which were of specially prepared designs, was left in the hands of the Orient Line. One major reason why *Ophir* had been chosen was the fact that she was a twin-screw vessel and, with her boiler rooms some 62 ft apart, plus a longitudinal watertight bulk-head dividing the engine rooms, she was considered to be extremely safe. The royal tour, although covering most of the Empire, was primarily aimed at Australia, and so it was fitting that a vessel belonging to one of the two great mail lines which served the Commonwealth

Ophir *in her role as a Royal Yacht* (P&O).

should be chosen as the royal yacht.

During the time *Ophir* lay at Tilbury, between 500 and 800 men were employed to undertake the numerous alterations to the ship. A shelter was built on the bridge for the steersman and officers on duty, and in the bridge house itself two of the cabins were converted into sitting rooms for the royal couple. On the boat deck a 30 ft gig took the place of one of the ship's lifeboats, whilst over the poop two 32 ft steam cutters were carried. On the promenade deck the first class public rooms were converted into the royal drawing room and smoking room. The former, with its rosewood and satinwood panelling with satinwood Sheraton furniture, upholstered in blue and white silk damask, and with a fawn-coloured deep-pile carpet, looked magnificent. Immediately aft was the grand staircase and then the royal smoking room. Further aft on this deck the former second class smokeroom became the ward room smoking room. Descending to the upper deck by the grand staircase, one found that the whole of the space forward of the foyer, which had been occupied by 19 first class cabins, had been converted into two suites of royal apartments. Each consisted of three rooms and a bathroom, and the two were divided by a central corridor with a staircase at the forward end leading to the royal servants' quarters which were on the main deck in the first class cabins. In the royal apartments themselves the theme of the decorations was simplicity, the paintwork throughout being a matt white relieved only by the satinwood and light-oak furniture and pale green upholstery and carpets. Immediately aft of the grand staircase was the royal dining saloon, the decoration and furniture of which remained unchanged. Although its primary function would be to accommodate official state banquets, it would also double as a concert room.

During this fitting-out period at Tilbury, the Duke and Duchess took a particular interest in the work and, on the morning of Thursday February 21 1901 they travelled by special train from St Pancras to 'O' shed at Tilbury Docks, a journey of some 50 minutes. There they were met by Mr Kenneth Anderson and Mr Frederick Green of the Orient Line's management, who welcomed them on board. After having lunch on the ship, the royal party spent some four hours touring her. Despite the heavy falls of snow that afternoon, quite a crowd gathered to see the Duke and Duchess leave Tilbury Docks, their train being hauled by the locomotive *Crouch Hill*. That same day 72 men of the Royal Marine detachment left Portsmouth to join *Ophir*.

By now work on the vessel was almost completed and the *Ophir* presented a splendid sight with her hull painted white with a broad band of royal blue. The two funnels and the ventilators

A souvenir postcard issued by the Orient Line to commemorate the Royal Tour of 1901 (P&O).

were painted a buff colour and the ship's boats were white with blue and gold lines at the top. The ship commissioned at Tilbury on the morning of Tuesday February 26 1901, under the command of Commodore A. L. Winsloe CVO RN. Her complement was made up of both naval and mercantile personnel, consisting of 27 officers and 125 naval ratings, 100 Royal Marines (including 37 bandsmen) and 20 boy seamen. The seven engineer officers and the engine and boiler room complement of 88 were provided by the Orient Line, as were the purser, stewards, cooks and galley staff. The total number of crew members was 525 and all the victualling arrangements were left in the hands of the Orient Line.

Ophir sailed from Tilbury at 6 am on February 27 1901, and she arrived alongside Railway Jetty in Portsmouth Dockyard at 12.40 pm the following day, after being delayed in the Solent by thick fog. The next two weeks were spent taking on coal and stores, and finally, at 4.30 pm on March 15, the ship was dressed overall ready for the arrival of the Duke and Duchess and their entourage, which took place an hour later. At 10 am the next day the King and Queen visited the ship, and at divisions held on board His Majesty presented South African War medals and inspected the vessel. Later that day, after making their farewells, the King and Queen left the ship and *Ophir* slipped from South Railway Jetty to start an eight-month cruise around the world. Despite the miserable weather, large crowds gathered on Southsea Common to wave them off, and as *Ophir* passed the Royal Yacht *Victoria and Albert* in the Solent, three cheers were given for King Edward VII and Queen Alexandra. Soon *Ophir* was out in the Channel and a course was set for Ushant. She had a rough passage through the Bay of Biscay, but the weather had improved by the time she reached Gibraltar.

One of the best accounts of the Empire tour is by Petty Officer Harry Price and is entitled 'The Royal Tour 1901—Or The Cruise of HMS *Ophir*'. It is interesting to note that on the first Sunday at sea on March 17 the ship's company went to church in the royal dining saloon and the Duke attended, although the Duchess, it seems, was still finding her sea-legs that day. After Gibraltar *Ophir* called at Malta, Port Said, Suez, Aden, Colombo, Singapore and then Albany in Western Australia before moving on to Auckland on June 6 1901. Just over three weeks later *Ophir* was back in Australia, and she did not finally leave the country until July 26 that year.

Ophir's homeward route took her to Mauritius, Durban, Simonstown, St Vincent and on across the Atlantic to Quebec, Halifax and St John's in Canada. She finally arrived in Plymouth on October 31 1901, and the Duke of Cornwall and York had invited Mr Kenneth Anderson of the Orient Line to join him there for the last leg of the voyage to Portsmouth. However, the weather was rough as Mr Anderson boarded *Ophir* and he was thrown into the water and found to be unconscious when he was rescued. Fortunately, he recovered and was able to accompany the Duke the next day for the final lap of the long cruise. *Ophir* arrived in the Solent at 10.30 am on November 1, where the royal couple were joined by their children and the King and Queen. Soon afterwards, the *Ophir* was safely berthed alongside South Railway Jetty once more, her commission in the Royal Navy completed. Exactly one week later she was back in Tilbury where she was converted to a passenger liner once again for the service to Australia. All the naval stores had been landed at Portsmouth, and the furniture from the royal apartments was bought by Messrs Waring & Sons. The remainder of the government property was sold by auction at the Sheerness Dockyard in March 1902, at a handsome profit.

Ophir made her first commercial sailing from Tilbury on January 3 1902, and her second sailing on April 25 that year. By now she was a household name in Great Britain, and there is no doubt that this helped to sell her summer cruises to the Norwegian fjords. In the summer of 1904 she sustained some minor keel damage while on one of these cruises, but this was quickly repaired and did not interrupt her itinerary. In the summer of 1907 she made three 13-day cruises from Tilbury, the first on June 14 that year. The fares

SS Ophir *at Sydney; she was the first twin-screw vessel on the Australian mail service* (P&O).

were advertized at prices from 13 guineas with calls at Bergen, Gudvargen, Balholmen, Loen, Naes and Odda. The programme ended on August 24 1907, and she sailed once again for Australia in the following month. However, owing to her high running costs, she was very often laid up off Southend during the low season.

In July 1914 *Ophir* was anchored in the Thames off Gravesend when the Admiralty requested either *Otranto* or *Otway* for charter as hospital ships. The Orient Line turned down this request but offered the *Ophir* which, they said, 'could be made ready for sea in about seven days'. The Admiralty took up the offer and chartered her for three months, but not as a hospital ship. They had decided to use her on the mail run, and she left London for Brisbane with the mails on October 23 1914 on what was to be her final voyage to Australia. She left Sydney for the homeward leg in late December that year, and on January 19 1915 she ran into trouble in the Suez Canal when she went aground. There was a delay of four days while her cargo was unloaded and she was refloated; she sailed again on January 23.

Meanwhile, in the Orient Line offices in London and at the Admiralty, decisions were being taken about *Ophir*'s future. On January 26 1915 the Admiralty decided that she was to be taken up by them as an armed merchant cruiser, and that to purchase her would be more economical than a continuous charter. On her return to London in early February that year the Admiralty carried out a full survey of the vessel, and they found that, although she had been well maintained, a number of minor repairs and adjustments were required to the main and auxiliary machinery. On March 8 1915 they made an offer of £25,000 to the Orient Line for the ship, and this was accepted.

At Tilbury Docks work had started as soon as she arrived from Australia to convert her to an armed merchant cruiser, and she was commissioned on March 3 1915. She left London 18 days later to patrol off the River Tagus as part of the 9th Cruiser Squadron in the mid-Atlantic. She was commanded by Commander J. M. D. E. Warren RN, and it was not long before she was intercepting suspicious merchant ships. It is interesting to note that soon after starting her patrol she stopped a British cargo ship, the SS *Cardiffian*. Although everything was in fact in order, it seems that her master had had the name *Cardiffiani* painted on her bows and stern and, in an attempt to avoid trouble with enemy submarines, he was flying the Italian flag. On April 23 1915 *Ophir* captured the Swedish ship SS *Marta* off Las Palmas. She was carrying cargo taken from the German ship *Cap Ortegal* which had been lying at Santa Cruz. The *Marta* was taken as a prize of war and sent to Gibraltar under armed guard.

During the next 11 months *Ophir* patrolled off the Atlantic Isles, and located six German nationals who were attempting to return home. On March 26 1916 she went into dock at Gibraltar for a long refit which was to last for three months.

It was June 30 1916 before *Ophir* was at sea again, and soon after that on August 12 she ran aground at Dakar. Fortunately she was refloated at 5.48 am the next day, only eight hours later, and soon after she left the port she captured two Germans from the Danish ship SS *Hulda Maersk*. The rest of that year passed uneventfully and, apart from a spell in Devonport, and Christmas in drydock at Gibraltar, she was on patrol continuously. Finally, on February 28 1917, she left Freetown escorting a convoy to Devonport, her days in the mid-Atlantic now over. Her next refit was started in Devonport, and during her stay there the 8,000-ton Union Castle liner *Galway Castle* collided with *Ophir* while the former was leaving harbour. Fortunately there was only minor damage to both ships. On May 26 1917 *Ophir* left Plymouth and arrived in the Mersey at Birkenhead two days later. Soon after that her ship's company were paid off and she remained in dockyard hands until early 1918.

It was March 1918 before *Ophir* recommissioned and she left the Mersey on the 22nd of that month, bound for the Far East by way of Cape Town. The first half of her final commission was spent patrolling from Singapore, a port she had not visited since the royal tour 17 years previously. In August 1918 she spent four days in dock at Hong Kong, before crossing the Pacific to patrol the east coast of South America for the remainder of the war. On Armistice Day she was in Taltal, Chile, and on December 26 that year she arrived at Cristobal and went through the Panama Canal. New Year's Day was spent at Colon, and three days later she left for Devonport, arriving there on January 19 1919. Two days later she left for the Clyde, arriving there on January 22, and three weeks later, on February 11 1919, she paid off for the last time.

For a year the *Ophir* lay awaiting her fate and then, in 1920, she was offered for sale by auction. Ironically the £45,000 which was bid for her was considered by somebody in the Admiralty as unsuitable as it was below the reserve price, so she was withdrawn. Two years later she was sold for £6,000 and scrapped at Troon: a sad end for a ship which had sailed the world as a royal yacht in the second year of this century.

Technical data

Gross tonnage: 6,814
Net tonnage: 2,920
Length overall: 481 ft 11 in (146.91 m)
Breadth: 53 ft 5 in (16.29 m)
Depth: 28 ft 6 in (10.39 m)
Main engines: Twin screw, two triple-expansion engines, 13,000 ihp, 18 knots
Boilers: Coal-fired, steam pressure 160 psi
Passengers: First class 230, Second class 142, Steerage class 520

Omrah 1899

The *Omrah* was completed in 1899 and she ushered in the 20th century for the Orient Line, for she was the first ship built for the company since the *Ophir* eight years previously. In October 1897 the contract for the vessel was placed with the Fairfield Shipbuilding and Engineering Company Ltd of Glasgow, and the price quoted was £215,300. In those days the Clyde shipbuilders always delivered their ships on time and sometimes, indeed, early, so *Omrah* was launched on schedule on September 3 1898. Her name was derived from the Arabic word 'Umara' meaning 'Lord', now used in Urdu in the sense of 'Grandee of the Court'. Unfortunately the launching ceremony did not go exactly to plan. As she slid into the water, instead of moving away she seems to have drifted back onto the slipway and stuck fast. It was the following morning before tugs were able to clear her and tow her into the fitting-out basin.

Omrah had accommodation for 350 first and second class passengers and 500 third class emigrants. The first and second class passengers were carried amidships, whilst the third class were accommodated on the main deck with an open deck space in the well decks. The standard of accommodation was a distinct improvement upon that aboard the *Ophir*. Like *Ophir, Omrah* was a twin-screw ship driven by triple-expansion engines, the steam being supplied by three double-ended and two single-ended boilers working at 180 psi and under Howden's forced draught. She had an ihp of 9,200 which gave her a service speed of 18 knots. All together *Omrah* was an imposing-looking ship, and her enormous single funnel, which stood over 70 ft high, gave the impression that she was much larger than her 8,282 gross tons.

On January 5 1899, just four months after the launching ceremony, *Omrah* ran her trials in the Clyde. Unfortunately the weather was rough at the time and during the speed trials she only managed to attain 17.3 knots. Everything else was successfully completed, but it was January 17 before she left the Clyde, arriving off Gravesend two days later. For some days after her arrival in London she was the cause of a dispute between the builders and the Department of Trade, regarding the numbers of cabins fitted per gross ton. However, it was decided that the regulations had not been breached and by the end of the month the civil servants had given her the 'all clear'. She was finally handed over to the Orient Line on January 30, eleven days after arriving in London, and four days later, on February 3, she left for Australia.

When she arrived 'down under', the *Omrah*, with her high freeboard, handsome hull lines and enormous funnel, caused quite a stir in the press. At this time the Orient Line service, in conjunction with the PSNCo service, was rather disorganized. Several ships had been taken up by the government as troop transports for the South African War, and it was 1902 before the service settled down again. In October that year *Omrah* was joined by the *Orontes*, a slightly larger

Above Omrah *ushered in the 20th century for the Orient Line* (P&O).

Below Omrah*'s enormous single funnel, which stood over 70 ft high, gave the impression that she was a muchlarger ship than was actually the case* (National Maritime Museum).

version of herself, and until 1909 the two vessels were the pride of the Orient fleet.

On March 25 1901 *Omrah* took on Lascar firemen and trimmers, and in the 1902–3 naval estimates she received an armed merchant cruiser subsidy, although, like her younger sister *Orontes*, she would never be employed in this role. During the unbroken years of her service to Australia in the first 14 years of this century she became a very popular ship, being much drier, more comfortable and, most important of all for the company, more economical than the *Ophir*.

However, 15 years after *Omrah* entered service, the situation changed. She sailed from London on July 17 1914, in the closing weeks of what was to become known as the Edwardian era. She was destined as usual for Brisbane and was in the Indian Ocean when war broke out. On her arrival in Brisbane she was requisitioned by the Commonwealth government and fitted out as a troop transport. It was September 20 before the work was completed and *Omrah* became HMT A5. She embarked the 1st Queensland contingent of the AIF, who were part of the 9th Battalion of that force, and members of the AAMC, including four nursing sisters. Also embarked were personnel of the 5th AASC. Many of the troops on board would eventually fight on the battlefields of Gallipoli. *Omrah* left Brisbane on September 24 1914 and sailed independently round the coast to Albany, where she was to join a large troop convoy bound for the Middle East.

The convoy consisted of 36 troop transports and included *Omrah* and the *Orvieto*, which had also been requisitioned by the Commonwealth government as a troopship. The convoy left Albany on November 1 1914, and in fact it was the first troop convoy to sail from Australia in the first few months of the war. Altogether there were some 20,000 Australian soldiers on board the ships, and with the *Emden* loose in the Indian Ocean a powerful escort of cruisers was provided. As they formed up on leaving Albany, *Omrah* took her place as number nine in the starboard column. The voyage was not without incident and, eight days out of Albany, one of the

Left Omrah *at sea. She had a service speed of 18 knots* (P&O).

Right *The magnificent splendour of the first class dining saloon* (National Maritime Museum).

Right Omrah's *first class drawing room* (National Maritime Museum).

Omrah's *second class smoking room* (National Maritime Museum).

escorts, HMAS *Sydney*, destroyed the *Emden*, making the Indian Ocean a much safer place. When the convoy arrived in Colombo the German prisoners were put aboard several of the troop transports, and two German officers together with 40 sailors were allocated to *Omrah* for the passage to Egypt. From Colombo the convoy sailed west for Suez, where both the Australian troops and German prisoners were disembarked, the Germans being transferred to HMS *Hampshire*. (She was lost in 1916 with Lord Kitchener on board.)

From Egypt *Omrah* proceeded to England and then returned to Australia where, on February 10 1915, she was discharged from government service as a troop transport and handed back to her owners. For almost two years she and the *Osterley* maintained some semblance of the Orient Line service and she left London for her last Orient Line voyage to Australia on November 3 1916.

Then, in January 1917, she was once again taken into government service as a troop transport when she conveyed Australian reinforcements, consisting of 7 officers and 730 men, from Sydney to England. In April 1917 she came under the government's Liner Requisition Scheme, but she continued to run in the Australian trade carrying government passengers, troops and cargo. In May 1917, while serving in this capacity, she carried 1,100 British troops from England to South Africa, then sailed on to Sydney, returning with 323 Australian officers and men. Later that year, in October, she took 1,000 British troops from England to Bombay via Cape Town, and from India she went to Egypt with 1,100 Indian troops. She was to remain in the Mediterranean Sea for the remainder of her career, and during this seven-month period she was to carry German and Turkish PoWs, the latter having been captured at Kut El Amara. She conveyed Greek and Armenian refugees as well as Allied troops. Between January 1918 and her sinking four months later she carried 500 officers and 4,000 men between Egypt, Taranto and Marseilles. During this time the Allies were making every effort to reinforce the Western Front in France and Belgium, at the expense of other theatres of war, and *Omrah*, along with other troop transports, was engaged in an attempt to fulfil this commitment.

At the end of April 1918 she, along with six other troop transports which included P&O's *Malwa* and *Kaiser-I-Hind*, embarked British troops of the 52nd and 74th Divisions at Alexandria and on May 1 that year sailed for Marseilles. The convoy arrived at the port safely and the troops were disembarked, after which, on May 10, the ships left once again for Alexandria. They were now empty of troops, but *Omrah* was carrying mail from Australians stationed in France.

All went well for the first day at sea, but at 6.30 am on May 12 1918, when the convoy was some 40 miles south-west of Cape Spartivento in Sardinia, disaster struck. The German submarine *UB 52* fired one torpedo, which the liner *Indarra* managed to avoid. The missile continued on its deadly way and slammed into the port side of *Omrah*, forward of the bridge between one and two hatches. There was a terrific explosion and a volume of water and sand, together with the hatch covers, split wood and glass, rose high in the air and descended on the boat deck and bridge. Almost immediately she went down by the head until the forward section of the main deck was under water. On examination it was found that two holds were flooded and another was rapidly filling. In addition to this, sections of the ship were on fire and great efforts were made to extinguish it, but without success. While this work was in progress the vessel suddenly lurched heavily to port and orders were given to abandon ship. This was carried out successfully and the survivors were taken on board an escorting destroyer and subsequently landed at Gibraltar. Just over two hours after she had been hit by the torpedo, at 8.50 am, *Omrah* rolled over onto her port side and took the final plunge, leaving behind a great circle of floating debris. One of her trimmers was killed and one was badly injured. The Orient Line was eventually paid £198,571 by the government as compensation. As for the German submarine *UB 52*, she herself was torpedoed and sunk later that year by the British submarine *H4*, in the Straits of Otranto.

Technical data
Gross tonnage: 8,130
Net tonnage: 4,419
Length overall: 490 ft 7 in (149.53 m)
Breadth: 56 ft 7 in (17.25 m)
Depth: 26 ft (7.92 m)
Main engines: Twin screw, two triple-expansion engines, 9,200 ihp, 18 knots
Boilers: Coal-fired, steam pressure 180 psi
Passengers: First and Second class 350, Third class 500

Orontes 1902

The Orient Line's first ship to be built after the turn of the century was the *Orontes*, and her keel was laid in 1901 at the Govan yard of the Fairfield Shipbuilding and Engineering Company Ltd of Glasgow. She was to replace the ageing *Cuzco*, and she was in fact an enlarged and improved version of the *Omrah*. The new vessel was named after the river in Syria which flows near the ancient city of Antioch, and the launching ceremony took place at just after 2 pm on Saturday May 10 1902, her sponsor being the daughter of an Orient Line manager, Mr Thomas Lane Devitt. Large crowds had gathered inside the yard and on the opposite bank to watch the launching and afterwards the Fairfield Company entertained about 250 guests in the company's drawing office, where the toast was 'Success to the *Orontes*'.

She was a vessel of 9,023 gross tons with an overall length of 513 ft and was the first Orient liner to be fitted with quadruple-expansion engines. She had six decks, from the boat deck down to the orlop deck, with accommodation for 323 first and second class passengers berthed on the main and upper decks and 320 third class passengers housed on the lower deck. The first class drawing room and smoking room were on the promenade deck. The former was panelled in bleached Italian walnut and satinwood, and the ceiling had white rafters and interspaces of white painted wood, forming panels on which was stencilled a design of stems and leaves in purple and green. The sofas and upholstery as well as the curtains were of silk brocade in blues and greens. The floor was laid with eastern carpets and there was a grand piano in a specially designed case of bleached Spanish mahogany. The smoking room had a floor area of 700 sq ft, with seats and settees grouped around small tables, 'where reading and card playing can be carried out in good light'. Between the two rooms were the main foyer and grand staircase down to the dining saloon. Both the foyer and staircase were very spacious with natural daylight coming through from a skylight on the boat deck above. The first class dining saloon was situated one flight down on the upper deck and seated 97 passengers. The general scheme of decoration in the saloon was mahogany with ebony moulded panels and pilasters of Coromandel wood, inlaid with devices in mother-of-pearl and green shell. The centre of the ceiling rose to a dome through the promenade deck and was fitted with stained glass.

The second class saloon was at the after end of the main deck and had seats for 126 passengers. Outside in the foyer the staircase led up to the promenade deck where the lounge and smoking room were situated, as well as a library which was shared by both first and second class passengers. The first saloon passengers had the use of most of the promenade deck and boat deck, while the after section of both decks was given over to the second saloon passengers.

The main propulsion machinery consisted of

Above Orontes *made her maiden voyage to Australia in October 1902. She is seen here at Sydney* (P&O).

Below Orontes *moored off Gravesend* (P&O).

two sets of four-cylinder, four-crank, quadruple-expansion engines, driving twin shafts. The propellers each had four blades of manganese bronze, the boss being of steel. Steam was provided by two double-ended and four single-ended multi-tubular marine boilers working on forced draught. The double-ended boilers each had eight furnaces and the single-ended four furnaces, making a total of 32 furnaces. The boilers had a working steam pressure of 215 psi. The whole arrangement developed 10,000 ihp and gave *Orontes* a service speed of 18 knots.

The new vessel ran her official trials in the Firth of Clyde on Monday September 9 1902. Leaving the Tail of the Bank, the *Orontes* was run over the measured mile at Skelmorlie for a series of progressive trials, and she worked up to a speed of 18.18 knots. On completion of the mile trials, a second test of four runs between the Cloch and Cumbrae lights was carried out at full speed, and when these were successfully completed, she then underwent continuous steaming for 12 hours at full speed. All the trials were carried out to the satisfaction of the managers of the Orient Line, and *Orontes* returned to the Tail of the Bank early the next morning, September 10. She was officially handed over to the owners on Thursday September 12 1902, and the following day she embarked a number of invited guests for the voyage down to Tilbury. One of these guests recalls the day thus: 'Arriving at Gourock Pier, we saw the new ship off the Tail of the Bank, looking bright and graceful, aglow with electric light, which has been fitted throughout. In a few minutes we were on board, assigned to our Bibby cabins and Hoskins berths; and betimes we were summoned by bugle notes to dinner, which was accompanied by good music.' And so 48 hours later, after a pleasant cruise, the *Orontes,* 'the last word in naval architecture and engineering', arrived in Tilbury.

Orontes sailed from London on her maiden voyage to Brisbane on Thursday October 24 1902, and she soon earned a reputation for comfort and steadiness. In 1904 she received an armed merchant cruiser subsidy from the Admiralty, and, of course, she had always been on their list of vessels suitable for conversion to armed cruisers. Like other Orient ships it was calculated that she would be able to stay at sea for about six months at moderate cruising speeds without re-coaling. Over the next 12 years *Orontes* made 53 round voyages on the Australian run without any serious incident. Among her distinguished passengers were the Australian cricket team under their captain M. A. Noble, travelling to the UK in March 1909 to defend the Ashes. Five years later on June 19 1914 she left London for another round voyage.

When war broke out, *Orontes* was in Australia and she returned to London in late September that year. Although she had received the Admiralty subsidy she was not in fact taken up by them, and she was left on the mail run. Two years later she was finally requisitioned by the government, but as a troopship, a role she was to keep for the remainder of the war. During her first year as a troop transport she was employed carrying British troops to South Africa and the Middle East and Australian troops to the Middle East. In August 1917 she came under the Liner Requisitioning Scheme on the North Atlantic shuttle service, and she ran between Liverpool and New York for the remainder of the war. In late September 1918 she was one of 12 liners which made up the convoy HX50 from New York to Liverpool, sailing in atrocious weather conditions. Towards the end of the voyage, the other Orient ship in the convoy, *Otranto,* was wrecked off Islay. In December 1918, with the war over, *Orontes* was employed to carry invalided Australian soldiers from convalescent camps in England and South Africa back home. These shattered men were the same troops who had been transported fit and healthy in those earlier years of the war. In late June 1919 *Orontes* finally completed this task and left Australia for the last time as a troop transport.

After a period under refit, she returned to the Australian mail run on October 25 1919, when she left Tilbury for Brisbane. Although she was less than 20 years old, sadly her career was drawing to a close. She made only five post-war round voyages to Australia, and assisted the company in those first few years after the end of the war when there was a desperate shortage of shipping. On February 19 1921 she sailed for Brisbane on her final Orient Line voyage, returning to London in June that year. Her war service as a troop transport had taken its toll and she was not up to the standard of other ships of the line. In order to bring her up to scratch an extensive refit would have been needed, and as this was considered uneconomic she was laid up off Southend with a seemingly bleak future ahead of her.

Eight months later, on February 16 1922, the situation appeared to look more hopeful when the British World Trade Exhibition Company took out an option to purchase *Orontes*. It was their intention to use her as a floating exhibition centre for British industrial products in a world tour, and she was renamed *British Trade*. She left the Thames for the last time bound for Hull where she was to be converted. But the company went bankrupt and the project failed, so the vessel reverted to Orient Line ownership and her original name of *Orontes*. She remained laid up in Hull for a time before she was moved to Gareloch and then, in 1926, she was finally sold to shipbreakers.

Technical data
Gross tonnage: 9,028
Net tonnage: 4,622
Length overall: 513 ft 7 in (156.54 m)
Breadth: 58 ft 2 in (17.73 m)
Depth: 34 ft 5 in (10.49 m)
Main engines: Twin screw, two sets of quadruple-expansion engines, 10,000 ihp, 18 knots
Boilers: Coal-fired, steam pressure 215 psi.
Passengers: First and Second class 320, Third class 323

Orsova 1909

In 1909 the Orient Line received five ships, all of over 12,000 gross tons, and designed to maintain the company's place on the Australian mail run following the withdrawal of their partners, the Royal Mail Steam Navigation Company. *Orsova* was the first of these vessels and her keel was laid in early 1908 at John Brown and Company's Clydebank yard. She was launched on Saturday November 7 1908 by Mrs R. Muirhead-Collins, the wife of the Australian Commonwealth representative in London. The new liner's name was taken from a small town and fortress on the Danube, which was in those days Hungary's southern outpost. For many years the rapids near the town, known as 'The Iron Gate', were a barrier to shipping and, with this in mind, *Orsova's* badge was in fact an iron watergate.

At that time there was never any doubt that a shipbuilding order placed in such a prestigious yard as John Brown & Co would be delivered on schedule, and six months after the launch she was ready to undertake her trials on the Clyde. She was handed over to the Orient Line on Thursday May 20 1909 at Tilbury, having been subjected to speed and consumption trials on the voyage down from the north.

Orsova's gross tonnage was 12,036. She was a schooner rigged with a straight stem and an elliptical stern and she wore the traditional Orient colours of black hull and white upperworks, with two buff-coloured funnels. She had berths for 288 first, 128 second class, and about 700 third and steerage class passengers, who were accommodated on six decks from 'A', or the boat deck, downwards. The first class passengers were placed amidships and the boat deck formed a spacious promenade for them, with a deck-house forward which contained the captain's and officers' cabins. The promenade or 'B' deck housed the first class public rooms and staterooms. At the forward end was the lounge and also the library and music room, which was decorated in the style of Louis XVI. The wall panelling was sycamore with a silver-grey tint, and the whole room was enhanced by the semi-circular bookcase which formed part of the panelling. The carpet was a rose colour, as was the upholstery of the furniture, which gave the room a handsome effect. Aft of this deck-house were the one- and two-berth staterooms, and grouped around the funnel casings were the bathrooms. At the after end of this deck was the smoking room where, according to a contemporary description 'the gentlemen may smoke without the society of the fairer sex'. The room was abaft the engine room skylight and was elegantly arranged in bays suitable for 'card parties'. Immediately aft of the smoking room was an open-air lounge, 'to further increase the comfort and facilities for those who wish to pass the time in smoking'.

The forward part of 'C', or the shelter deck, formed the forecastle, and amidships were more first class cabins. Abaft the engine casings on this deck were the second class music room and smoking room and right aft were these same

Above Orsova *was schooner-rigged with a straight stem and an elliptical stern* (A. Duncan).

Right *The second class smoking room,* Orsova (P&O).

Right *The third class smoking room,* Orsova (P&O).

facilities for the enjoyment of the third class passengers. On the upper deck, or 'D' deck, were the dining saloons for both first and second class passengers, with the galleys and pantries. The first class saloon was panelled in white and the furniture was mahogany, which together with a rich red carpet gave the room warmth. Up above the saloon a spacious well and gallery went all the way round, the railing of which was wrought iron decorated with ornaments of bronze gilt. At the after end of the gallery a charming effect was obtained by the use of mirrors which reflected the whole decorative scheme. Down below in the boiler and engine rooms *Orsova* was quite conventional for her day, with twin screws driven by quadruple-expansion engines, and her coal-fired boilers providing steam at 215 psi. The machinery fitted developed 14,000 ihp, and gave her a service speed of 18 knots, which was well in excess of the 17½ knots required by the builder's contract.

On the afternoon of Saturday May 29 1909, she left the Thames on a Whitsun cruise to Plymouth, with a large number of Orient Line guests on board, including *Orsova's* sponsor and her husband, Captain R. Muirhead-Collins RN. The new liner steamed directly to Plymouth, arriving there 24 hours after leaving London and anchoring overnight. Early on Monday morning she left for Cowes, which was reached shortly after midday, and in the afternoon she sailed for Tilbury. She encountered thick fog on this last leg, and speed was much reduced, but she still managed to arrive in Tilbury early in the morning of June 1 1909. Just over three weeks later, on June 25, *Orsova* left London for her first voyage to Brisbane via Gibraltar, Marseilles, Naples, Port Said, Colombo, Fremantle, Adelaide, Melbourne and Sydney. She was commanded by Captain Ruthven, and she arrived at her destination in mid-August that year. She introduced stiff competition for the well-established P&O Line, for she was some 1,200 tons larger and marginally faster than P&O's 'M' class ships. Early in her career she was given two masts and Admiralty funnel cowls, setting a precedent for all the company's ships through to the *Orontes* of 1929.

The first of the 1909 12,000-tonners, the Orsova (P&O).

Just two years after that maiden voyage, in June 1911, *Orsova* was on another outward trip to Australia. Ten days before she reached Melbourne, a baby girl was born on board, and the grateful parents named her after the ship's nurse, purser and captain, calling the child Orsova Nina Ingram Staunton Hodgson. It was to be 25 years before the little girl saw *Orsova* again.

Orsova made her final pre-war voyage to Australia on February 13 1914, and she was back in Tilbury by the middle of May that year. Just three weeks later on June 6 she left London once again, and when war broke out she was in Melbourne. The events in Europe did not affect *Orsova's* routine immediately and she made two more scheduled mail voyages to Brisbane, leaving London on September 25 1914 and January 15 1915. However, on her return to Tilbury on April 15 1915 she was requisitioned by the government and fitted out as a troop transport for the conveyance of troops to the Mediterranean. On May 2 that year she sailed from Devonport with 1,300 British officers and men, calling at Malta, Alexandria and Mudros. After this voyage she resumed the Australian service, and on her arrival in Sydney she was transferred to the Australian government for the conveyance of that country's reinforcements to Egypt and Europe. She sailed from Sydney on July 14 1915 as Australian transport A67, and she arrived in London just over one month later on August 25. Two more regular Australian voyages on government service followed, with calls at Mudros and Basra on the outward leg. On the homeward lap of her third trip to the antipodes she carried troops to the Persian Gulf and then returned to London via Cape Town. Between July 1915 and March 1917 she carried 6,500 Australian reinforcements and 9,000 British troops.

On Monday March 14 1917 *Orsova* was homeward bound from Australia, and in the English Channel off Eddystone, when at 4.50 am she was torpedoed by a German submarine. The missile penetrated the port side of the engine room killing six of the crew on duty there. However, the vessel herself was not disabled and with the skilful handling of Captain A. J. Coad RNR, her master, she was successfully beached in Cawsand Bay, just inside Plymouth Sound, at 9 pm the same day. Some days later naval tugs towed her round to the Naval Dockyard at Devonport where temporary repairs were carried out. From there she sailed to Liverpool for permanent repairs, but due to urgent naval construction at the shipyard the work became very protracted and in fact was not completed until September 1918, only two months before the end of the war. As soon as she was fit for service *Orsova* came under the Liner Requisition Scheme and she was allocated to the North Atlantic to assist with the conveyance of US troops and essential cargoes from North America to Europe. She was employed in this capacity for three months until the end of 1918, during which time she carried 1,700 American soldiers across the Atlantic. At the end of December 1918 *Orsova* was released from this role and transferred to the Australian route, but still on government service. She made two round voyages and transported 2,850 troops and personnel to Australia for demobilization. On May 12 1919 she returned to Tilbury from Sydney and was then released from government service. She was one of the three 1909 sisters to survive the war, but it had been a very close thing.

It was November 1919 before *Orsova* was fitted out once again for her peacetime role in the Australian mail service, and originally she was scheduled to sail for Brisbane on November 14 that year. In the event this sailing was cancelled, but she left eight days later on November 22. On her sixth round voyage to Australia, when *Orsova* was in Adelaide, the contents of the ship's safe were stolen—some £1,500. The offender, as it transpired, was an assistant purser on board, and all the money was later recovered from lodgings he had ashore.

Orsova's post-war career lasted for nearly 17 years, and by June 1936 she was 27 years old and very outdated, being the last of the Orient Line's coal burners. The five vessels of the 1920s rebuilding programme were in service, as was the *Orion*. In the following year the new *Orcades* would be ready to take her place in the mail service, and the time had come to dispose of the now elderly *Orsova*. She left London on her 70th voyage to Brisbane on June 20 1936, commanded by Captain L. F. Hubbard. On August 6 that year she left Brisbane for the last time, flying a 200 ft paying-off pennant. She was given a rousing send-off from all the Australian ports, and in Melbourne on August 17, Miss Orsova Nina Hodgson, who had been born on board 25 years earlier, and her mother, were guests of the captain at a farewell dinner before the liner sailed from the port for ever. After leaving Toulon her speed was regulated to ensure an early morning arrival in London, the company instructions to the master being, 'You should not arrive at Tilbury after 4 am on September 24 1936'.

Orsova lay at Tilbury for a week before she left Bo'ness on the Firth of Forth, her engine room stanchions still bearing indentations caused when she was torpedoed in 1917. She had been sold to Douglas & Ramsey of Bo'ness for breaking up.

In her 27 years *Orsova* had steamed nearly two million miles at an average speed of 15.3 knots, and had carried 14,000 tons of mail without ever being late. She had also carried 70,000 passengers, not counting troops, and 300,000 tons of cargo.

Technical data

Gross tonnage: 12,036
Net tonnage: 6,831
Length overall: 536 ft 3 in (163.45 m)
Breadth: 63 ft 3 in (19.29 m)
Depth: 34 ft 3 in (10.45 m)
Main engines: Twin screw, two sets of quadruple-expansion engines, 14,000 ihp, 18 knots
Boilers: Coal-fired, steam pressure 215 psi
Passengers: First class 288, Second class 128, Third and steerage class 700

Orsova *passing under Sydney Harbour Bridge later in her career* (P&O).

Otway 1909

The second of the 12,000-tonners to enter service in 1909 was the *Otway*. She had been built by the Fairfield Shipbuilding Company of Glasgow, and she was launched on Saturday November 21 1908. The naming ceremony was performed by Mrs Frederick Green, wife of one of the managers of the line, and the ship herself was named after the Cape on the coast of Victoria, south-west of Melbourne. She was powered by two sets of quadruple-expansion engines developing some 14,000 ihp which, driving her twin screws, gave her a speed of 18 knots. She started service with two classes of accommodation, with berths for 400 first and 700 third class passengers, but 115 second class berths were later provided by down-grading some of the first class cabins.

Just over six months after the launching ceremony on May 29 1909, *Otway* was handed over to her owners, and four days later on Wednesday June 21 1909 she arrived in Tilbury. She left the port on her maiden voyage to Brisbane in the following month on July 9, taking the traditional route via the Mediterranean and Suez. Her career prior to the First World War was largely uneventful, and she made 17 mail voyages to Australia. Her last peacetime voyage started on April 10 1914, and by mid-July that year she was back in London.

Two days before she was due to sail once more, and with the declaration of war with Germany only six days away, the Admiralty requested *Otway* to be chartered as a hospital ship. But it was only a request, and the Orient Line turned it down outright, saying that she was obligated to the Australian government and was about to sail with the mails for that country. This was accepted by the authorities and *Otway* left Tilbury on schedule at noon on Friday July 31 1914, just four days before the lights went out all over Europe. She arrived in Gibraltar at 9 am on that fateful day, August 4 1914, and she should have departed after a stay of only a few hours. However, soon after her arrival her master was informed that immediate departure was out of the question and that no passengers were allowed ashore. By this time the government in London had delivered the ultimatum to the German government warning them to respect Belgian neutrality and, as *Otway* lay at anchor in Algeciras Bay, rumour and speculation were rife on board. The following day the Governor of Gibraltar made a proclamation regarding the declaration of war, and of course it soon became the chief topic of conversation on board. As *Otway* lay awaiting orders, the rumours abounded. How long would the war last? Would it be over by Christmas? How would it affect *Otway*'s movements? The most favoured story was that the ship was to be re-routed via Cape Town, and that German cruisers were lying in wait off the Canaries. After six days most of the speculation was ended when *Otway* was released by the Admiralty and she was left to continue her voyage via Toulon, Naples, Taranto and Port Said. However, things were not the same on

board, as all deck lights were put out at night and deadlights covered all the portholes. She made a brief call off Malta on August 12, and three days later she arrived in Port Said where the passengers were allowed ashore for the first time. She arrived at Fremantle on September 5 1914, and later that month she made her final visits to Sydney and Brisbane.

Otway arrived back in Tilbury on November 8 1914, and two days later, at 11 pm on November 10, a telegram was received at the Orient Line offices requisitioning her for use by the Admiralty as an armed merchant cruiser. Work on the conversion began at Tilbury Docks two days later and she was scheduled to be commissioned into the Royal Navy on November 19. However, when the day came she was far from ready, as work on the gun positions had not been finished and no searchlights had been received. But more importantly, there was no captain or senior lieutenant on board, so the ceremony was deferred. On November 23, with her guns fitted and with coaling completed, *Otway* was commissioned with Captain E. L. Booty RN as her commanding officer, and all that remained to be done was to strip the ornate woodwork from her foyers and public rooms.

Otway left Tilbury on November 29 1914, to join the 10th Cruiser Squadron and the Northern Patrol. Her duty was to enforce the blockade of the German ports, and the patrolling ground was approximately the area between the Shetlands and Skerries to Norway, south of Iceland and north of minefields laid by the enemy in the North Sea. She was armed with eight 6-in guns, which were situated on 'C' deck, four in the forward section and four aft. She also had two 6-lb guns which were fitted on 'B' deck forward. After several days in Birkenhead, *Otway* left for the icy northern waters on December 16 1914. During the period January to December 1915 the squadron patrolled an area of 220,000 square miles and intercepted 3,018 vessels, of which 677 were carrying contraband and were ordered into British ports. There is no doubt that right from the start *Otway* was one of the busiest ships of the squadron. When she first arrived in the area, she and the *Teutonic* were the only ships on the patrol, and with such a large area virtually unguarded, a German collier managed to pass through to Germany with survivors of the *Karlsruhe* on board. On March 10 1915 *Otway* intercepted the 10,000-ton Norwegian-America liner *Bergensfjord*. She had been a particular problem to the patrol by carrying German nationals and doing her best to evade the patrol line. But now

Left Otway *was launched on November 21 1908 and she entered service in June 1909* (National Maritime Museum).

Right Otway *was requisitioned as an armed merchant cruiser during the First World War, and she was sunk in July 1917* (P&O).

a prize crew was put on board and she was sent into Kirkwall. Apparently there were 17 Germans of military age on board but they avoided capture as they had false Norwegian passports.

By October 1915 *Otway* had intercepted 14 vessels which she had sent into port with armed guards on board. On June 11 that year she suffered a fire on board in the blacksmith's shop, and in the following month she underwent a short refit at Birkenhead. While there, on September 28, another fire broke out, this time on the navigating bridge, but fortunately there was only minor damage. On October 16 1915 she was sent to assist in salvaging the Norwegian ship, SS *Corona*. The *Corona* had been intercepted by the AMC HMS *Hildebrand*, but she was found to have sprung a serious leak and her crew were taken aboard the *Hildebrand*, which took her in tow. *Otway* stayed with the two ships for some hours before the *Corona* became a dangerous derelict and the tow-line was parted. The *Corona* was then sunk by gunfire from HMS *Hilary*.

On January 3 1916, *Otway* was entering Birkenhead again for another short refit when she collided with the SS *Dominion* at anchor, resulting in damage to *Otway*'s port quarter. She went into drydock the same day and stayed there for two weeks, before leaving the port towards the end of the month for the patrol line once again. By the end of October that year she had intercepted 21 vessels and sent them under guard to Lerwick or Kirkwall. On November 18 1916 *Otway* was in a position 59°18′N, 11°58′W, when she intercepted the British ship SS *Older* flying the Norwegian flag. The signals which the latter vessel gave in reply to *Otway* made Captain Booty suspicious and he sent a boarding party across to her. To their surprise they found a German prize crew on board who had been taking her to Kiel. Apparently she had sailed from Newport, South Wales on November 11 bound for Gibraltar with a cargo of coal. Two days later she was captured by a U-boat in the Western Approaches. The same submarine had also sunk the Italian steamship *Lela* bound from Glasgow to Genoa, and had taken her crew of 25 on board. They were then transferred to the *Older*, along with the eight-man crew of the British trawler *Hatsuse* which was sunk on November 14. Fortunately the U-boat and *Older* had parted company on November 17, and the next day the latter vessel was intercepted by *Otway*. When *Otway*'s boarding party embarked on *Older* the German prize crew, which consisted of an officer, an NCO and seven ratings, claimed they had set bombs which were timed to explode in half an hour. The crew of the *Older,* the 25 Italians, the eight-man crew of the *Hatsuse* and the nine Germans were taken on board *Otway,* which then steamed round the *Older* all night. Next morning, with the collier still intact, her master and crew, and the crews of the *Lela* and *Hatsuse,* were sent back to the *Older* with an armed guard for her journey to Stornaway, where she arrived on November 21. The German prisoners remained on board *Otway* and were eventually landed at Loch Ewe on November 26. Ironically the SS *Older* was sunk by a U-boat soon after she left Stornaway to continue her voyage.

Towards the end of January 1917 *Otway* went into Birkenhead again, and in early February Commodore Booty was relieved by Commodore P. H. Colomb RN, who was to command her for the few brief months she had left. She left the Mersey once again for northern waters in mid-February 1917, but she was soon back again for a week for repairs to her machinery. On April 7 that year she was visited while at sea by Vice-Admiral Sir Reginald Tupper, who was in command of the 10th Cruiser Squadron. Two days later on April 9 she came across the Norwegian steamer *Augusta* which was leaking badly and in trouble. The crew were taken off and *Otway* circled the ship all night. The following day an engineering officer and a party of stokers boarded the *Augusta* in an attempt to raise steam, but without success. *Otway* continued to stand by the Norwegian vessel, but on April 11 she finally foundered. On the following day the Norwegian crew were transferred to the SS *Granfos*, for a passage home.

In the latter half of April 1917 she was in drydock at Liverpool once more, before leaving again for her patrol at the end of the month. On May 21 1917, whilst at Loch Ewe, she was involved in a minor collision with the collier SS *Simeon,* but fortunately once again she sustained only minor damage. On June 13 1917 she was back in Liverpool for the last time. Her visit lasted ten days before she sailed on what was to be her final patrol in northern waters.

In early July 1917 the German minelaying submarine *UC-49* left Germany on a mission to lay three separate fields of mines around the Orkney Islands. At 10 pm on July 22 1917 the *Otway* was in the Atlantic, north-west of the Isle of St Kilda, on patrol line 'D', when she was sighted and torpedoed by *UC-49.* The torpedo hit *Otway* on the port side under the funnels, causing a considerable amount of destruction. Ten ratings, who were all in the third class saloon, were killed outright in the explosion, and the vessel's port shaft was broken. It soon became obvious that *Otway* was sinking fast and the remainder of her crew were got safely away in the boats. The ship gradually turned on her end with the forward section remaining out of the water. *Otway*'s Chief Officer, who was in charge of a large lifeboat, took several other boats in tow, one of them with several badly scalded engineers and stokers on board. The submarine surfaced and was in the act of sighting the boats with searchlights, presumably with the object of taking any officers prisoner. Then fate intervened, when one of *Otway*'s forward guns on the now rapidly sinking ship fired of its own accord. In the darkness of the night this obviously frightened the U-boat captain and he submerged and was not seen again. *Otway* herself sank by the stern before midnight and the survivors were subsequently rescued by destroyers.

Otway was the third ship of the 10th Cruiser Squadron to be lost. The last word on the subject was contained in a brief letter from the Admiralty to the Orient Line management which said, 'HMS *Otway* is to be regarded as formally paid off on the 4th August 1917'.

Technical data
Gross tonnage: 12,077
Net tonnage: 6,690
Length overall: 535 ft 10 in (163.32 m)
Breadth: 63 ft 2 in (19.25 m)
Depth: 34 ft 2 in (10.41 m)
Main engines: Twin screw, two sets of quadruple-expansion engines, 14,000 ihp, 18 knots
Boilers: Coal-fired, steam pressure 215 psi
Passengers: First class 400, Third class 700; 115 second class provided prior to August 1914 by downgrading from first class

Osterley 1909

The third of the 1909 sisters to enter service with the Orient Line was the *Osterley*, and she was built by the London & Glasgow Iron Shipbuilding Company Ltd of Govan. The launch was scheduled to take place at noon on Thursday January 21 1909, which turned out to be a bitterly cold day with a severe frost. The ceremony was performed by Lady Jersey who named the ship after her home, Osterley Park, in Middlesex. (The house is now a National Trust property and lies between the A4 and M4 on the route from London to Heathrow Airport.) However, after sliding just 40 ft down the slipway, *Osterley* stuck fast and despite great efforts she would move no further. It seemed that the cold had solidifed the tallow on the launching ways, and as the tide was receding fast the whole operation was postponed. Over the next few days the sliding ways were removed and fresh grease was applied. Finally, five days later on the afternoon of Tuesday January 27 1909, *Osterley* took to the waters of the River Clyde. Five months later, on June 23, she had completed her trials and arrived at Tilbury.

The accommodation for 274 first, 126 second and 750 third class emigrants followed generally the same arrangement as the first two Clyde-built ships of the class and embodied the long experience acquired by the managers of the line. A special feature was the number of single- and two-berth cabins, and also the decoration of the staterooms and public rooms. The first class dining saloon, which seated 150 passengers at small tables instead of the customary long refectory-style ones, was furnished in Austrian oak, relieved with burnished gold. On the promenade deck the lounge was decorated in white and green, with a decorative skylight fitted into the ceiling. Surrounding the companion-way, which opened into the lounge, was an oil painting of a Venetian scene, and with its profusion of plants the lounge proved to be a most popular room. The library abaft the companion-way and also on the promenade deck was in white and blue with white plaques, relieved with gold. Aft on the same deck was the smoking room, in Georgian style, the wood used here being walnut with bands and mouldings of rosewood, giving a simple charm to walls, ceiling and furniture. The whole was topped by a central decorated glass dome. In all five vessels of the class the third class accommodation was greatly improved and the 'open steerage berths' were abolished. All the third class passengers had much more privacy in enclosed cabins with six berths being the maximum.

Osterley was a twin-screw vessel of 12,129 gross tons, powered by quadruple-expansion engines which developed 14,000 ihp and gave her a service speed of 18 knots. In fact, on her progressive speed trials on the measured mile at Skelmorlie she had achieved a speed of 18.76 knots. On her 24-hour coal consumption trials she had steamed 390 miles and consumed 105 tons of coal—well within the requirements of the contract.

Osterley *was named after her sponsor's residence, Osterley Park in Middlesex* (Orient Line).

Osterley left Gravesend Reach for her maiden voyage on August 6 1909, a hot summer's day, and she arrived in Australia in the middle of September. At the beginning of October 1909 she left Sydney on her return to London. She passed the island of Perim, at the entrance to the Red Sea, at 9 pm on October 27 and three days later she was at Suez. After an overnight transit of the Suez Canal she moored at Port Said, along with another ship in the same convoy, the Russian steamer *Roman*. The *Roman* was on a voyage from the eastern port of Vladivostok to Riga in Latvia, and she was due to leave Port Said ahead of *Osterley*. As she manoeuvred to leave the port she collided with *Osterley*, which was still at her moorings, causing damage to her stem which immediately flooded the forepeak. *Osterley* was only very slightly damaged, and at 5 pm on November 1 1909, as divers struggled to plug the holes in the other vessel's bows, she left the port for Naples. She arrived in London without any further incident on Saturday November 13 that year, and sailed on her second round voyage to Brisbane on Christmas Eve 1909. In June 1911 *Osterley* took part in the Coronation Naval Review for King George V. For her passengers it was a three-day event with fares starting at eight guineas. She was fully booked for this mini-cruise, and passengers embarked at Southampton on June 23. The next two days were spent at Spithead, and for the review itself *Osterley* anchored in line 'H', opposite Ryde Pier. On the evening of June 25 she left the Solent for Tilbury and arrived there early the next morning when her passengers disembarked.

In April 1917 *Osterley* came under the Liner Requisition Scheme, and so was on charter to the government permanently. For the remainder of the year she was left on the Australian run and she conveyed 3,000 British troops from the UK to South Africa and 1,246 Australian reinforcements to England. In January 1918 *Osterley* was employed on a triangular service between Australia, Egypt and South Africa. She conveyed British troops from Egypt to Mombasa, and afterwards she went on to Cape Town where she

The third class dining saloon, Osterley (P&O).

embarked 1,500 wounded Australian troops and returned them to their homeland. In July 1918 she was transferred to the North Atlantic for the transport of US troops and essential cargo to Europe. Between then and the end of the war she carried over 3,000 'doughboys' from New York to Liverpool. When Armistice Day came *Osterley* was in New York and her ship's company celebrated the occasion in the city. She remained on the North Atlantic until the end of the year when she was released from requisition, but then was immediately chartered by the government for one Australian voyage. After embarking 977 Australian troops and their dependants, *Osterley* sailed from Liverpool to Brisbane on January 10 1919. The outward passage was made by way of Cape Town, and her passengers received a rapturous welcome back in their home country.

Osterley arrived back in London in May 1919 and she was finally released by the government, after which the company sent her into dock for reconditioning. It was September 27 1919 before she made her first peacetime sailing from London to Brisbane, once more in the Orient Line mail service. She soon settled back into her old routine and in September 1920 she carried the MCC team, which included Jack Hobbs, to Sydney. On February 18 1922 she made one round passage to Brisbane and on her return to London she was chartered to a US tourist agency for summer cruises from New York to the Norwegian fjords and the northern capitals. The charter lasted from June to September 1922, and it was October that year before she resumed her place in the mail service.

In 1924 *Osterley* was stranded for a time in a serious position in the Brisbane River. However, her cargo was unloaded into lighters and, with the assistance of tugs, she was refloated with no damage. In November 1928, during a severe storm with gale-force winds, *Osterley* answered the SOS call of the German barque *Pommern* in the Indian Ocean. It took *Osterley* one and a half hours to turn and she reached the barque after three hours to find a tug in attendance and another steamer standing by. The crew of the

Pommern had lashed themselves to the poop rails because of the severity of the weather. The ship's fore and main masts, although steel, had been buckled and were bent over the vessel's side, making it impossible to get alongside. The other steamer in attendance launched one boat which was immediately broken up by the heavy seas, and the rescuers only just managed to save the boat's crew. In the event the tug got a line on board and managed to rescue *Pommern*'s crew. *Osterley* then turned around to continue her voyage and while carrying out the manoeuvre she herself was badly hit by heavy seas, resulting in ladders and skylights being smashed. She reached Australia soon afterwards, but her troubles were not yet over. On Christmas Eve that year she was scheduled to sail from Sydney on her return passage. However, only hours before sailing time, over 100 members of her crew walked off the ship in a protest about the food on the outward journey. Happily the dispute was resolved and *Osterley* left for England.

It was in fact her final voyage, for on her arrival in Tilbury in February 1929 she was withdrawn and laid up. With the new tonnage in service she and *Orvieto* were now surplus to requirements. Just over a year later, in March 1930, *Osterley* was sold for £26,000 to the Scottish shipbreakers, P. & W. Maclellan of Glasgow, and she was broken up on the Clyde 21 years after she first left the river to join the Orient fleet.

Technical data
Gross tonnage: 12,129
Net tonnage: 6,781
Length overall: 535 ft (163.07 m)
Breadth: 63 ft 2 in (19.25 m)
Depth: 34 ft (10.39 m)
Main engines: Twin screw, two sets of quadruple-expansion engines, 14,000 ihp, 18 knots
Boilers: Coal-fired, steam pressure 215 psi
Passengers: First class 274, Second class 126, Third class 750

Osterley *in the Thames off Tilbury* (P&O).

Otranto 1909

Without doubt the most famous Orient liner of the pre-1914 era was the *Otranto*, the fourth of the 1909 sisters. Her fame arose not from her service with the Orient Line, but from her brief and extremely active service with the Royal Navy. She was built by Workman Clark & Co Ltd of Belfast, a company later taken over by Harland & Wolff. The new vessel was named after the fishing town in southern Italy, also the straits between Italy and Albania, and she was to have been launched on March 23 1909, but the proceedings that day came to the same end as *Osterley*'s had just two months previously. *Otranto* slid only 20 ft down the launching way and stuck fast. Despite the pressure of hydraulic jacks she did not move again that day and the ways had to be rebuilt. It seemed that once again frosts had hardened the tallow which was used as lubrication. However, four days later *Otranto* finally took to the water.

With a length of 554 ft and a gross tonnage of 12,124, *Otranto* provided accommodation for 300 first, 140 second and 850 third class passengers. The first class cabins were amidships on three decks, and they included a large number of single-berth rooms with beds rather than bunks. On the shelter deck the 'Bibby' tandem system was used to enable both inner and outer cabins to have the benefit of natural light through portholes in the ship's side. The first class dining saloon on the upper deck catered for 156 passengers at one sitting, at tables which were arranged on the restaurant plan. The lighting was by large patent ventilating ports arranged in pairs, and by a central lighting well. The whole room was panelled in oak which had been bleached to give it a silvery grey colour. The decoration was in the style of Louis XVI, and the main feature was a series of balconies and lounges going up through three decks to a vaulted ceiling. The music room and lounge, which were forward on the promenade deck, were both lofty and spacious rooms, connected by folding glazed doors. The lounge was, of course, the centre of after-dinner entertainment and social conversation, while the music room was 'available for ladies' use only'. The style of both rooms was a tasteful rendering of Georgian decor, and the furniture consisted of reproductions of some of the finest models of the 18th century. A lift running down to the dining saloon foyer was sited in one corner of the lounge. The smoking room was aft on the same deck and was also very spacious, again with panelling in oak relieved by carved patterns in some of the sections. Here a unique effect was obtained from a large wagon roof lit by dormer windows. The seats and chairs were wide and deep and upholstered in hide for optimum comfort. At the after end of the room the doors led out to a sheltered alcove on the deck, fitted with tables and chairs, thus creating what could almost be called an open-air lounge.

The second class accommodation was on the upper and shelter decks. Once again the 'Bibby' tandem system was adopted in the cabins, many of which were two-berth rooms. There was a

Above *The first class lounge,* Otranto (P&O).

Left *The first class drawing room,* Otranto (P&O).

Right Otranto *presented a very handsome yacht-like appearance, being imparted by her schooner rig* (P&O).

promenade provided on the shelter deck, very similar to that given to the first class on the deck above. The second class dining saloon was aft of the first class saloon on the upper deck, and separated from it by the galley. It extended the full width of the ship and seated 150 persons at refectory-style tables. The lighting was effected by a well over the centre of the room and by large round ports in the ship's side. The stairway from the upper deck to the shelter deck above gave access to the foyer and the music room. Again this was a comfortable room, the furniture consisting of settees, chairs and small tables in mahogany, upholstered in leather. There was also a bookcase which contained a wide selection of subjects and authors. Access to the bridge deck was gained by a continuing stairway, at the head of which was the main entrance hall and second class smoke room. The latter was panelled and furnished in oak and leather, with a sofa running round the room. As in the case of the first class smoke room, there was an out-of-doors sheltered alcove abaft, with tables and chairs. One contemporary publication described the second class part of the ship thus: 'The style and finish of the berths and cabins, which is similar to that in the first class, together with the promenade, induces the query as to whether it is worth going first class when such accommodation is provided in the second.'

The third class passenger accommodation was also much better than that in earlier ships. It was situated on the lower, upper and main decks with a promenade space on the boat deck aft. The dining saloon, which seated 200 passengers, was on the lower deck, and on the upper deck was a ladies' room and smoking room.

Like the other ships of the class, *Otranto* was powered by two sets of quadruple-expansion engines, each driving a three-bladed propeller. The boiler installation consisted of four double-ended and two single-ended boilers, designed for a working pressure of 215 psi. The boilers were arranged in two boiler rooms with double funnels of oval section to each group, and with forced-draught fans powered by electric motors.

By the end of June 1909, *Otranto* had been fitted out and she left Belfast on Tuesday June 29, commencing her trials on the Clyde the following day, during which she attained a speed of 18.975 knots. That same afternoon she left the Tail of the Bank for London, and during the

Otranto *was renowned for her cruises in the years before the First World War* (J.K. Byass).

passage she carried out a 24 hours' coal consumption trial. With the ship running at 17 knots for 409 miles, 127 tons of coal were used—well within the contract requirements. She arrived at Tilbury on Friday July 2 1909, and presented a very handsome appearance, her schooner rig giving her a yacht-like look. There were some changes from the earlier Clyde-built ships, in that her superstructure was about four feet higher and her beam was slightly wider. There were also differences in her cargo spaces: three of her hatches were forward of the passenger accommodation, whereas in the Clyde vessels the third hatchway descended through the first class rooms.

It was to be the autumn before *Otranto* made her maiden voyage to Australia, and before that she made a series of five cruises, in conjunction with *Ophir*, to the Norwegian fjords and the northern capitals. Apart from the first cruise which left from Tilbury, the passengers embarked at Immingham. The last of these cruises ended at that port on September 9 1909, and the following day the liner arrived at Tilbury. Exactly four weeks later, on Friday October 1, *Otranto* left London for Brisbane, where she arrived on November 17. It was early January 1910 before the ship arrived back in Tilbury, and she made one more round voyage to Australia that winter before undertaking a 17-night cruise from London into the Mediterranean. Following this cruise she returned to the mail run and made two round voyages that year, arriving back in Tilbury on January 6 1911. Another full voyage to Brisbane followed and then a 20-day Whitsun cruise from London to the Atlantic Isles, which ended on June 16 that year. A week later the managers of the line despatched *Otranto* to the Coronation Naval Review for King George V, which was held at Spithead. Passengers embarked during the morning of Friday June 23 and the liner sailed for the Solent that same afternoon. The review took place the following day and *Otranto* took her place in line 'E' off Alverstoke. On Sunday June 25, *Otranto* left Spithead for Scheveningen in Holland, where her passengers could spend a day at The Hague or Rotterdam, and the mini-cruise ended on Tuesday June 27 at Tilbury. Among the guests on board were the High Commissioner for Australia and several state premiers. For the rest of the summer of 1911 *Otranto* was employed on cruises to the Norwegian fjords, until mid-September when she rejoined the mail service.

Otranto remained on the Australian run during 1912, and on November 12 she left Brisbane for London on her final passage home that year. Unfortunately, in the Indian Ocean she suffered a breakdown in her refrigeration machinery, resulting in a large quantity of her cargo being ruined. Throughout 1913 and for the first half of 1914 *Otranto* remained on the mail service, and between January 1913 and July 1914 she made five round voyages. Her final passage for the Orient Line commenced from Tilbury on April 24 1914 and she arrived in Brisbane on June 8, just over six weeks later.

In Europe the great powers were drawing inexorably towards war; the Archduke Franz Ferdinand of Austria and his consort had been assassinated at Sarajevo on June 28, and a month later Austria declared war on Serbia. On July 29 1914 *Otranto* was between Gibraltar and Plymouth on her homeward journey and on that same day the Admiralty contacted the managers of the Orient Line and requested that both *Otranto* and *Otway* be chartered to them for service as hospital ships. Although it was only six days before Great Britain declared war on Germany, there was obviously no urgency in the request, for the following day the managers sent a reply that stated, '*Otranto* is due in Tilbury from Australia next Saturday (1.8.1914). She is under obligation to the Australian government to sail on Friday August 14 1914 with the mails and she cannot be offered as a hospital ship'. They went on to say that the *Ophir* could sail within ten days and they offered her instead. However, the next telegram to Anderson, Anderson & Co left no choice. It was sent on August 4, the day war broke out, and read thus: 'Urgent & Confidential. *Otranto* is requisitioned under Royal Proclamation for service as armed merchant cruiser. Owners required to supply coal full bunkers engine room and deck stores for four months mens traps and utensils for full complement. Admiralty prepare ship but will require all assistance possible from you also in obtaining engine room complement which will be signed on from mercantile. Capt Hunt RN c/o P&O Tilbury appointed to superintend fitting. Please acknowledge letter follows.' This time the managers could only hand over their ship, and the fitting out for naval service started on the same day.

Exactly a week after she had been requisitioned she was commissioned into the Royal Navy as HMS *Otranto*, and three days later she sailed from London never to return. The story of her voyage south into the Atlantic is perhaps best told by a crew member, Mr G. M. McCarthy, who has left a very graphic account in the Orient Line records at the National Maritime Museum in London. 'After two hours' steaming we arrived at Sheerness, stopping there for three hours in which time we saw submarines, aeroplanes and battleships, making a lovely sight in all.' After a brief stop at Dover they reached Portsmouth, where 'there were several battleships and gunboats near us and their bands were playing as if there wasn't any war on at all.' Eight days after leaving Tilbury *Otranto* arrived at St Vincent in the Cape Verde Islands to coal ship, after which she continued steaming on her south-westerly route. On August 27 she met HMS *Monmouth* and *Glasgow*, the two cruisers she would be attached to until the Battle of Coronel. After patrolling for some days she arrived at the Abrolhos Rocks off the coast of Brazil which was to be a coaling and supply base for the South Atlantic Squadron. For the next few weeks *Otranto* patrolled the coast of South America enforcing the contraband blockade. According to Mr McCarthy, the weather conditions were varying from one extreme to the other: 'For instance one day it would be lovely and the next day it would rain

HMS Otranto *on naval service off the coast of South America* (Imperial War Museum).

as hard as it could and then it would suddenly turn cold. We find it terribly cold at the present moment and the sea is running very high which is making the poor old *Otranto* pitch and roll.' In mid-September *Otranto* joined HMS *Good Hope, Glasgow* and *Monmouth* to search for the German cruiser *Dresden* and the auxiliary *Cap Trafalgar*. One interesting incident happened on September 20 1914, when the four ships were off Montevideo. 'We were taking in stores when a gunboat belonging to the Argentine Republic named the *Buenos Aires* passed us and fired a salute to which our flagship the *Good Hope* responded.'

On October 15 1914 *Otranto* was at Port Legunas in Chile, and after coaling she was leaving the bay when, in the words of Mr McCarthy, 'We hadn't been under steam for ten minutes when all of a sudden the ship gave a mighty jerk and shook like a leaf.' She had struck a rock but fortunately damage was slight, and *Monmouth*'s diver gave her the 'all clear'. At the end of the month *Otranto* called at Port Montt in Chile, where the captain found many of the inhabitants to be of German origin. She left the port at 6 am on Saturday October 31 1914. The following day, at 1.15 pm, she rejoined Admiral Craddock's squadron, and during the afternoon they carried out manoeuvres in a position 36°41'S, 74°12'W, off Coronel.

Late in the afternoon at about 4.30 pm, lookouts on *Otranto* sighted smoke and reported it to the flagship *Good Hope*. It turned out to be coming from Admiral von Spee's powerful fleet of German cruisers, *Scharnhorst, Gneisenau, Dresden, Nürnberg* and *Leipzig*. The British squadron was hopelessly outnumbered and outgunned, but Admiral Craddock manoeuvred his vessels into line for action thus: *Good Hope, Monmouth, Glasgow* and *Otranto*. According to *Otranto*'s log the German ships opened fire at 7.12 pm, and in the words of another of *Otranto*'s crew members, Mr N. W. Douglas, 'The first salvo of the Germans fell about 200 yards short. I think from the time I saw the first flash from the Germans until the shots dropped in the water was the most awful moment I have ever spent. The second salvo from the Germans fell in a line about 100 yards ahead of us and took the *Good Hope*'s forward 9.2-inch clean off the deck and set fire to her. The third went over the top of us with such a rotten whistling noise, caught the *Monmouth* on fire amidships, took the *Good Hope*'s foremast away. At this time we were a little out of line and the *Good Hope* was just making a signal for us to leave but she never finished it. At 7.40 pm the *Good Hope* and *Monmouth* blew up.' Mr McCarthy describes the sight: 'The Monmouth again caught fire and then there was an explosion on her and the flames leapt a height of 200 ft. It was one of the finest but most awful sights it was my lot to see. We started away and from the distance we could see that another explosion had occurred and the flames lit up the skies.' By this time *Otranto* was making good her escape. She had been unable to open fire, her eight 4.7-inch guns being totally ineffectual. During the action both the *Good Hope* and *Monmouth* were sunk and the *Glasgow* had been damaged but, like *Otranto*, had managed to escape. All that night *Otranto* steamed hard to the south and on November 7 she rounded Cape Horn, arriving in Montevideo on November 10. There she joined the new flagship HMS *Defence* and other ships, including the *Orama*.

Towards the end of November 1914 *Otranto* crossed the Atlantic to Sierra Leone, where the crew were given their first leave since she was commissioned. She remained in the West African port until December 3 that year when she sailed for the Falkland Islands, arriving there two weeks later. By this time the Battle of the Falkland Islands had been fought and the defeat at Coronel avenged. Four of von Spee's cruisers had been sunk and the British fleet were engaged in searching for the sole survivor, *Dresden*. *Otranto* was ordered to stay in the vicinity of the Falklands to carry out the duties of guardship, and Christmas that year was spent at San Carlos. She remained in the area until early February 1915, and Mr McCarthy says of the time spent there, 'We were granted leave once or twice and we went ashore; we found the people very sociable and the only fault that can be found with the place was, that it is always cold.'

It was while *Otranto* lay at the Falkland Islands that problems arose with her crew. Most of the mercantile men on board had signed on in London and their contracts were due for renewal, so the captain mustered them on the boat deck and asked them whether they were prepared to sign on again. To a man they refused, and on January 17 1915 the Governor of the Islands signalled to the Admiralty requesting that *Otranto* be allowed to return home where the Orient Line men would sign on for another voyage. The Admiralty replied that she must remain as guardship to the colony until relieved by HMS *Macedonia*. On February 4 *Otranto* left the islands to patrol off the River Plate, but the trouble was not yet over and on February 13 that year the Governor of the Falklands once again signalled the Admiralty, 'Civilian crew of *Otranto* agreements expired 11.2.15. The captain reports they will certainly refuse duty if ordered to sea except for the purpose of proceeding to England.' This stark message obviously had some effect on the Admiralty for on March 10 1915 *Otranto* berthed in Alfred Dock, Birkenhead, for a refit. As part of the overhaul the 4.7-inch guns were replaced by 6-inch ones and her crew were paid off.

It was May 6 1915 before *Otranto* was at sea once more, and she set course for another commission in the South Atlantic off the coast of South America. All that year she patrolled the coast in the Atlantic and Pacific Oceans, but this time it was largely uneventful. On December 19 she left South America for Sydney and on Boxing Day she was off Easter Island, arriving at Garden Island, Sydney, on January 14 1916 for a long refit. With the work completed she left Sydney on March 5 that year and returned to South America to continue patrolling the coast and enforcing the contraband blockade. Again the months passed by uneventfully, and on October 13 1916 she arrived in Esquimalt, Canada, for another overhaul. The crew spent Christmas in Canada before *Otranto* sailed south again on December 28 that year, for a nine-month patrol mainly off the west coast of South America. On October 2 1917 she was once again at Esquimalt for another period of maintenance. She was too large for the graving dock and there were underwater repairs to be effected, so after the work had been commenced on the main engines, *Otranto* went to Prince Rupert and was docked in the floating drydock there. Craftsmen from Yarrows in Esquimalt went along to carry out the necessary work, which involved drawing the tailshafts, repairing the stern bearings, and overhauling the sea connections. The ship then returned to Yarrows for extensive main engine repairs and alterations to magazines and guns, which had new mountings fitted. *Otranto* left Esquimalt for the last time on December 21 1917, once again for South America and the contraband patrol. It was the start of a new commission with a new crew, most of whom were from Chatham. However, she spent only five more months in the southern hemisphere before she left Rio de Janeiro for Devonport, where she arrived on June 16 1918. After a short spell in dock she left the port on July 8 for New York.

In these last months of the war, with America now well and truly involved and providing fresh divisions to reinforce the Western Front, there was a great need for troop transports. *Otranto* was pressed into service in this role, but she was destined to make only one full voyage in this employment.

Otranto arrived in New York for the first time on July 20 1918 and berthed at Pier 95 on 55th Street. She left the Hudson River at 3.35 pm on August 8, arriving at the Brocklebank Dock, Liverpool, 12 days later at 11.25 am on August 20. An hour later the US troops on board started to disembark, and eight days later *Otranto* left Liverpool once again bound for New York. After a voyage of 11 days she arrived back in 'The Big Apple'. She was just one of a large number of passenger liners, now troop transports, which were to be seen alongside most of the piers in the Hudson River. They were embarking the many thousands of US troops who were to break the deadlock in France and win the war for the Allies.

There were to be 12 troopships in the convoy HX50 for the return voyage to Liverpool, and *Otranto* was one of these. She was commanded by Captain Ernest J. W. Davidson, and she was to be commodore ship of the convoy. Originally the convoy had been scheduled to leave New York on September 24 1918, but there was a delay as 12 officers and 691 troops plus two YMCA representatives embarked on board *Otranto*. The troops' quarters were in the ship's cargo holds with staircases down from the well decks. Rows of tables ran crosswise across the ship and the hammocks were packed in. One American soldier wrote of this voyage, 'Descending the stairs, one met a strong, sickening odour of phenol used in disinfectants; and this odour, reminding one of a hospital, seemed to pervade the whole ship. That first night shipboard, while the *Otranto* still lay at the pier, many of the men developed symptoms of colds and there was much coughing. The next day, September 25, at 12.30 pm, the *Otranto* cast off and after being nudged out in the channel by tugboats, sailed down the harbour to join the main body of the convoy anchored in the bay. It was a cold raw day and the fog was so thick that the outline of the Statue of Liberty could only be made out dimly. As the *Otranto* passed the statue there was silence among the soldiers.' Sadly, hundreds of the troops on board would never see their beloved homeland again, and were doomed never even to see their destination.

The convoy consisted of two lines of six ships, with the escorts, which were US Navy vessels, screening them. The vessels were positioned thus:

SS *PLASSEY* (P&O)	SS *SAXON* (Union Castle)
SS *OXFORDSHIRE* (Bibby)	SS *BRITON* (Union Castle)
SS *CITY OF YORK* (Ellerman)	SS *KASHMIR* (P&O)
SS *TEUGER* (Blue Funnel)	HMS *OTRANTO* (Convoy Commodore)
SS *RHESUS* (Blue Funnel)	SS *ORIANA* (PSNCo)
SS *ORONTES* (Orient)	SS *SCOTIAN* (Allan)

Otranto was in the front line, flanked on the port side by P&O's *Kashmir* with the PSNCo liner, *Oriana*, to starboard. The battleship USS *Louisiana*, the cruiser USS *St Louis* and the destroyer USS *Dorsey* made up a formidable escort and a French ship, SS *La Lorraine,* stayed with convoy HX50, as it had been numbered. Soon after leaving port there was a report of enemy submarines ahead and a northerly route was chosen. The colds mentioned by the US soldier soon developed into a severe outbreak of Spanish influenza; that and rough seas soon laid low many of the troops. Conditions on board were vividly described by that same American soldier, 'Entertainment on the *Otranto* consisted mainly of movies shown in a dining saloon by the two "Y" men. They had also brought aboard a phonograph and some books and magazines. The food served to the soldiers on all ships was about the same, mutton, fish, cheese, white bread, black tea—much disliked by everyone—and weak coffee. This had to be consumed in the same quarters where the men slept, and the smell of phenol, mixed with the sickening odour of *mal de mer*, handicapped many an appetite.'

Six days out of New York, at 9.30 pm on October 1, the blacked-out convoy found itself among a fleet of 22 French fishing barques, returning home from the Grand Banks. *Otranto* collided with one of the vessels, the *Croisine*, severely damaging her. Captain Davidson stopped his ship and picked up the *Croisine*'s 37-man crew, sinking the derelict by gunfire before steaming on to rejoin the convoy, and by daylight on October 3 she was in position again. By now the first death had resulted from the 'flu outbreak, and from then on *Otranto* encountered severe gales and very heavy seas. On Friday October 4 the USS *Louisiana* turned and left for home, and the following evening the USS *St Louis* followed her as scheduled. The next day was Sunday October 6 1918, and with winds of storm force 11 and mountainous seas it was no wonder that the ships of the convoy were not exactly sure of their position. In fact the convoy was about to enter the North Channel between Scotland and the north coast of Ireland, but owing to the foul weather conditions they were further north than they thought. At 5 am that day the destroyers HMS *Mounsey* and *Minos* relieved the USS *Dorsey* as escort, and the latter vessel left for Buncrana. At just after 8.30 am land was sighted, and the officer of the watch on board *Otranto* thought it was the north coast of Ireland, whereas the master of *Kashmir* thought it was the coast of Scotland, which in fact it was, being the island of Islay.

The events are best described by Mr Justice Hill, who, sitting in judgement at the court of inquiry, said, 'In this position each sighted land and took helm action to avoid it. The *Otranto* first sighted land on the starboard bow. The *Kashmir* first sighted land ahead on the port bow. Various estimates of the distance of the land were formed and given in evidence; but it was common ground that land was so near that it was a matter of urgency to take action for it. The *Otranto* hard-a-starboarded and stopped the port engine to assist the helm. The *Kashmir* hard-a-ported and stopped the starboard engine with the like object. The other ships of the convoy, so far as observed—they were not all in sight—did as the *Kashmir* did and turned to starboard. The effect of wind and sea upon the ships was such that the swing under port helm was more rapid than the swing under starboard helm. The effect of starboard helm upon the *Otranto* was all the slower because she was already carrying starboard helm. Whether the two ships took action precisely at the same moment is a matter which cannot be determined. But there came a time when the *Kashmir,* turning to starboard, was heading for the *Otranto*, turning more slowly to port. When they were in that position, most unfortunately each began a change of manoeuvre. I say began, because, so far as the *Kashmir* was concerned, the change was quickly countermanded. It came about in this way: the *Otranto*, at a late stage, observed the *Kashmir* heading for her, and sounded two short blasts, and almost at the same time hard-a-ported and put the port engine full ahead. The two short blasts were heard on board the *Kashmir* and her helm was ordered hard-a-starboard and was actually put over, but immediately the order was changed to hard-a-port again and both engines were reversed. The collision followed soon afterwards.'

At about 8.45 am that morning *Kashmir*'s bows crashed into *Otranto*'s port side amidships between the funnels. One eyewitness, the troop storekeeper on board *Kashmir*, recalls that moment, at which time he was busy preparing

Wreckage from Otranto *fills the gullies on the rocky coast of Islay. The cross in the top left-hand corner shows the position of the wreck* (A.M. Aitken).

thousands of boiled eggs for the troops' breakfast that morning for which there was little demand. 'I was just about fed up with things, wondering however we were going to manage at dinner time, when looking over the starboard side on the after well deck, I saw a sight that I shall never forget. "Good God," I said looking forward and seeing that our bows were rammed into the port side of the *Otranto* amidships, and then I felt our engines going astern and we slowly backed away leaving a large hole in the shape of a letter V, from under the waterline up to her top decks. As she rolled away I could see men hanging on for dear life and then having to give up and being washed into the sea. We could do nothing to help them.' Fortunately *Kashmir* reached the Clyde safely with no casualties.

On *Otranto* the situation was extremely grave. Her boiler and engine rooms were flooded and the ship was drifting helplessly, with no power, in the mountainous seas. It was impossible to lower the boats or to let the anchor go, and as *Otranto* drifted closer to the shores of Islay, great efforts were made to prepare the sick for abandoning ship. Then at 9.30 am HMS *Mounsey*, commanded by Commander F. W. Craven RN, managed to manoeuvre alongside *Otranto*, which enabled men to jump onto the little destroyer. Many were lost as they misjudged the distance as the two ships lurched sickeningly against each other. Almost 600 men were saved in this way before *Mounsey*, very badly damaged herself, finally had to abandon her mercy mission and make for Belfast. She had rescued 27 officers, 300 American troops, 239 crew members and 30 French sailors from the *Croisine*.

The funerals of the victims of the Otranto *at Kilchoman, Islay. The American flag-bearer is Sgt McDonald, one of the* Otranto *survivors* (A.M. Aitken).

Meanwhile, back on board *Otranto*, which was now close in to the rocky shore, the situation was desperate. A message signalled to the Admiralty summed up the situation: '*Mounsey* reports that she embarked survivors by going alongside lee of ship. When she left *Otranto* was close in to beach which apeared to be steep to.' At about 11 am that morning the unfortunate vessel grounded on a reef off the rocky shore at Kilchiaran on Islay, and very soon after that she broke in two. The forward half was quickly overwhelmed by the sea and sank; the after section remained for a time gripped on the rocks, and at about 3.30 pm only her stern was visible, sticking up among the fury of the waves. Of the 400 or so left on board, only a handful survived, most of them being killed by the crashing about of heavy floating wreckage in the violent sea. Despite valiant efforts by the coastguard and local people, only 21 men reached the shore safely.

One of the few residents of Islay who remembers that stormy day is Mr Gilbert Clark of Port Charlotte, and he has set his memories down in a letter to the author. 'I was 14 years old at the time so I can well remember that Sunday when my father and myself walked over to the scene of the *Otranto* a few hours after it had struck on a reef about 300 yards from the shore, called Botha na Caillieach, "Old Woman's Reef", one of the worst places on the west coast. We met one of the survivors on the road being taken to Kilchiaran Farm. When we got to the shore there was only a part of the stern to be seen above water. It was such a stormy day that the vessel was torn to pieces in a short time. In those days these liners were all done up in wood panelling,

Above *A section of the* Otranto *cemetery at Kilchoman. Captain Davidson's grave is in the foreground* (A.M. Aitken).

Below *The* Otranto *cemetery at Kilchoman* (A.M. Aitken).

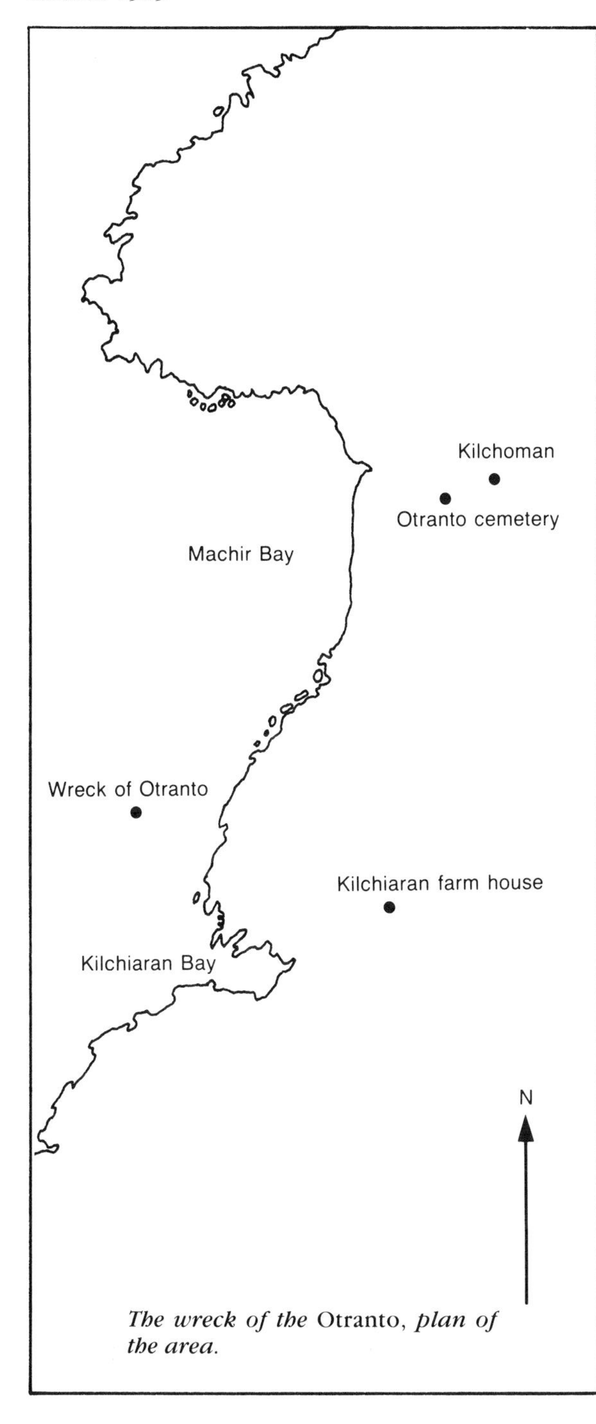

The wreck of the Otranto, *plan of the area.*

so the shore and the sea had so much wood and wreckage floating. We could see so many people swimming or being swept by the heavy seas along the shore to a large gulley that was full of wreckage, where the poor soldiers and crew had no chance of being rescued. They must have been killed within moments, and all the local people waiting on the shore had to look on helpless as it was impossible for anyone to reach them owing to every gulley and all the shore being covered with floating wood. No wonder so few survivors got ashore.' Among those who lost their lives was Captain Davidson, and the last body recovered was that of Signalman James Brennan on November 13 1918, two days after the Armistice. The dead were buried with full military honours in a cemetery adjoining the churchyard at Kilchoman on Islay, and so it remains to this day, a monument to that tragic day in the closing weeks of the First World War.

The legal wrangle went on for 18 months after the end of the war, when it was decided that both ships were equally to blame for the collision. The position of the wreck of the *Otranto* is given as 55°46′N, 6°30′W; over the years several items have been recovered, and these are now displayed in a museum at Port Charlotte.

On the southernmost tip of this lonely island, at the Mull of Oa overlooking the sea, is a monument erected by the American Red Cross and dedicated to the dead of the *Otranto* and the *Tuscania,* which had been torpedoed in the same area some months earlier. It is clearly visible from the sea and is a constant reminder of the hazards still faced by seafarers the world over.

Technical data
Gross tonnage: 12,124
Net tonnage: 7,433
Length overall: 554 ft (168.85 m)
Breadth: 64 ft (19.51 m)
Depth: 38 ft 7 in (11.76 m)
Main engines: Twin screw, two sets of quadruple-expansion engines, 14,000 ihp, 18 knots
Boilers: Coal-fired, steam pressure 215 psi
Passengers: First class 300, Second class 140, Third class 850

Orvieto 1909

Orvieto was the second of the 12,000-tonners to be built by Workman Clark & Company of Belfast, and she completed the 1909 building programme. She was launched on Tuesday July 6 1909, and exactly four months later, on November 6, she was delivered to the Orient Line.

The new ship was named after the town in Italy, on the River Paglia north of Rome. Like *Otranto, Orvieto* had accommodation for 235 first, 186 second and 696 third class passengers. The first class passengers had access to five decks, from the boat deck down to the upper deck. The first class suites and cabins were situated on the bridge and shelter decks, with the main public rooms on the promenade deck which lay directly beneath the boat deck. Here were housed the lounge and music room and, at the after end, the smoke room. In addition to the first class cabins on the bridge deck there was the second class smoke room, which was aft and overlooked the shelter deck. The shelter deck itself was mainly given over to cabin accommodation with the first class suites amidships and the second class entrance foyer and music room aft. Both the first and second class dining saloons were on the upper deck, situated forward and aft respectively. One notable feature of the first class saloon was the arcaded well which rose through two decks to the bridge deck, with a skylight to give natural light and ventilation. The decoration was cheerful, and as in the other ships of the class, the tables were provided for four, six, eight or ten passengers. The smoking room was some 18 ft high, the central part having an arched roof, lit by dormer windows. The whole room was in oak with leather upholstery, the chairs being reproduced from a Jacobean design. The lounge, as in other ships, was *en suite* with the music room, separated only by a glass door. The decoration was in Georgian style, predominantly pale grey and white, with notes of rich colour being given by prints of famous French paintings. The furniture was in Italian walnut and richly upholstered. The music room, which was in fact a retreat for the ladies, was decorated with golden satinwood and its furniture was reproduced from antique models in the possession of Waring & Gillow, who were responsible for all the furnishings.

As with the other four ships in her class, *Orvieto*'s propelling machinery was designed to give a service speed of 18 knots. She was fitted with quadruple-expansion reciprocating engines driving twin screws, and the two single-ended and four double-ended coal-fired boilers provided steam at 215 psi. On her trials she achieved her required speed without difficulty.

Orvieto's maiden voyage began in London on November 26 1909, and ahead of her lay four full years of service on the mail run to Brisbane, and cruising. These were the untroubled, heady years of the British Empire, and on May 24 1911 'Empire Day' was celebrated in style on board *Orvieto*. The ship was dressed overall from truck to deck as she neared the end of a round voyage, and as she passed Cape Trafalgar and Cape St Vincent that day the band turned out to play the national anthem. By the end of November 1913 much progress had been made in the development of the port of Brisbane. New wharves were opened within the boundaries of the city, and *Orvieto* was the first Orient Line vessel to berth at New Farm Wharf. A luncheon to celebrate the event was held on board and the guests included Sir William Macgregor, the Governor of Queensland, and the State Premier, Mr Denham. The Governor, referring to Brisbane as a port, stated that Queensland, and indeed the whole of Australia, owed a great debt of gratitude to the Orient Line which had done more to make Australia known to the outside world than any other agency. *Orvieto* returned to London in February 1914, and on March 13 that year she made her last full peacetime trip to Australia and back. On July 3 1914 she left Tilbury on her second passage of the year and she reached Australia soon after the start of the First World War, when she was immediately requisitioned by the Commonwealth government. For the next two months she lay in dock at Sydney being fitted out as a troop transport. On November 1 1914 *Orvieto* sailed from Sydney with 91 officers and 1,347 men of the AIF. She was part of a convoy of 36 ships, all of them bound for Egypt, and escorted by Royal Navy and Japanese cruisers which included HMAS *Melbourne* and HMAS *Sydney*.

Meanwhile, in the Indian Ocean, the German cruiser *Emden*, commanded by Captain von Müller, was sweeping the seas, creating havoc for Allied shipping. The cruiser had left the port of Tsingtau soon after the outbreak of war and had sailed into the Indian Ocean by way of the Banda Sea and Bali. Then in the course of 70 days she captured 23 vessels and bombarded British ports. So concerned were the Admiralty that they ordered all merchant shipping to stay in harbour, which had a severe effect on trade in the area.

On November 9 1914, the *Emden* arrived at the Cocos Islands and put a landing party ashore to destroy the radio station there. Von Müller had not reckoned on the alert Superintendent of the Telegraph Company who, as soon as *Emden* was sighted, put out an alarm call. These signals were

A painting by W.M. Birchall which shows the graceful lines of Orvieto (P&O).

intercepted by HMAS *Melbourne* which, with the rest of the convoy including the *Orvieto*, was only 55 miles to the north of the Cocos Islands, on passage to Colombo. The convoy's senior officer, Captain M. L. Silver, ordered HMAS *Sydney* to investigate, and just three hours after the first signals from the Cocos Islands were received the *Sydney* intercepted *Emden*. In a short action the *Emden* was disabled and grounded, and von Müller surrendered his crew, which included 56 wounded. All together there were 202 German prisoners, and the injured were transferred to the AMC *Empress of Russia*. The convoy arrived in Colombo on November 15 and that same day the able-bodied prisoners were transferred to other ships. A number of them, including Captain von Müller and Prince Franz Josef von Hohenzollern, *Emden*'s torpedo officer, were embarked on board *Orvieto* for the passage to Egypt. The senior officers were given their own cabins on the upper deck and their prison section was separated from the rest of the officers' quarters by a wire grating, which was manned by sentries. They were allowed to exercise on the promenade deck twice a day, and they ate in the first class saloon accompanied by British officers. On arrival at Suez the Australian troops and the PoWs were disembarked, the latter continuing their journey to Malta in HMS *Hampshire*.

Orvieto then proceeded to London, arriving in January 1915. Originally she had been scheduled to sail for Australia on February 12 1915, and in fact she was shown in *The Times*' sailing lists for that date. But shortly after her arrival she was requisitioned by the Admiralty as an armed merchant cruiser and she was fitted out at Millwall, being armed with eight 6-inch guns. She was commissioned as HMS *Orvieto* on March 8 that year, commanded by Captain Smyth RN who joined the ship that same day. A week later she was drydocked at Tilbury for two days before leaving for Scapa Flow where she arrived on March 21. For the next two months she remained at Scapa, spending very little time at sea, and on June 8 she left for Immingham where she was to be based for the next ten months. Her role while based on the east coast was that of a minelayer and her duties took her all along the coast between Sheerness and Rosyth, often in company with HMS *Princess Margaret*, a 6,000-ton vessel which had been built as a coastal ship for the Canadian Pacific, but which had been taken by the Admiralty on completion. On February 18 1916, *Orvieto* was slightly damaged when she was involved in a collision with the Swedish *Abiska* at Immingham. Then in the following month, on March 20, she went aground for a time off Sheerness. On April 24 that year she was off the Thames Estuary when her guns were fired in anger for the first time as she opened fire on enemy aircraft, but no hits were recorded. Finally, on May 25 1916, she was at the Royal Albert Docks in London when her first commission came to an end and her ship's company were paid off.

By the end of July 1916 she had been recommissioned and left London at the end of that month for the Northern Patrol. Over the next six months she intercepted over 30 foreign merchant vessels and sent them into northern ports to be searched. In September that year she spent a week in dock at Glasgow, and the New Year was spent in the cold northern waters with Vice-Admiral Tupper on board to witness gunnery trials. On the last day of February 1917 she was at Busta Voe when she collided with the fishing vessel, *Drifter 32*. The smaller ship unfortunately had her masts and funnel carried away, but there were no casualties. *Orvieto*'s refit in the summer of that year was carried out on the Tyne during July and August, and she left Hebburn on September 21, once again for the Northern Patrol. Her base during the autumn of that year was Liverpool, and on January 9 1918 she arrived back in that port to be refitted in the Queen's Graving Dock. During the refit there was a series of mysterious small fires on board. The first of these was on January 16 when a blaze was discovered in number three lower hold, which took about three hours to extinguish. The last was ten days later and this took just over three hours to put out.

Orvieto left Liverpool on March 23 1918, but

Orvieto *arriving at Tilbury* (P&O).

she did not return to the Northern Patrol for she was to spend the rest of the war on convoy duties across the Atlantic. Her first two voyages were to Rio de Janeiro escorting convoys, and she berthed at Cardiff on her return on August 13. The next two passages were to Canada, sailing to Quebec and Halifax and then back to Devonport. She left Halifax on the return leg of the second trip on October 20, and eight days later she arrived back in England. It was her last voyage as a Royal Naval auxiliary and on her return she was visited by HRH Prince Arthur of Connaught, one of Queen Victoria's sons, accompanied by the Japanese Ambassador. *Orvieto* was at Devonport when the war ended and at the close of that year she was paid off and returned to the Orient Line to be reconditioned for peacetime service.

It had been hoped to get *Orvieto* ready for the mail service by mid-October 1919, but as the date approached it was clear that she would not be completed, and she finally sailed for Brisbane on November 1 that year. For the next 11 years she remained on the mail run without serious mishap, apart from running aground in the Brisbane River. By 1930 she was outdated, having never been converted to burn oil fuel, and with new tonnage in service she was no longer needed. She made her last voyage to Australia in August 1930, and on her return she was laid up off Southampton. She remained there for five months until, at the end of March 1930, she was sold to Scottish shipbreakers. She arrived at Bo'ness at the end of her final voyage on April 3 1931, having served the company and her country for almost 22 years.

Technical data

Gross tonnage: 12,133
Net tonnage: 7,421
Length overall: 528 ft 7 in (161.15 m)
Breadth: 64 ft (19.51 m)
Depth: 38 ft 7 in (11.76 m)
Main engines: Twin screw, two sets of quadruple-expansion engines, 14,000 ihp, 18 knots
Boilers: Coal-fired, steam pressure 215 psi
Passengers: First class 235, Second class 186, Third class 696

Orama 1911

On June 28 1911 the last Orient liner to be built before the First World War was launched at John Brown and Company's Clydebank yard. She was a vessel of some 12,927 gross tons and she was named *Orama*, after a small town in South Australia. She was slightly larger than the 1909 series of ships, and in her design a number of improvements were embodied. The most important difference was that she was a triple-screw vessel propelled by a combination of reciprocating engines and steam turbines which gave her a speed of 18 knots. She had accommodation for 293 first, 145 second and 867 third class passengers. All the principal first class public rooms were on the promenade deck. Forward were the lounge and music room, which were decorated in Louis XVI style, and aft were the smoking room and verandah café. The first class dining saloon was on the upper deck. Apart from a well deck forward she was very similar in profile to the 1909 ships, but sadly her career was all too brief.

Orama was handed over to the Orient Line on the morning of Sunday November 5 1911 at Tilbury Docks, and at the end of the week she left London on her maiden voyage to Brisbane. She had a full complement of first and second class passengers, and 900 in the third class. They were described at the time as 'mainly farm worker class', and were would-be emigrants. *Orama*'s first landfall off Fremantle was on December 12 that year, and she arrived in Brisbane at noon on Christmas Day 1911. She left Gravesend Reach on her second Australian mail voyage on March 1 1912, and in the following year she was involved in her first mishap. She had sailed from London on October 10 1913, and after arriving in the Brisbane River went aground in mud while berthing. All her cargo was discharged into lighters and with the aid of tugs she was refloated the following day, after which she was able to return to England on schedule.

Orama had only two more peacetime voyages as a mail liner before the outbreak of war. She left London on the second of these on May 22 1914 and she arrived back there just after the declaration of war. She was in fact scheduled to sail once again on September 11 that year, but soon after her arrival at Tilbury she was requisitioned by the government for service as an armed merchant cruiser. She was commissioned into the Royal Navy on September 12 1914, commanded by Captain J. R. Seagrave RN. Six days later she left Tilbury for South America, coaling at St Vincent on the way. She arrived at Abrolhos Rocks off the coast of Brazil on October 10, and there she joined a squadron which included the AMC and former Orient liner HMS *Otranto*, the cruisers HMS *Defence, Carnarvon, Kent* and *Cornwall* and the ex-Union Castle liner, HMS *Edinburgh Castle*. She immediately went out on patrol, and at 1.12 pm the next day she received a signal that a German cargo ship, SS *Santa Catarina*, was on fire in a position 18°2'S, 38°44'W, just south of Abrolhos Archipelago. *Orama* was quickly on the scene and a fire party was sent across to try

Above Orama *on her full power trials, November 1911* (P&O).

Below *A port side view of* Orama. *Her name was taken from a small town in South Australia* (Orient Line).

Above *An Orient Line postcard showing the third class dining saloon* (Orient Line).

Below *HMS* Orama *as an armed merchant cruiser flying the White Ensign* (P&O).

to subdue the blaze. However, the crew of the German ship had laid their scuttling charges well and the task was impossible, so the sea cocks were opened, and the would-be blockade runner sank the following day.

On November 11 1914, *Orama* was patrolling off the mouth of the River Plate when, at 4.10 pm, she saw a strange ship being set on fire. She was the 5,700-ton German cargo ship *Navarra*. She had been built in 1905 for the Hamburg America Line, for the South America service, and on the outbreak of war she had been converted for use as a German auxiliary. However, on sighting the more powerful *Orama*, her crew had set off scuttling charges. When *Orama* arrived alongside, the German ship was blazing fiercely and her crew had taken to the boats. At 5.15 pm *Orama* took the German crew on board, and then manoeuvred into a position to open fire on the *Navarra*. *Orama*'s gunfire was decisive and at 7.58 pm that evening the derelict auxiliary turned turtle and sank. The following day *Orama* arrived back at Abrolhos Rocks where the German prisoners were transferred to the *Edinburgh Castle*.

Later that month *Orama* escorted British colliers to Port William in the Falkland Islands, and then, in company with HMS *Kent*, she searched the west coast of South America for the German auxiliary *Prinz Eitel Friedrich* and the cruiser *Dresden*, which had escaped from Tsingtau just before the outbreak of war. For the next two months the two ships patrolled fruitlessly, and on January 26 1915 *Orama* went into Mollendo where she heard news of a 'fight between the battlecruisers in the North Sea'. It was the Battle of the Dogger Bank, which had been fought some three days previously. Then a few weeks later she was in action once again. The German cruiser *Dresden* had finally been tracked down to Mas Afuera in the Juan Fernandez Islands in the Pacific off Valparaiso. On the evening of Sunday March 14 1915, *Orama* and *Kent* were ordered to the islands at full speed.

Perhaps the best account of the action that followed has been given by Surgeon T. B. Dixon RNVR of HMS *Kent* in his diary, published as *The Enemy Fought Splendidly*. 'Full speed in night ordered and so we arrived within sight of Juan Fernandez (Mas Afuera) at daylight. As we approached island I saw it to be composed of high volcanic walls, the remains of an old crater evidently, and thickly wooded in places. The walls very thin for their height of about 3,000 ft. Soon we picked up the smoke of the *Glasgow* and later the *Orama*, 20 miles away straight ahead of us. The island lay ahead of us on our port bow. All three of us converged on the island. As we rounded several points and nothing appeared the news went round that routine was to be as usual and so I went below to change my clothes. Halfway through the act action was sounded and in a second the ship was in a turmoil of sound. Never had I known the men respond so quickly. Then I heard the news shouted, "The *Dresden* is lying in the bay at anchor! Hastily getting my water bottle I rushed on deck and there, sure enough, lying in Cumberland Bay, half hidden against the cliffs behind her was a three-funnel cruiser. I heard the order, open fire. The first salvo roared out above us but in four minutes all was over. The *Dresden* had hoisted the white flag and the crew were leaving the ship in boats and going ashore. She was on fire aft amidships. Her after guns were dismantled. There was a huge hole in her starboard waterline aft, and her casemates were blown to pieces in two places. She was still at anchor and between her and the shore were a stream of boats filled with half-dressed men. A steam boat flying a huge white flag came towards us carrying Captain of *Dresden* and we directed him to the *Glasgow* as senior ship. The *Glasgow* had by this time got into the bay followed by the *Orama*, and we all anchored about 1,000 yards from the *Dresden*. Order came, all doctors ashore, went ashore. As I was leaving ship there was a huge explosion on *Dresden* and smoke came from port side forward. Ten badly wounded, set to work operating. Later, orders were received to remove the wounded to *Orama*. The *Dresden* was close inshore and sitting around her were our three ships watching her death struggles. She was visibly sinking, smoke came out in curls from amidships and she was nearly awash when suddenly her nose plunged downwards. She gave a big heave to port and we could see the water pouring down into her funnels, then her stern went under and the water boiled with the rush of escaping air, then slowly her masts disappeared. German steam boat towed our boats with us and wounded aboard to *Orama*. Operating continually all way to Valparaiso.'

Orama's log book describes the whole incident thus: '8.50 am off Juan Fernandez, observed German cruiser *Dresden*. 9.15 am—9.21 am opened fire with port guns. Enemy hoisting white flag. 10.30 am *Dresden* blew up forward. Sank 11.38 am. Embarking wounded from *Dresden*, 15 PoWs in all.'

Dr Dixon gives an insight into life on the *Orama* at this time. 'Thursday March 18 1915. To meet *Kent* at Mas Afuera tomorrow. Life on *Orama* a pleasant change and a holiday after *Kent*. To begin with the large decks give plenty of exercise. The food was scrumptious and all officers were kind in making me at home. Every officer in ship complained of Captain Seagrave RN who treated them all without slightest tact or respect for experience.' On April 10 1915, both ships were anchored at Port San Nicholas, and Dr Dixon again visited *Orama*. 'Arrived San Nicholas at dawn. *Orama* finished coaling. In the evening went across with some officers and 200-odd men to *Orama* to an entertainment they were giving. Held in their first class saloon. It was first class all the way through. The one-act farce quite good too. After the show we adjourned to smoking room and drinks flowed along. We started dancing to bagpipes and finished up about midnight with a football scrum after lancers. Great night and improved relations between two ships.'

In late April that year *Orama* called at James Island, one of the Galapagos Islands, where her crew reported, 'The island covered with very dense scrub, populated with wild donkeys, snakes, lizards, sea lions, and sharks.' A number of the men suffered from sunstroke and apparently very few of the ship's company enjoyed their visit. *Orama* remained off the west coast of South America until the end of June 1915, when she steamed across the Pacific to Sydney and into dockyard hands for a long refit. On September 3 that year Captain Baillie-Hamilton RN took over command from Captain Seagrave and in the following month on October 9 *Orama* left Sydney for the Falkland Islands and the River Plate. On November 28, just over a month after leaving Sydney, *Orama* was on patrol off the mouth of the River Plate when she intercepted the German ship SS *President Mitre* and took her as a prize.

Orama remained off South America until March 10 1917 when she arrived in Simonstown, South Africa, for another long refit. She remained there until June that year when she left in convoy for Halifax, Nova Scotia, loaded with 553 crates of specie. From Canada she crossed the Atlantic and arrived in Liverpool on August 12 1917. It was the first time she had returned to Britain since September 1914, an absence of almost three years, and it was also to be her last visit.

After a further spell in dockyard hands *Orama* recommissioned at Liverpool and left the port on September 22 1917, bound for Dakar where she arrived eight days later. Orders were received to proceed to sea once again on October 7 1917, as escort to a convoy of 21 merchant ships, and they sailed at 6 am that day. From daylight on October 8 until they met the destroyer escort, *Orama* steamed ahead of the convoy. On board preparations had been made to minimize any damage in case she were attacked by a submarine. All watertight doors were closed, and all available timber was used to shore up bulkheads. On deck all guns were kept fully loaded ready for instant use and 11 lookouts were permanently stationed round the ship. At 7 am on the morning of October 19 a destroyer escort, made up of eight vessels including the USS *Conyngham* and the USS *Jacob Jones*, met up with *Orama*. She now took her position as leading ship in the second column. At 9 am that day one of the destroyers detached from the convoy in response to an SOS from the American merchant ship *Luchenbach* about 70 miles away. It was an exceptionally clear day, and several 'submarine

HMS Orama *in early 1917* (Imperial War Museum).

warnings' had been received during the course of the voyage. At 10.30 am a merchant ship, SS *City of Chester*, dropped out of the convoy with engine trouble, and at 4 pm the *Luchenbach* and the destroyer joined the convoy. Although *Luchenbach* was well down by the head she was able to keep station astern of the fourth column.

At 5.55 pm, when the convoy was only 217 miles from the Scilly Isles, *Orama* was struck by a torpedo on the port bow abaft the bulkhead which separated numbers two and three holds. There was a terrific explosion and immediately afterwards the wake of a torpedo appeared on the surface. A keen lookout aboard the USS *Conyngham* spotted a periscope only a few inches out of the water, and the destroyer went for it at full speed. When they reached the spot, officers and men sighted a green cigar-shaped object in the clear waters which was submerging rapidly. The destroyer crew were equal to the occasion and a depth charge was dropped directly on top of the submarine. After the water had subsided, pieces of wreckage and debris floated to the surface. Although it was not absolutely certain that the submarine had been destroyed, there is little doubt that the decisive action of USS *Conyngham* prevented any further casualties.

The British government decorated Commander Johnson of the *Conyngham* for his achievement. The citation read, 'At 5.50 pm HMS *Orama* was torpedoed in convoy. *Conyngham* went full speed, circled bow of *Orama*, saw submarine between lines of convoy, passed right over it so that it was plainly visible, and dropped depth charge. Prompt and correct action of Commander Johnson saved more ships from being torpedoed, and probably destroyed the submarine.'

Meanwhile, back on *Orama*, immediately after the explosion the engines were stopped and steps taken to ascertain the damage. The ship was listing to port and sinking considerably by the head, in view of which orders were given to lower the starboard boats just clear of the water. There was great difficulty in passing such orders because of the roar of escaping steam. It soon became clear that number two and three holds were filling rapidly, and the pumps were found to be useless as the piping had been wrecked. Commander Moorsom gave orders for his passengers, approximately 121 merchant seamen paid off from SS *Caronia*, and all the wounded, to take to the boats which were to be lowered and kept close to the ship. As daylight was now fading he ordered that the ship be darkened, and that a radio message be sent to Queenstown requesting tugs to be despatched. At 8 pm, with a third hold taking water fast, Commander Moorsom gave the order for the ship's company, with the exception of 50 ratings for whom there were no places in the boats, to abandon ship and make their way to the destroyers *Conyngham* and *Jacob Jones*. He then requested *Conyngham* to come alongside to evacuate the remainder. Once again Commander Johnson USN was equal to the task and he skilfully placed his little vessel alongside the sinking *Orama*, taking off more than 50 men without accident or casualty. Commander Moorsom was himself taken on board *Conyngham* and, after they had put off, a light was seen on board *Orama* which it was thought might indicate that someone had been left behind. Together with two volunteers, Commander Moorsom returned to *Orama* in one of the destroyer's boats and carried out a thorough search, but no one was found. By this time *Orama* was well down by her head with her well deck awash, and so the three men left her quickly. At 9.50 pm, 20 minutes after Commander Moorsom left his ship for the last time, *Orama* finally foundered, with her stern upright out of the water as she went down.

The two US destroyers steamed to Pembroke where the survivors were landed at 6 pm on October 20 1917, just over 24 hours after *Orama* had been hit. In his report to the Admiralty, Commander Moorsom described the hospitality on board the destroyers thus: 'The kindness and attention shown by the officers and crews of these American destroyers under most trying circumstances was beyond all praise.'

Technical data

Gross tonnage: 12,927
Net tonnage: 8,179
Length overall: 551 ft (167.95 m)
Breadth: 64 ft 2 in (19.56 m)
Depth: 39 ft (11.89 m)
Main engines: Twin screw, two sets of quadruple-expansion engines, 14,000 ihp, 18 knots
Boilers: Coal-fired, steam pressure 215 psi
Passengers: First class 293, Second class 145, Third class 867

Ormonde 1917

In May 1913, just 18 months after the *Orama* entered service, the keel was laid for the next Orient liner. She was to feature several innovations, including the fact that she was the first vessel of the line to have a cruiser stern, and the first to be fitted with geared turbines for her main propulsion machinery. Sadly it was to be five years before she sailed to Brisbane for the Orient Line. She was built at John Brown & Company's Clydebank yard, on the slipway which had recently been vacated by Cunard's *Aquitania*, and it was intended that she enter service in the spring or summer of 1915.

Over the next 15 months work on the new ship progressed according to schedule and the hull was almost ready for launching when the First World War broke out. Suddenly work on merchant ships took second place to that on naval vessels and the construction of the new Orient liner came to a halt. For over two years the uncompleted hull lay idle on the stocks, but by early 1917 there was a great need for troopships and work started once again on yard number 425 at John Brown's. On February 10 1917 the new ship was launched without any ceremony, being named *Ormonde*, and in the following month the Orient Line's most experienced officer, Commander Baynham RNR, was transferred from the armed merchant cruiser *Otranto* to stand by and then take command of the *Ormonde*.

By November 1917 *Ormonde* was completed with very spartan trooping accommodation, and she was immediately requisitioned by the government as a troopship. At 14,982 gross tons she was the largest ship to be built for the company, and she was easily identified by her two raking masts fore and aft, two tall, slender raking funnels amidships, her straight bow and cruiser stern. She also had a raised forecastle, well decks forward and aft of the superstructure, tall, slender ventilators forward, and a straight-fronted stepped bridge. Although she was powered by steam turbines, her boilers were coal-fired and she had a service speed of 18 knots. Instead of the usual Orient Line colours she entered service with her hull dazzle-painted.

She made her first voyage down the Clyde to Greenock on November 13 1917, and she lay at the Tail of the Bank for six days before sailing to Australia. It was to be 19 months before she returned to the UK. She arrived in Sydney on February 14 1918, and left the port in early March that year with Australian troops bound for Port Said. From Suez she took British troops up the Persian Gulf to Shat Al Arab, the river which runs into the Gulf from Basra and forms the border between Iraq and Iran. It was the ship's only passage into the Persian Gulf. From there she conveyed Indian troops to Suez, and then carried French troops to Marseilles before returning to Egypt. In July 1918 she made two voyages between Egypt and Taranto, and until the Armistice she remained in the Mediterranean, calling frequently at Kantara in the Suez Canal, Taranto and Salonika. In December 1918 she

Ormonde *makes her first voyage down the Clyde to Greenock on November 13 1917, dazzle-painted and fitted out as a troop transport* (P&O).

went through the Dardanelles to Constantinople (Istanbul) and on into the Black Sea to Batoum (Batumi), on the Turkish-Russian border. She remained in that area all through January 1919, before returning to Port Said at the end of the month. During February and early March she made three trooping voyages between Egypt and Marseilles, and then on March 16 1919 she left Suez carrying 2,000 Indian troops back to Bombay. She left Bombay on April 8 1919 with 347 first class passengers and 607 second and third class passengers on board, mainly wives and families of servicemen. Sadly two little children died of pneumonia during the journey.

She arrived in Tilbury at the end of her last voyage on government service on May 1 1919, to some rather adverse publicity which ended with questions being asked in Parliament. Among her first class passengers had been six Indians who were, according to a government minister, Mr Montague, 'coming to England to agitate on the subject of the proposed Indian Reform Scheme'. The complaint from another Member of Parliament was that sick women and children had been accommodated in the third class, while the Indian deputation travelled in the first class. In fact the company had tried hard to make conditions better by allowing the third class passengers to use second class facilities and fitting their cabins with electric fans. However, this controversy was soon forgotten and shortly after arriving in London she was discharged from government service. In her brief period as a troopship she had carried 2,400 officers and 20,000 men.

Some six weeks later, on June 14, *Ormonde* sailed for her builders' yard at Clydebank to be refitted for the Orient Line mail service to

With her war service over, Ormonde *became well known for her fjords cruises in the 1920s* (P&O).

Australia. Originally she was scheduled to leave for Brisbane on October 31 1919, but this was delayed for 11 days and she finally sailed on her maiden voyage with the mails and passengers on November 11. She now had accommodation for 278 first, 195 second and 1,000 third class passengers, and from the very outset she was a popular ship with both passengers and crew. She sailed from Tilbury on her second round voyage to Australia on March 20 1920, and 12 days later on April 2 she was in the Suez Canal when her stern hit the bank, damaging two blades of the port propeller. She was able to make Colombo at a reduced speed and once there went into drydock where the propeller was changed. She sailed once again on April 22, some days behind schedule. She reached Brisbane without further incident, but her troubles were not yet over. During the return voyage, on May 26 1920, she developed engine trouble between Melbourne and Adelaide, which resulted in a further delay at the latter port. It was July 9 1920 before she finally reached Tilbury again.

Over the next two and a half years *Ormonde* made eight round voyages to Australia, and in the summer of 1922 she cruised to the Norwegian fjords. On her return from Brisbane on Wednesday April 25 1923, *Ormonde* went up to John Brown's Clydebank yard where she was converted into an oil-burning vessel, and at the same time her accommodation was re-planned to cater for first and third class passengers only. No sooner was this work completed than she started a series of four cruises to Norway. The first was from Greenock on July 21 1923, with fares starting at 20 guineas for the 13-day trip. The following three cruises were from Immingham, and the last ended on September 14. At the time

Ormonde was described as 'the largest steamer hitherto employed on pleasure cruises to the Norwegian fjords'. One month later she left Tilbury for Australia again.

The next ten years passed without incident for *Ormonde* and in 1933, when she was the next oldest ship in the Orient Line fleet after *Orsova*, she was converted into a 'one-class' tourist ship carrying 770 passengers. Three years later, on September 23 1936, when she was nearing the end of a voyage from Tilbury to Sydney, and off Gabo Island near Cape Howe on the boundary between Victoria and New South Wales, fire broke out in number four hold. The blaze had started in a cargo of bales of tightly-packed fibre and *Ormonde* went into Twofold Bay, an old whaling anchorage. At 10.30 am the Commonwealth liner *Murada*, which was a few miles away, was asked to stand by in case *Ormonde*'s 320 passengers had to be evacuated and assistance was needed from ashore. At 1 pm the fire was brought under control so *Murada* continued her voyage, and by 5.30 pm the fire was almost out. At 3 pm the next day *Ormonde* continued her passage to Sydney, the damage being confined to the deck plates around the hold, although the deck tiles in the forward dining saloon were badly charred. There was also a fair amount of water damage to storerooms, and once she arrived in Sydney she was taken into dock for repairs.

Two years after this incident *Ormonde* left Tilbury for Brisbane again, at 11.30 am on December 3 1938, on her last full pre-war voyage, and she arrived back in London again on March 9 1939. She spent the summer cruising to

Left *The first class lounge,* Ormonde (P&O).

Below left *The second class dining saloon,* Ormonde (P&O).

Below Ormonde *at Sydney on January 26 1931, when she was the flagship at an Anniversary Regatta* (P&O).

the Norwegian fjords and then on August 12 1939, at 12.40 am, she left for Australia once more, commanded by Captain Sherbourne, and three days later Britain and France informed Germany that each would go to war automatically if Germany invaded Poland. When war was declared *Ormonde* had just left Colombo, and on September 23, the day that Germany announced all organized resistance in Poland had ended, she arrived in Brisbane. On November 18 that year she arrived back in Tilbury, having returned via Suez, and a week later she was requisitioned by the government, for the second time in 22 years, as a troop transport.

During the next two weeks she underwent conversion work in preparation for her new role, which required the provision of 1,560 berths for the troops she was to carry. These 'berths' included 686 hammocks on 'F' deck. On December 8 1939 she sailed from London to Halifax, Nova Scotia, and she returned to Greenock with Canadian troops. On January 7 1940, she left the Clyde and anchored off Cowes in the Solent where she remained until mid-February when she went into Southampton Docks. She stayed there for the remainder of the month before sailing to Australia as a requisitioned liner on March 2. Her passenger berths and cargo space were allocated by the government, and she sailed via the Mediterranean, calling at Naples for six hours on March 10. She left Sydney in mid-April that year once again returning through the Mediterranean; but this time the call at Naples was omitted because by now Mussolini had abandoned all public pretence of staying out of the war and had declared that he intended to ally Italy with Germany. *Ormonde* arrived back in London on May 27 1940, and as she came up the Channel she passed through the massive evacuation fleet, as the BEF was taken off the Dunkirk beaches.

The 'Phoney War' had come to an end, and *Ormonde* was to be fully occupied over the next two months with the evacuation of Allied troops from Europe. Three days after her arrival in London she sailed for Norway to assist with the British withdrawal from Narvik. No sooner had she landed her troops at Gourock on June 13, than she left for St Nazaire where she embarked tired units of the BEF and landed them at Plymouth on June 16. She then made one more voyage to the French Atlantic ports where she evacuated more troops before taking them to Morpeth Dock in Liverpool. In July 1940 she made a trooping voyage to Reykjavik to land garrison troops on the island. By now Allied land operations in Europe were effectively at an end for four years, and *Ormonde* was to undertake more orthodox trooping voyages.

With Tilbury 'out of bounds' to the big troopships, *Ormonde* left Liverpool on August 5 1940 with 2,592 troops for Bombay and Suez. She returned to the Clyde in late December that year with a much-needed cargo of food from Bombay and South Africa. She made one further voyage to Bombay and Cape Town, which kept her away from home until the end of April 1941. In the following month she sailed for Loch Fyne, where, for most of May and the first week in June, she carried out invasion exercises. During July that year she lay at anchor off Gourock at seven days' notice awaiting orders. When they came they were for more invasion exercises off Inverary, and then in late August she lay off Gourock once more awaiting orders.

In late September she was prepared for a voyage to Iceland, which in the event was cancelled, and she left instead for Southern Africa and the Middle East. This time her troop accommodation was limited to 2,100 on account of inadequate cooking facilities on board. During this voyage she added yet another new port to her list when, in early December, she called at Takoradi on the Gold Coast (Ghana). She arrived back in Glasgow just in time for the New Year, when she went into dock and was fitted to carry 3,587 troops, 2,390 of them in hammocks. She made two more voyages to Durban which kept her away from February until September 1942, before carrying out further exercises in preparation for the invasion of North Africa. In November 1942 *Ormonde* took part in 'Operation Torch', disembarking her troops at Algiers between November 12 and 21. Then followed four trips in quick succession to the Mediterranean, one to Oran, one to Borne and two to Algiers.

The war in North Africa had now ended and the ship was detailed to take part in the invasion of Sicily. She sailed from the Clyde on June 29 1943 and landed her troops at Augusta. Her next voyage was to Algiers and then on to the west coast of Africa to take West African troops to Bombay to join the 14th Army in Burma. The return voyage was made via the Suez Canal and she was one of the first ships to use this regular route since May 1940, and she was the first to make a night transit. After two short runs to the Mediterranean, she finally arrived in the UK on January 4 1944, having brought home the 7th Armoured Division of the 8th Army from Naples. For them there was more important work to be done.

After another short voyage to Algiers, she again took West African troops from Takoradi to Bombay, this time via the Mediterranean, finally bringing home a full ship of leave troops in time for Christmas. A voyage to Bombay followed and then, on July 16 1945, she sailed from Tilbury on what was to be her last wartime voyage, taking troops to the Far East. *Ormonde* had taken part in all the big ship evacuations and invasions, but there was still operational work for her to do. Although VJ day occurred while she was in Bombay, the plans still went ahead and she was earmarked to land troops in Malaya. She left Madras on September 12 1945, and five days later disembarked her troops at Morib before sailing to Rangoon to embark released prisoners-of-war. She arrived in Tilbury on October 25 with her very grateful passengers, and for the second time in her career she was discharged from government service at the end of a war.

During the Second World War *Ormonde* had on several occasions been subjected to air attack or been closely threatened from the air and sea; off Norway, during and after the North African landing, at the Sicily landing, and at times in the Atlantic and Mediterranean. Although she had some near misses she never sustained any damage. Her armament, which started in a modest way with one 6-inch gun and one 3-inch high angle, was increased as the war went on, by two 12-pounder guns, one Bofors, 12 Oerlikons, and one Lewis gun. She had steamed over 300,000 miles and carried more than 120,000 troops.

For the second time *Ormonde* went into a shipyard for conversion to peacetime service, only this time she was not the crack ship of the fleet. She was 28 years old, and as she went to Birkenhead for refitting it was obvious that her future was limited. One factor which was to play a major part in her career was the enormous demand for passages to Australia, by emigrants from England. The majority of these were sponsored by the Australian government, and there were some 180,000 people waiting to start a new life 'down under'. Negotiations were under way between the Australian Minister of Immigration, the British government and various shipping companies. The Australian government wanted to charter the *Aquitania*, but the British government would not release her. In the event they offered *Ormonde* and the two P&O ships *Chitral* and *Ranchi*, which the Australians agreed to. Meanwhile, work was progressing at Birkenhead to prepare *Ormonde* for her new role, but it was early 1947 before she was ready.

The new accommodation for 1,050 passengers was officially described as 'austerity class'. Basically the public rooms were the same as pre-war, but more seating was provided and all passengers had the run of the whole ship. The division between the forward and after dining saloons was made by the purser, and usually it depended on the accommodation occupied by the individual passengers. A few cabins on 'B' deck still had the old bedsteads and Pulman berths, and they were fitted with fans. All the cabins on 'B' and 'C' decks were fitted with a wardrobe and chest of drawers. On 'D' deck the cabins were fitted with wardrobes only, and on 'E' and 'F' decks there was no furniture fitted in the cabins at all apart from wall hooks. The absence of furniture in the majority of the cabins enabled the refit to be completed by October 1947, for with the shortages of those years the complete fitting

Left *A stern view of the* Ormonde (P&O).

Below Ormonde *in the Suez Canal in the last few years of service* (P&O).

out would have taken at least another 12 months. The liner's crew accommodation had been much improved, with the addition of a recreation room and a separate mess.

By October 8 1947 *Ormonde* was in Tilbury Docks and preparing for her first voyage in her new role. That day a large selection of British and Australian members of the Press were invited aboard. Mr Colin Anderson told them that the refit had cost £270,000, just over half the original cost of her building, but the state of the hull was as good as many ships built 15 years later. *Ormonde* was commanded by Captain T. L. Shurrock, and for her first voyage the whole of the accommodation was taken up by the Australian government, who had selected all the passengers. She was carrying some 1,068 emigrants, 400 of these being children, including one baby only 11 weeks old; 23 of the youngsters were returning to foster parents who had cared for them during the war. The highest fare for the voyage was £95 for a two-berth cabin on 'B' deck, and the lowest fare was £59 for a six-, eight- or ten-berth cabin on 'F' deck. *Ormonde* sailed from Tilbury on October 10 1947, delivering all her passengers to Australia well before Christmas, and the ship herself was back in Tilbury at the end of January 1948. The emigrant ships normally returned home with only a few passengers on board, usually carried on the company's account. In May 1950 *Ormonde* was one of five liners chartered by the Dutch government to evacuate their nationals at Jakarta and the voyage was continued to Rotterdam where they were disembarked.

By August 1952 the demand for migrant passages to Australia had fallen dramatically, and at 35 years old it was clear that *Ormonde*'s career was coming to an end. On August 20 1952 a farewell luncheon was held on board at Tilbury, and on the following day she sailed on her 75th and final voyage to Australia. She had made 17 migrant voyages since October 1947, and had carried 17,500 passengers. She left from berth 34 of Tilbury Dock, not far away from the newest Orient liners. She was flying her 210 ft paying-off pennant when she left and a full orchestra of ships' whistles did her honour. Three members of her crew had totalled 53 years continuous service between them, and her purser remembered that when he first served in *Ormonde*, access to the smoking room was forbidden to ladies. The room itself was from another age, completely panelled in dark wood and, with its leather chairs, providing the sedate atmosphere of a gentlemen's club. In Australia there were farewell dinners held on board before she left Brisbane, Sydney and Melbourne, and on November 19 1952 she arrived at Tilbury Landing Stage for the last time. She had been sold to the British Iron & Steel Corporation, and on December 1 1952 she left the London River for the last time to be broken up at Dalmuir. She arrived there three days later, and so ended her long career, only a few miles from where it had started 35 years previously.

Technical data

Gross tonnage: 14,981
Net tonnage: 9,021
Length overall: 580 ft 5 in (176.92 m)
Breadth: 66 ft 7 in (20.29 m)
Depth: 40 ft 5 in (12.32 m)
Main engines: Twin screw, four sets of Parsons single-reduction geared turbines, 17,000 shp, 18 knots
Boilers: Coal-fired, steam pressure 215 psi; 1923, boilers converted to burn oil fuel
Passengers: First class 278, Second class 195, Third class 1,000; 1947, Austerity class 1,050

The German Trio of 1920 and 1921 *Ormuz, Omar* and *Orcades*

The years immediately following the end of the First World War were difficult ones for Britain's shipowners. Their losses during the war had been heavy and the demands on them in the first months of peace were great. The Orient Line was no exception, for during the war it had lost four vessels totalling some 45,200 gross tons, which was half the fleet as it had stood in 1914, and although *Ormonde* had come into service with them in the closing months of the war, she could not compensate for the lost tonnage. The answer to the problem was partly provided by large numbers of German merchant ships which were taken over by the Allies after the Armistice in November 1918. The Allied Control Commission was the body responsible for the allocation of the German war prizes and they handed over the lion's share of the ships to the British government. These were then sold on behalf of the government by the Shipping Controller. The Orient Line purchased three ex-German vessels, the *Königin Luise* of 11,103 gross tons, the *Prinz Ludwig* of 9,764 gross tons and the *Zeppelin*, a reasonably modern ship of 14,167 gross tons.

The *Königin Luise* was the eldest of the trio, having been launched on October 17 1896 from the A. G. Vulkan Shipyard at Stettin which was in the Prussian province of Pomerania. She was built for the Norddeutscher Lloyd's service from Bremerhaven to New York and originally she carried 225 first, 235 second and 1,940 steerage passengers. She made her maiden voyage to New York on March 22 1897 and between then and a major refit, which she underwent in 1902, she sailed both the North Atlantic and to Australia. Between 1904 and 1914 she served the Norddeutscher Lloyd route between Trieste and New York, and in 1910 she rescued 19 men from a sinking British sailing ship, *Harvard Queen*. In 1912 she had another major refit during which the well decks forward and aft were plated up and decked over. It seems her war service was completely uneventful as she lay at Bremerhaven for the duration, a victim of the British blockade.

The *Prinz Ludwig* was also built at the A. G. Vulkan yards in Stettin, for Norddeutscher Lloyd's Far East service. She made her maiden sailing in 1903, and during the 11 years before the First World War she sailed to Japan and Australia. In early 1914 she carried German troops to Tsingtao, the port in the northern Chinese province of Shantung which Germany had occupied since 1897, and which had been turned into a fortified naval base. She too remained at Bremerhaven during the First World War, although at one stage she was equipped as a troopship for the projected invasion of Britain.

The most modern of the three ships was the *Zeppelin*, and she was launched on June 9 1914 at the Bremer Vulkan Shipyard at Vegesack on the River Weser. The ceremony was actually performed by Count Zeppelin who gave his name to the vessel. She was intended to be the first of a series of 15,000-tonners for the Norddeutscher Lloyd Australian service which, had they all been built, would have proved formidable opposition for the Orient Line and the P&O. She had accommodation for 319 first, 156 second, 342 third and 1,348 steerage class passengers. When war was declared in August 1914 it seems that *Zeppelin* was still not completed, and work was temporarily halted. Her proposed maiden voyage from Bremerhaven to Sydney had actually been advertised, but with the tight blockade of Germany there was no chance that she would leave her home port. She was eventually completed on January 21 1915 but was immediately laid up for the next four years.

After the Armistice in November 1918 the *Zeppelin* left the River Weser for the first time, bound not for Australia but for England. Initially she was managed on behalf of the Shipping Controller by the White Star Line, and in early 1920 she was purchased by the Orient Line who sent her to Belfast for major alterations to meet their requirements. During the refit, which was completed at Rotterdam, the three forward holds were fitted for frozen cargoes and the accommodation was altered to cater for 293 first and 882 third class passengers. As a result of the changes her gross tonnage was increased to 14,588, and she was transferred to her new owners, the Orient Line, as the *Ormuz* on March 28 1921.

The *Königin Luise* was handed over to the British government, and she was managed by the Orient Line for the Shipping Controller. *Prinz Ludwig* was handed over in early 1919, being managed by the P&O Company on behalf of the government. She made two voyages to Australia with P&O before being sold to the Orient Line on March 21 1921. She was renamed *Orcades* and refitted to carry 123 first class and 476 third class passengers.

Königin Luise made a number of voyages under her German name carrying only cargo. On

The Zeppelin *was transferred to the Orient Line on March 28 1921 and renamed* Ormuz (National Maritime Museum).

S.S. KONIGIN LUISE
Leaving Sydney Harbour 6th March 1920.

Left *The* Königin Luise *leaving Sydney on March 6 1920. At this time she was being managed by P&O* (P&O).

Below left *In January 1921* Königin Luise *was renamed* Omar (National Maritime Museum).

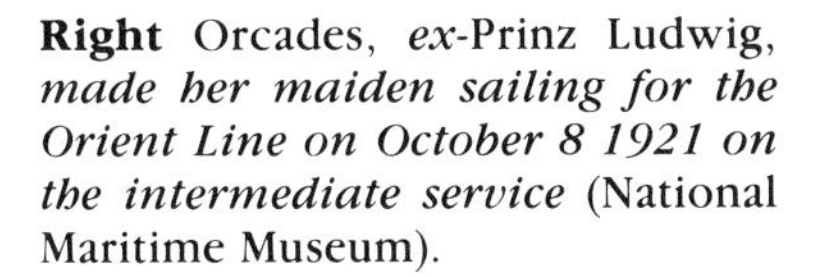

Right Orcades, *ex*-Prinz Ludwig, *made her maiden sailing for the Orient Line on October 8 1921 on the intermediate service* (National Maritime Museum).

one of these voyages fire broke out in one of her holds while she was loading copra. In the event two holds had to be flooded in order to extinguish the blaze. She made her first Orient Line passenger sailing from Tilbury to Brisbane on September 4 1920 and four days later she was in collision with the 3,000-ton British steamer *Loughborough*. The two vessels were in dense fog off Lisbon at the time and, although there was no serious damage to the *Königin Luise*, the *Loughborough* was leaking badly and she had to be beached at Belem on the River Tagus just outside Lisbon. *Königin Luise* was able to continue her voyage and she arrived in Gibraltar at 2 pm on September 9 1920, the day after the accident. She returned to Tilbury at the end of that year and in January 1921 she was renamed *Omar*. It is probable that she was purchased by the Orient Line at this time. The name *Omar* is Arabic, being the title given to the second of the Mohammedan Caliphs.

Thirteen weeks after being handed over to the Orient Line *Ormuz* resumed the company's cruises to Norway, which had been in abeyance since 1914. She sailed from Immingham with a large complement of passengers for the first two-week cruise to the fjords on Saturday June 25 1921. She continued to run her northern cruises until the end of the season in October that year and in the following month, on November 12 1921, she made her first voyage to Brisbane for the Orient Line. She then settled into the route and by the spring of 1924 she had made seven round voyages interspersed with cruises to the fjords.

Orcades made her maiden sailing to Australia for the Orient Line on October 8 1921 and in conjunction with *Omar*, which sailed for Brisbane on October 22 that year, she maintained what was described as the intermediate service. Both ships were routed by way of Naples, Port Said and Colombo and, although their cargo space was adequate, their passenger accommodation was not up to the company's standards and their speed was too slow for the mail run. Although the two vessels spent a good deal of time laid up off Southend, they provided a useful stop-gap for the line until the new tonnage of the

1920s could be brought into service.

On March 8 1922, while *Orcades* was laid up in the Thames Estuary, her anchor cables parted and she went aground on mud flats about one mile south-east of Southend Pier. It took six tugs three days to refloat her and then she was towed to Tilbury where she remained until she sailed for Australia once again on September 22 that year.

Omar made only nine voyages to Australia for the Orient Line and she left Tilbury on the last of these on February 9 1924. On March 10 that year, while in the Indian Ocean, she hit a submerged object and lost a propeller. However, she was able to continue the voyage at reduced speed and she was only 24 hours late arriving at Fremantle. On her return to London in June 1924 she was put up for sale and on July 4 1924 she was purchased by the Byron SS Co, a British subsidiary of a Greek company. She was used for an emigrant service between Greece and New York and she was renamed *Edison*. In 1928 she was sold to the Greek National Shipping Company, and she survived for another six years before being broken up in Italy in 1935.

Orcades made her last sailing to Australia on September 20 1924. On March 30 1925 she was sold to Stern Aktiengesellschaft of Bremen to be broken up, so ending her days not far away from her pre-war home port.

Although *Ormuz* had been by far the most successful of the German trio, she was not really suited for Orient Line service, and on November 27 1926 she sailed on her final voyage for the company. It was her 14th Australian trip since her first voyage to Brisbane in 1921, and on her return to London on April 22 1927 she was sold to her original owners, Norddeutscher Lloyd, for £25,700. She was given an overhaul and renamed *Dresden* before being put onto their Atlantic service. Seven years later she was sailing on the 'Strength Through Joy' cruises organized by Dr Ley, the leader of the Labour Front in Germany. On May 16 1934 she was on a cruise off the coast of Belgium when she rescued the crew of a French military seaplane which had been forced to ditch in the sea.

One month later she was on a fjords cruise near Stavanger when, at 7.18 pm on Wednesday June 20 1934, there was a sudden heavy shock to the vessel, just as she was passing the Aresgounen sea-mark, about 400 metres away. Immediately after the incident the *Dresden* took a heavy list and Captain Petermöller tried to run his ship aground on Karmoy Island. Unfortunately it was not possible because within minutes of the shock the ship's furnaces were extinguished by the inrush of water. The lights went out and there was a certain amount of panic among the passengers on board. Captain Petermöller gave the order to abandon ship and as the first lifeboat was lowered it capsized, throwing all the occupants into the water. Three women were drowned, but fortunately there were no further casualties. The survivors were taken on board the Danish steamer *King Haakon* and landed at Stavanger. Among the ships which rushed to the scene was the battleship HMS *Rodney*, but she was too late to render any assistance. It seems that *Dresden* had struck uncharted rocks near Utsira Island, and by the following day she had rolled onto her port side in 26 fathoms of water with her stern completely submerged and her bows out of the water. She was declared a total loss and in the following month the wreck was sold to a local company to be broken up.

Technical data

Gross tonnage: 14,588 (*Ormuz*), 11,103 (*Omar*), 9,764 (*Orcades*)
Net tonnage: 8,082 (*Ormuz*), 6,790 (*Omar*), 5,704 (*Orcades*)
Length overall: 550 ft (167.64 m) (*Ormuz*), 523 ft 1 in (159.44 m) (*Omar*), 492 ft (149.96 m) (*Orcades*)
Breadth: 67 ft 4 in (20.52 m) (*Ormuz*), 60 ft 1 in (18.31 m) (*Omar*), 57 ft 7 in (17.55 m) (*Orcades*)
Depth: 35 ft 1 in (10.69 m) (*Ormuz*), 34 ft 10 in (10.62 m) (*Omar*), 35 ft (10.67 m) (*Orcades*)
Main engines: Twin screw, two sets of quadruple-expansion engines, 10,000 ihp, 16 knots (*Ormuz*), 6,000 ihp, 13½ knots (*Omar*), 7,000 ihp, 14 knots (*Orcades*)
Boilers: Coal-fired, steam pressure 215 psi (*Ormuz*), 125 psi (*Omar* and *Orcades*)
Passengers: First class 292, Third class 828 (*Ormuz*), First class 170, Third class 757 (*Omar*), First class 123, Third class 476 (*Orcades*)

Orama 1924

Orama was the first ship to be constructed for the Orient Line after the First World War, and she was also the first of the five 20,000-tonners built in the 1920s. The keel for the new vessel was laid in 1920 at the Barrow-in-Furness yard of Vickers Ltd, who went on to build a long series of vessels for the Orient Line.

In April 1923 it was announced that in future there would be no second class accommodation on board, and all new ships would carry only first and third class passengers. *Orama* was to have berths for 582 first and 1,244 third class passengers. Originally she was to have been named *Oriana*, but this was changed and *Orama* chosen, reviving memories of the first ship of that name which entered service in 1911 and which was sunk during the First World War. The launching ceremony was arranged for Tuesday May 20 1924, and was to have been carried out by Lady Cook, the wife of Sir Joseph Cook, the High Commissioner for Australia. However, on the day she was unable to attend and so her daughter, Miss Winifred Cook, graciously deputized. It was quite an occasion at Barrow and was, according to contemporary reports, reminiscent of big launches in pre-war days. Tramcars lined up outside the Town Hall, and Michaelson Road was bustling with activity as hordes of people walked towards the shipyard. Crowds of workmen joined the throng of onlookers and hundreds of others chose Walney Island as their vantage point. After a dull morning the sun broke through at midday to grace the proceedings, and at 12.15 pm *Orama* was sent down the slipway to her natural element.

Orama's design was very similar to *Ormonde*'s, with passengers accommodated on eight decks from 'A' deck down to 'H' deck. The first class cabins were situated amidships on 'A' to 'F' decks, 'A' deck being a large games area beneath the funnels. Below this on 'B' deck, overlooking the bows, was the first class lounge, with a dance space, smoking room and café aft overlooking 'C' deck. One of *Orama*'s features was the large number of single-berth cabins, and a lot of these were on 'C' deck, the first class promenade area. Also forward on this deck was the first class reading and writing room. For the third class there was open deck space aft on 'D' deck, with a promenade below on 'E' deck, and the lounge and smoking room on 'F' deck. Dining saloons for both classes were also on 'F' deck, the first class being amidships with the sculleries and galleys aft of it, and then the third class saloon aft again.

Orama was a twin-screw ship powered by six single-reduction geared turbines, with the steam being provided by six double- and four single-ended, oil-fired boilers. She had an nhp of 3,836 and a service speed of 18 knots, which made her the fastest ship on the Australian mail run until P&O's 'Straths' took this honour in the 1930s.

On Saturday October 12 1924 work on *Orama* was completed and she left Barrow for Belfast and Thompson's Graving Dock on Queen's Island where the underwater hull was scraped

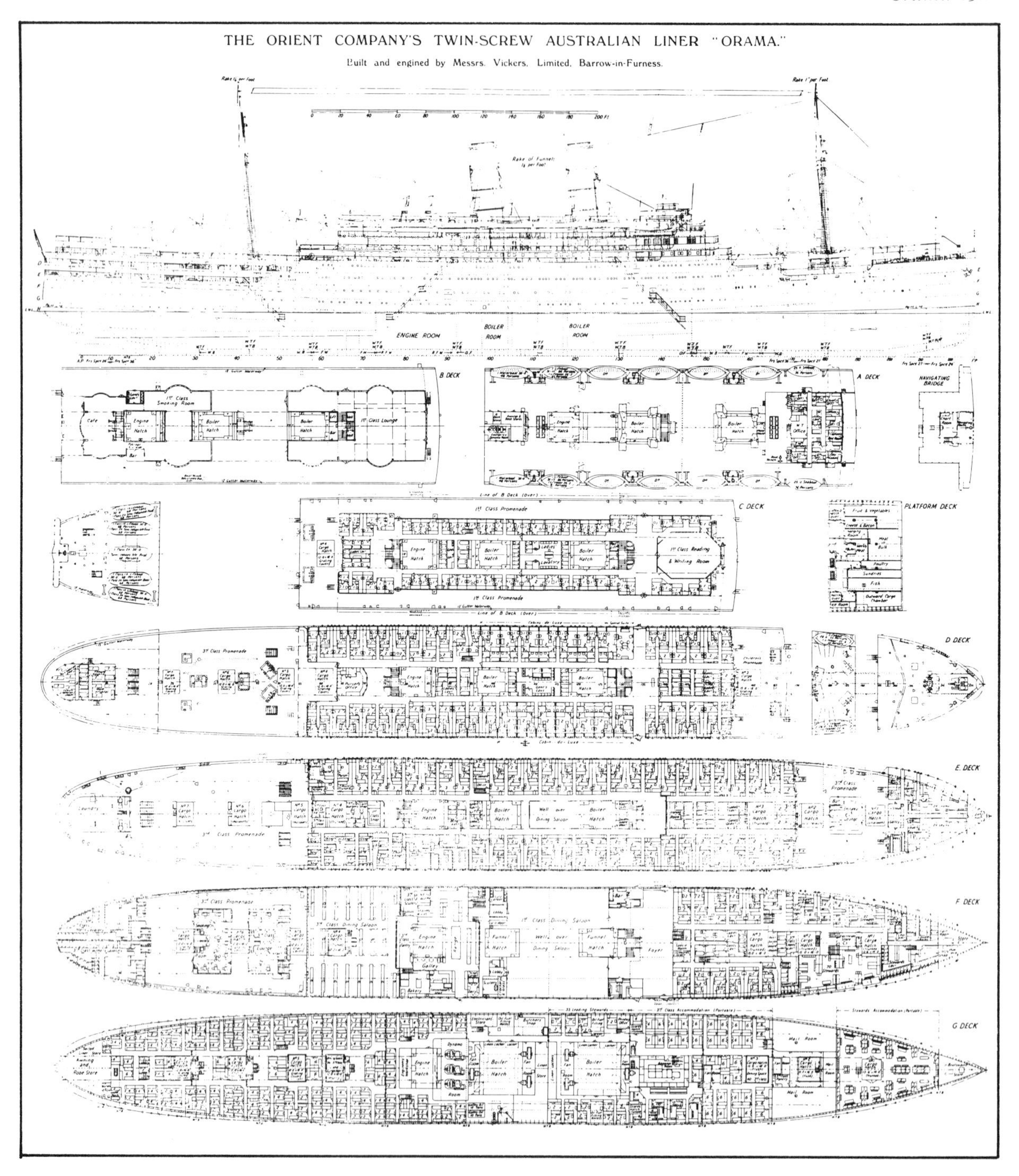
THE ORIENT COMPANY'S TWIN-SCREW AUSTRALIAN LINER "ORAMA."
Built and engined by Messrs. Vickers, Limited, Barrow-in-Furness.
ENGINE ROOM
BOILER ROOM
BOILER ROOM
B DECK
1st Class Smoking Room
Cafe
Bar
1st Class Lounge
A DECK
NAVIGATING BRIDGE
C DECK
1st Class Promenade
1st Class Reading & Writing Room
Line of B Deck (Over)
PLATFORM DECK
D DECK
3rd Class Promenade
Cabin de Luxe
E. DECK
Laundry
Well over Dining Saloon
F DECK
1st Class Dining Saloon
3rd Class Dining Saloon
Galley
Bakery
Foyer
G DECK
Awning and Rope Store
Mail Room

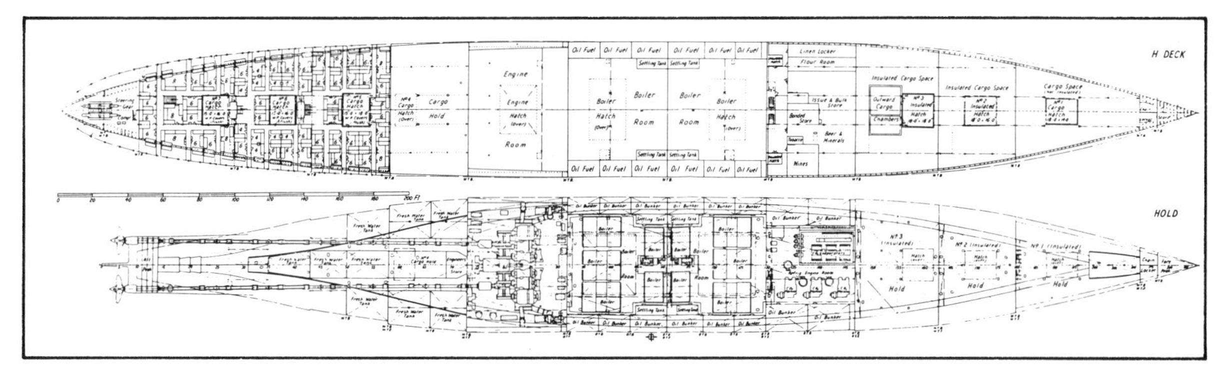

Left and above *Deck plan of RMS* Orama, *1924* (Marine Publications International Ltd).

Right Orama *entering Tilbury Docks for the first time, in October 1924* (Vickers).

Right Orama *at Tilbury, October 25 1924* (Vickers plc).

Orama *in corn-coloured livery. The new hull colour was tested on* Orama (P&O).

and painted. Four days later she left Belfast for the Clyde where she underwent trials, before finally arriving in Tilbury on Friday October 25, 13 days after leaving Barrow. *Orama* made her maiden sailing to Brisbane on November 15 1924, with first class fares starting at £92 per person. In February 1926 she called at Southampton on her outward voyage to Australia and became the first Orient liner to make regular calls at the port. A year later, in February 1927, Sir Alan Garrett Anderson, a director of the managing company, returned home from Australia in *Orama*. It was the ship's eighth round voyage and in a report written on board he says, 'The ship is now in her third year of service and it distresses me to find that in so fine a ship—so well run in general—there remain minor defects which should have been corrected in her trial runs. Why should *Orama* satisfy passengers less than, say, *Oronsay*?' It seems that Sir Alan's main complaints centred around the poor ventilation in the first class dining saloon and lounge, and excessive vibration in the verandah café and smoking room on 'B' deck.

Despite these problems *Orama*'s career continued uninterrupted, with voyages to Australia and cruises to the Mediterranean and the Norwegian fjords. In the New Year of 1936 *Orama* went up to Barrow-in-Furness to be refitted by her builders. By late April that year, with the refit completed, she left Barrow for Tilbury with just a skeleton crew and no passengers. Just over 24 hours later, at 5.34 am on Saturday April 25, *Orama* was off the East Goodwin lightship in very thick fog and only a few hours from her destination, when she was rammed on the starboard side amidships by the 3,200-ton Yugoslav steamer *Sveti Duje*. *Orama* anchored

Orama *at Sydney in March 1931* (Southampton City Museums).

off the Goodwins to assess the damage, and to render any assistance necessary to the smaller ship. Fortunately damage to *Orama* was limited to a pierced oil bunker on the starboard side above the waterline. The *Sveti Duje* was more severely damaged in her stem and bows, and her forepeak was flooded. However, both vessels were able to proceed under their own steam, and they arrived in Tilbury late that same afternoon. *Orama* was quickly repaired and she sailed for Australia on May 23 1936 on schedule.

In the following year *Orama* made two 17-day cruises in the late summer to Egypt and what was then Palestine. She left for the first voyage on September 3 1937, with fares starting at £18 in tourist and £40 in first class. Even then the seeds were sown for future conflict in those countries, as a government study of Palestine had recommended a partition of the country with neither the Arabs nor the Jews ruling absolutely.

Seventeen months later, in February 1939, *Orama* set sail on her last peacetime round voyage to Brisbane, arriving there on March 27. On her return through the Mediterranean she called at Naples, Villefranche, Toulon and Gibraltar, arriving in Tilbury on May 18 that year. She sailed once again for Australia on June 17 1939, commanded by Captain L. V. James DSC RNR. Her route took her through the Mediterranean, calling once again at Naples where she embarked a number of Italian emigrants bound for Australia. On July 3 she had passed Aden and was in the Indian Ocean, when at 9.40 am the 'man overboard' alarm was sounded on the bridge. A lifebuoy with calcium flare was thrown into the sea and the vessel circled the area at slow speed, but no one was found. At 10.20 am the search was abandoned

Left *A starboard bow view of* Orama (P&O).

Below right *Shells poured into* Orama *and her plight was hopeless; she is on fire and listing to port, June 8 1940* (W.Z. Bilddienst).

Bottom right Orama *takes the final plunge as the crew of a German destroyer look on* (Imperial War Museum).

and *Orama* resumed her course. It transpired that an Italian emigrant, Alfio Grasso, was the passenger who had jumped overboard. Five minutes after the first alarm, at 9.45 am, the surgeon was summoned to the after end of 'E' deck, where he found Mrs Grasso seriously wounded with her throat cut. It seems that husband and wife had had a dispute and Mr Grasso had stabbed her, before throwing himself over the side of the ship. She survived her wounds, but he was lost in the Indian Ocean. It was a small drama which was soon forgotten, compared to the terrible events that were to overtake the world.

On her arrival in Sydney *Orama* made a cruise from the port to Noumea and Fiji. It was the liner's last pleasure cruise, and by August 10 1939 she had sailed once again for London. On September 2, the day before war was declared, *Orama* was off Minicoy Island after leaving Colombo for the Red Sea. She received orders to proceed homewards via Cape Town, and a week later she called in to Mombasa. On September 18 she arrived at Cape Town, and on the last day of the month she left Freetown, arriving in Tilbury just two weeks later, having been routed well out into the Atlantic. As soon as she reached London *Orama* was requisitioned by the government and was partially converted to carry troops, leaving Tilbury on December 12 1939 bound for Halifax, Nova Scotia, where she arrived ten days later. In Halifax she embarked 900 Canadian troops and loaded 500 tons of much-needed cargo, sailing for Greenock on Christmas Eve. She disembarked the troops on the Clyde on New Year's Eve and then left Greenock for Tilbury again.

On her return *Orama* lay at Tilbury for over a month before she sailed for Australia, as a requisitioned liner, on February 10 1940. This time she sailed through the Mediterranean and called at Gibraltar and Naples. It was only four months before Italy declared war on the Allies, and *Orama* was one of the last British liners to call at an Italian port before the Sicilian landings in July 1943. It was *Orama*'s last visit to Australia and she called at Fremantle, Melbourne, Sydney and Hobart before sailing once again for England by way of Cape Town. It was May 15 1940 when *Orama* arrived in the Solent and anchored off Cowes for degaussing.

By now the war in Europe was escalating and in the previous month Hitler had invaded Denmark and Norway in a swift series of land, sea and air strikes. Germany had thus extended the war, claiming it possessed 'documentary proof that England and France had jointly decided, if necessary, to carry out their action against the will of the Scandinavian countries... Germany has thus preserved the Scandinavian countries and peoples from destruction, and will until the end of the war defend true neutrality in the North'. On April 15 1940, a combined British, French and Polish force landed near Narvik, and on the following day British troops landed at Andalsnes and Namsos, about 100 miles north of Trondheim. However, the Allied forces were rapidly rendered helpless by German aircraft which had established a mastery of the skies, and in early May the Allied forces were evacuated from all parts of Norway except Narvik. By the end of May plans were in hand to evacuate that port as well.

On May 19 1940 *Orama* had arrived in Tilbury from the Solent, and 11 days later, on May 30, she sailed north to assist the evacuation of the British troops from Narvik. She was commanded by Captain F. M. Sherbourne, and after leaving the Thames she joined a northbound convoy. The passage up the east coast was full of incident, with enemy aircraft and submarines taking their toll of nearby ships. On June 2 the convoy arrived in Scapa Flow, where *Orama* went aground. However, she was refloated at 7 pm that same evening and the convoy sailed under escort towards the Norwegian coast. Late in the afternoon of June 6 the convoy was dispersed to various destinations, and *Orama* and two other ships were ordered to a rendezvous which was reached the following evening. *Orama*, together

with the hospital ship *Atlantis*, was then ordered to return to the UK unescorted. Next morning at about 8 am she was sighted by enemy reconnaissance aircraft. Soon afterwards, at 9.20 am, the mastheads of unknown vessels were sighted; their identity was firmly established ten minutes later when a salvo was fired, falling just ahead of *Orama*.

With the evacuation of Narvik in full swing, and with little or no protection available for the numerous vessels which were crossing the Norwegian Sea, the Germans had embarked on 'Operation Juno', specifically designed to sink as much of the Allied shipping as possible. They therefore sent a powerful surface force which included the battleships *Scharnhorst* and *Gneisenau*, the heavy cruiser *Admiral Hipper*, with the destroyers *Karl Galster, Hans Lody, Erich Steinbrinck* and *Hermann Shoemann*. On the morning of June 8, in an attempt to locate the main evacuation convoy, the *Scharnhorst* and *Admiral Hipper* launched scouting planes, which reported seeing a cruiser and merchantman to the south, and a liner and hospital ship to the north. The *Admiral Hipper*, together with the destroyers, was sent north to locate the latter two ships, and so the fate of the *Orama* was sealed.

The *Atlantis*, obeying the rules of war, made no signals and so obtained the immunity due to a hospital ship. The first salvo fired at *Orama* was quickly followed by further attacks, the liner being freely hit. Shells poured into *Orama* and her plight was hopeless. Vital hits in the engine room and on the waterline necessitated abandoning ship. All the boats on the port side had been destroyed, so the crew had to get away in those from the starboard side. The German force picked up 279 survivors, and the *Orama*, listing badly and on fire, was finally sunk by a torpedo from the destroyer *Hans Lody*. Twenty members of *Orama*'s crew were killed in this forlorn engagement in which an isolated and defenceless Allied liner was sunk by surface ships.

The only glimmer of light in the affair was that *Orama* had no troops on board; had it been otherwise the casualty list would have been horrific. The surviving crew members became the largest block of Merchant Navy prisoners from any one vessel, and the 'Orama Band' became well known throughout the camps in northern Germany. In the early days of their internment the presence among the seamen of a highly qualified surgeon was invaluable in negotiating for proper sanitary and medical conditions in the camp.

Most of the crew were held in Stalag XIIIA in Germany, and on April 9 1942 the staff commander sent a seemingly innocuous postcard to the managers to let them know how they were faring. In order to get it past the German censors he worded it thus: 'Dear Colin, [Sir Colin Anderson] We are together again, the whole crew, officers and men except Sherbourne, who is still with the Senior Service. Everyone seems to be in the best of health. Received seven clothes parcels sent in October, which I have distributed. The men were very grateful. We have quite a few theatrical shows in which our men are in the majority and plenty to read. Sincerely, Addison.' For most of the men from *Orama* there were still three long years of captivity to endure, until they were liberated on April 28 1945 by a British division. They had been prisoners-of-war for five years, after which nine officers and men received personal thanks from the Ministry of War Transport and six were decorated.

Technical data
Gross tonnage: 19,840
Net tonnage: 11,896
Length overall: 632 ft (192.63 m)
Breadth: 75 ft 2 in (22.91 m)
Depth: 32 ft 10 in (10.01 m)
Main engines: Twin screw, six single-reduction geared turbines, 19,310 shp, 18 knots
Boilers: Oil-burning, steam pressure 215 psi
Passengers: First class 582, Third class 1,244; 1935, First class 484, Tourist class 498

Oronsay 1925

Just three months after the launch of *Orama* at Barrow, the second ship in the post-war rebuilding programme was launched on the Clyde. On Thursday August 16 1924 the *Oronsay* was sent down the slipway of John Brown & Company's yard at Clydebank. The christening ceremony was performed by Viscountess Novar, the liner being named after one of the Hebridean Islands off the west coast of Scotland. Her badge, symbolic of her Scottish name, was the targe and broadsword and it could be seen displayed on her funnel casing and stern. At the time of the ceremony she was the largest vessel to be launched on the Clyde since the Cunarder *Franconia* took to the water from an adjacent berth in the same yard two years previously.

Oronsay's design was almost the same as that of the *Orama*, and she was designated a two-class ship—first and third. This enabled a greater amount of space to be devoted to the public rooms and promenading areas. In the first class there were 14 special state rooms, and a luxury suite with private sitting room and separate bathroom. The first class lounge on 'B' deck had walls which were panelled in veneered mahogany with no fewer than 41 windows and a large skylight. The furnishings were based on the Louis XVI period, as were those of the dining saloon on 'F' deck. The third class accommodation included an exceptionally large dining saloon, two smoking rooms and a lounge, all very comfortably furnished. She had more berths for first class passengers than *Orama*, carrying 600, but only 1,200 third class compared with *Orama*'s 1,244.

Oronsay was a twin-screw ship, being powered by two independent sets of Brown-Curtis high-reduction geared turbines capable of developing 20,000 shp, and giving her a service speed of 20 knots. She was fitted with six double-ended and four single-ended cylindrical boilers which produced saturated steam at 215 psi. The boilers were oil-fired and arranged in two watertight compartments, with six electrically-driven fans for supplying air to the furnaces.

On January 14 1925 *Oronsay* ran successful trials on the Firth of Clyde, and in the following month on February 7 she left Tilbury for Brisbane. Later that year, in the summer months, she made a series of cruises from Tilbury. For the next 14 years she ran regularly to Australia without any major incidents, and in 1936 she made the first Orient Line passenger call at Hobart in Tasmania, disembarking 250 passengers at the port.

In the summer of 1939 *Oronsay* arrived back in Tilbury at 8 am on July 27, and made her next sailing to Australia as scheduled on August 26. She was eight days out of London in the Mediterranean when war was declared, and the ship was blacked out until clear of Suez. She arrived back in London on December 3 that year, and sailed once again for Australia 17 days later. It was to be her final voyage for the Orient Line and on her way out she called at Southampton, Naples and Suez, arriving in Brisbane on February

Above Oronsay, *the second ship of the 1920s building programme* (P&O).

Below Oronsay, *cruising in the 1930s* (Orient Line).

Gourock, April 20 1940: Oronsay *was used as a troop depot ship for 18 days* (Imperial War Museum).

10 1940. Her return voyage, also through the Mediterranean, was completed at Tilbury on April 2 1940 and at noon on April 6 she was requisitioned by the government as a troop transport.

Minor alterations had already been made to accommodate troops, and now further work was done so that she could carry an additional 1,274 troops as well as her normal complement of passengers. On April 13 she sailed empty for Gourock, where she arrived three days later. For the next 18 days she lay anchored in the Clyde awaiting orders, and during this period she was used as a troop depot ship at the port. Finally on May 3 1940 she left the Clyde for Southampton and Cherbourg, where she embarked troops for Gibraltar and Malta before returning to Liverpool on May 28. The following day she, like other liners, became caught up in the campaign in Norway, and she sailed for Narvik via Gourock. The whole of the month of June was taken up with evacuations, and she survived the return voyage from Norway to Gourock, packed with troops, without any problems. Two days after arriving from Narvik, on June 14 1940, she left the Clyde in company with *Ormonde* and *Otranto* bound for St Nazaire on the Biscay coast, to assist with the evacuation of Allied troops from France.

She arrived at St Nazaire early on June 17 1940, and started to embark troops. Some hours later, at 1.48 pm, she came under very heavy air attack, as did other ships in the port. The embarkation was still going to take some four hours to complete and she was unable to leave. One bomb hit *Oronsay* in the chartroom, wrecking the radio and wheelhouses and destroying all communication to the engine room. Eight crew members were injured, including the Staff Commander, Mr I. E. G. Goldsworthy. Although she suffered this one direct hit, luck was with *Oronsay*, for the Cunard liner *Lancastria*, which was also embarking troops, was sunk with considerable loss of life. Many of her survivors were taken on board the *Oronsay* for the voyage to safety, which now presented Captain Nicholls with a most unusual problem as all his navigational instruments and charts had been destroyed. He succeeded, however, in bringing his ship safely to Plymouth Sound on May 18, with the aid of a French motoring map and a penny ruler! Once at Plymouth the troops and injured were landed, and on the following day *Oronsay* sailed for Liverpool to have the damage

Left *April 1940: troops relaxing on the Promenade Deck of* Oronsay (Imperial War Museum).

Below *June 17 1940:* Oronsay *under heavy air attack at St Nazaire* (P&O).

Right Oronsay *at St Nazaire, June 17 1940, showing the damage to the navigating bridge and wheelhouse* (P&O).

Below right *St Nazaire, June 17 1940: damage to the after part of the chart room. Staff Commander Goldsworthy and the carpenter survey the mess* (P&O).

repaired. For his initiative and coolness in action Captain Nicholls was awarded the OBE.

Oronsay's next mission of mercy was entirely different but just as dangerous. On August 10 1940, with only makeshift repairs to her bridge, she was anchored in the Mersey ready to embark passengers. She was to carry 351 children to Halifax, Nova Scotia, under the government 'Children Overseas Reception Scheme'. She had been hurriedly converted from a troopship to a nursery for the 27 groups of children, and they were accommodated in the first class section of the ship on 'D', 'E' and 'F' decks, with easy access to lifeboats being the priority. Her precious charges were embarked at 10.45 am on the morning of August 10, and, according to one of their conductors, 'The children were settled in and had a midday meal, then lifeboat and fire drills which they thought was enormous fun, although they were a bit mystified by the long menus.' Altogether there was a total of 799 souls on board, which included, as well as the children, 35 conductors, 95 passengers and 318 crew members—the potential for disaster was enormous. *Oronsay* sailed on August 12 and, mercifully, arrived safely in Halifax seven days later.

Oronsay made her return voyage to the Clyde a week later with Canadian troops on board, and then sailed down to Liverpool where further repairs were carried out to the bridge. By October 3 1940 she was back on the Clyde, at Glasgow, and embarking troops for Egypt. She sailed from the Tail of the Bank as part of convoy WS3 during the evening of October 7, commanded by Captain F. L. Butler and carrying 3,000 British and Colonial troops. At 10 am the following morning the convoy was off the north-west coast of Ireland in a position 56°N, 10°W, in brilliant sunshine, ploughing its way into a heavy westerly gale. Suddenly a lone Focke-Wulf four-engined bomber came straight out of the sun with its engines shut off, and carried out a low-level bombing attack along the port side of the *Oronsay*, approaching from the stern and spraying the decks with machine-gun fire and cannon bullets. There were a number of casualties among the troops and Able Seaman Donald Folkes, the masthead lookout who was on duty in the crow's-nest, was shot through the base of the skull and killed instantly. The bombs were near misses and exploded under the ship abreast the after end of the promenade deck. The force of the explosions seemed to lift the vessel clean out of the water and put the engines out of action. However, the ship's armament was quickly in action and put up a heavy barrage of fire which prevented another attack.

The German aircraft then turned their force on the SS *Winchester Castle*, another ship in the same convoy. The remaining ships proceeded on their way and *Oronsay* was left lying helpless in the trough of the sea while radio messages were sent for assistance. The Admiralty made preparations for the liner to be taken in tow, but thanks to magnificent work by the ship's engineers, temporary repairs were effected and *Oronsay* was able to limp on at very slow speed under her own power. Meanwhile moves were under way to escort her back to the Clyde, and by 1.30 pm that day the destroyers *Arrow* and *Ottowa*, together with the AMCs *Salopian* and *Cheshire*, were all standing by the crippled liner. The *Salopian* then left to escort convoy WS3, and later that evening the cruiser HMS *Cairo* joined *Oronsay*. With HMS *Cheshire* ahead and HMS *Cairo* on station astern, *Oronsay* made her way slowly back to the Clyde at around 10 knots. At noon the following day she anchored off Gourock and disembarked her troops, before going up the Clyde and into King George V drydock for repairs.

Oronsay remained in dockyard hands at Glasgow and Liverpool until June 28 1941, when she sailed once again from the Clyde to the Middle East via Cape Town. When she arrived at Suez it was to find the bay there very congested with shipping and net obstructions. Air raids were very frequent and at night she and other large troopers left the harbour to cruise in the Gulf of Suez, returning in time for sunrise the next morning. This proved to be fairly successful at first, but it soon became obvious that the ships were an easy target in the narrow navigable channel of the Gulf of Suez, a fact which was clearly demonstrated when, in mid-July, the White Star liner SS *Georgic* was bombed and badly damaged. Fortunately *Oronsay* came through unscathed and on October 21 that year she berthed at Avonmouth.

Her next voyage took her to Halifax, Nova Scotia, once again, and it was reassuring for those on board to find that, on arrival at the 20th Meridian West, a substantial US Navy escort was there to accompany them the rest of the way to Halifax. This was a generous act by the USA which was still neutral at the time. On arrival at Halifax the British troops were transferred to American troopships and taken to the Far East. On her arrival in Liverpool *Oronsay* was again taken into dockyard hands before sailing once more for another theatre of war.

Oronsay left Liverpool on the morning of March 23 1942 in a convoy bound for Sierra Leone. At Freetown the convoy was regrouped and *Oronsay* became part of 'Assault Force F' for the invasion of Madagascar. The force left Durban in the early afternoon of April 28, sailing in a north-easterly direction, and after five days they joined up with a slower convoy. The offensive was scheduled to start at 4.30 am on May 5, and the assault force had to enter Ambararata Bay south of Diego Suarez, a Vichy French stronghold, which entailed negotiating a minefield in the hours of darkness. At 3.10 am *Oronsay* led the ships of her group into the bay, and the next few hours were very tense with everybody at action stations awaiting attack from the air or shore batteries. At daylight a signal was received to say that the batteries had been captured. At 9.50 am *Oronsay* was ordered close in to the landing beaches, and the escort HMS *Auricula* struck a mine just ahead of her. By nightfall disembarkation of troops was completed, and they were in action outside the town.

As dawn broke on May 7, *Oronsay*'s master and officer of the watch saw a Swordfish aircraft swoop out of the sky and bomb a dark object in the water. It proved to be the French submarine *L'Héros*, trying to get in between two reefs to torpedo one of the invasion fleet. *Oronsay* was the nearest and a sitting target—fortunately the submarine was sunk and *Oronsay*'s luck held once more. Soon prisoners from the submarine and from ashore were arriving on board. It was an extremely nerve-racking time, for mines kept exploding perilously close to the ship and, in view of the fact that part of her cargo consisted of high explosives, this was of great concern to all on board.

Finally, early on the morning of May 8, *Oronsay* left Ambararata Bay in convoy for Diego Suarez. During the voyage another hostile French submarine paid the penalty for its excessive boldness, and the convoy arrived at its destination that same afternoon. During the next 12 days the ship was moved to various parts of Diego Suarez Bay, close in to beaches where the deadly cargo of ammunition was discharged. More batches of French prisoners, together with their wives and children, were still arriving on board and *Oronsay* finally embarked 114 French officers, 688 Senegalese troops, 33 women and 42 children. A detail of 150 British troops also came on board to guard the prisoners and prevent sabotage.

On May 20, together with two other liners and a destroyer escort, *Oronsay* sailed for Durban and Cape Town. The South African authorities refused to accept the Vichy French as PoWs and in Cape Town the military guard was unfortunately replaced with naval ratings. These men, who were survivors from ships which had been sunk in the Indian Ocean, were not up to the task, and shots were accidently fired several times every day during the voyage to Freetown, at times causing near panic among the prisoners. On his arrival at Freetown Captain Roberts, master of *Oronsay*, protested strongly to the authorities and the naval guard was replaced by Royal Marines. Just before the ship sailed, security police came on board and removed ten French officers, who, it seems, were conspiring to seize the ship. With the arrival of the new guard confidence was restored and the remainder of the voyage passed without incident. *Oronsay* arrived back in Glasgow on July 1 1942 after an eventful voyage, and Captain Roberts himself received a message of congratulations from the senior officer in charge of the landings. The whole operation had gone extremely well and the Prime Minister, Mr Winston Churchill, praised all those who had taken part.

Only 13 days after she arrived in the Clyde, *Oronsay* sailed once again for Suez via South Africa. The outward voyage passed without incident, but *Oronsay*'s long run of good luck was soon to end. At Durban, on the homeward leg of her voyage, all the passengers had landed and nearly 5,000 RAF personnel were embarked for Cape Town. In addition the holds were fully loaded so that at Cape Town there would be no more to do once the troops had disembarked, and the ship could proceed homeward with only 50 passengers aboard, mainly civilians. The route she had been given took her southward, then about 800 miles due west to the middle of the Atlantic and then north. The submarines in the area were so thick that numerous diversions were ordered which left her with just enough fuel to reach Freetown.

At 5.30 am on October 9 1942 she was in a position 4°29′N, 26°52′W. It was a dark, wet morning with no moon or stars, and a large swell running from the south-easterly trades, when she was hit by a torpedo. The ship heaved away from the terrific explosion and then fell back some 27 degrees and stayed there. The torpedo, fired by the Italian submarine *Archimede*, struck between *Oronsay*'s boiler rooms which quickly flooded, causing the vessel to come to a standstill. As it grew light it was possible to see that the force of the explosion had destroyed the ship's radio and, even worse, the emergency radio aerial as well. Captain W. Savage, her master, decided to have the boats lowered, but before this could be done a second torpedo struck, blowing to smithereens one boat which was half-lowered, so that some of it actually went over the top of the funnels while other pieces fell onto the bridge where the captain and officers had to run for shelter. Captain Savage now gave orders for the abandonment of the ship, which was completed with all the boats well away before a third and fourth torpedo hit the vessel. The final one struck at 8 am, some two and a half hours after the first, indicating that the submarine commander may have been giving the ship's company the opportunity to get away, for he must have been in a position to continue firing from the time of his first attack. On the fourth hit *Oronsay* swiftly dipped below the water and glided down, stern first, at an angle of about 30 degrees, disappearing very quickly and leaving surprisingly little trace behind her.

Eight days later, on October 17, the main party of survivors, some 266 in all, were picked up from their lifeboats by Royal Navy ships which were searching for them; more were rescued a day later. One boatload, however, in the charge of the fourth officer, had become separated from the rest and they were eventually found at 2 am on October 14 by a French naval vessel, the *Dumont Durville,* and a merchantman she was escorting, the SS *Lipari*. This was 300 miles off Sierra Leone, and unhappily the men were put ashore at Dakar where, owing to the pressure of the Germans upon the French authorities, they were interned in degrading conditions, until the Allied landings in North Africa brought about their release.

The sinking of *Oronsay* was a disaster for the Orient Line, and within 48 hours *Orcades* was also lost some several hundred miles to the south. It was one of the war's most concentrated and massive blows against any one shipping company.

Technical data

Gross tonnage: 20,001
Net tonnage: 11,441
Length overall: 633 ft 7 in (193.12 m)
Breadth: 75 ft (22.86 m)
Depth: 47 ft (14.32 m)
Main engines: Twin screw, two sets of high-reduction geared turbines, 20,000 shp, 20 knots
Boilers: Oil-fired, steam pressure 215 psi
Passengers: First class 600, Third class 1,200; 1935, First class 501, Tourist class 482

Otranto 1926

The third vessel of the post-war rebuilding programme was the second *Otranto*, and she was launched in 1926 just a year after the first of her sister ships, *Orama*. The launching ceremony was a spectacular affair at midday on Tuesday June 9 1925, with brilliant summer sunshine sizzling over Vickers' shipyard at Barrow-in-Furness. The ceremony was performed by Mrs L. C. Amery, wife of the Secretary of State for the Colonies, and there was a distinguished list of visitors present, including the Governor of the Bank of England.

Like her two older sisters, *Otranto* was designed to carry only two classes of passengers, first and third, and she was propelled by two sets of Parsons single-reduction geared turbines. She developed 20,000 shp and had a service speed of 20 knots. The first class accommodation, for 600 passengers, was amidships on 'A' to 'F' decks and boasted remarkably fine public rooms and luxurious cabins, many of which were single-berth. The lounge on 'B' deck, which formed the centre of social life on board ship, was at the head of the grand stairway. It was a spacious room, nearly 2,059 sq ft in area, with bow windows on both sides, and decorated in the traditional English style. The ornamented plaster ceiling formed a feature of the room, together with small painted panels of decorative figure subjects, the work of Mr Paulsen Townsend. The smoking room on the same deck was also thoroughly English in character, offering elegance and refinement. The sense of ease and comfort was obtained by the use of unpolished cedarwood panelling on the walls, and the centre was carried to greater height than the rest with ornamental bronze grilles in the upper part for light and ventilation. Large bay windows looked out to port and starboard. Adjoining the smoking room was the café, a place for light refreshment and for shelter from the sun and open air.

The writing room, forward on 'C' deck, also known as the promenade deck, was a restful room where a sense of elegance was achieved by the quiet decoration. The walls were wood-panelled between supporting columns and pilasters, and blue lacquer panels with Chinese figure decoration were cleverly introduced— all the work of English artists. The dining saloon on 'F' deck was approached through a spacious foyer, designed *en suite* with the saloon, in a free English classic manner. The lofty centre part was carried up the height of two decks and was decorated by broad pilasters which supported an ornamented ceiling, the centre panel of which contained a group of sculptured bas-relief figures representing 'The Flight of the Planets'. Below the cornice and between the pilasters in the well was a series of perforated bronze grilles forming a frieze, with classic figure groups in bas-relief representing various subjects from Homer's *Iliad*. These were the work of the sculptor Mr Richard Garbe. Photographs of the panels with their descriptions were hung in the foyer. The facilities for the 1,114 third class passengers were of the same standard as the second class accom-

Above Otranto, *the third ship in the 1920s building programme* (A. Duncan).

Below Otranto *on full power trials, December 1925* (P&O).

modation in pre-war years, and were situated aft on 'D' to 'H' decks, with the dining saloon, lounge and smoking room on 'F' deck.

The fitting out took just six months, and by early January 1926 *Otranto* was lying at Tilbury ready to sail for Australia. Her maiden voyage was brought forward by several weeks as *Oronsay* had been temporarily withdrawn from service with a broken tail shaft. *Otranto* left London on Friday January 9 1926 and sailed by way of Gibraltar, Toulon, Naples, Suez, Aden and Colombo. She encountered heavy weather in the Mediterranean, but passengers spoke highly of the ship's behaviour. She arrived back in London in early April 1926, and she was then scheduled to undertake a series of cruises, the first of which was a month in the Mediterranean. She sailed from London on April 26 that year and arrived at Siracusa in Sicily on May 10. There were light south-westerly winds, and near Siracusa the sea was rough with a confused swell. At 8.20 pm the next day *Otranto* was off the Greek coast just north of Cape Grosso, near Cape Matapan, making for her second port of call, Athens. Land lights were not visible. It was the captain's intention to go in close to Cape Matapan, and if nothing had already been sighted, to take soundings at 8.40 pm. At 8.29 pm the sky became obscured, and the captain saw what appeared to be a low, dark cloud similar to others seen during that day. The speed of the ship was about 14 knots, and the next thing the captain saw was broken water. What he had thought to be cloud was, in fact, land.

Orient Line ships regularly carried the Australian test cricket team, as this souvenir of Otranto *shows* (P&O).

The next few minutes are best told in Captain Gordon L. Simner's own words. 'As soon as I saw the broken water I put the engines full steam astern. We struck at 8.38 pm. The port bow of the ship came into impact with the cliffs and was damaged. Then the ship swung round and her port side was scraped, and at once she was brought away from the rocks into deep water. The passengers were at once got to their stations and the discipline of all was magnificent. By 9.05 pm the boats were lowered, and by 9.30 pm everything was examined on the ship and she was reported dry. Immediately the vessel struck, an SOS was sent out and a German ship and a number of other vessels replied. There was no injury to anybody aboard.'

Otranto had suffered severe damage to her bows but she managed to reach Piraeus under her own steam two days later. Here her 550 passengers were disembarked and returned home by rail. Temporary repairs were carried out in the port, and on May 25 she left Piraeus for Southampton, where she arrived eight days later on June 2 1926 in the middle of the General Strike. Once in Southampton she was drydocked and permanent repairs were made to the bows. On July 17 that year a court of inquiry found: 'The casualty was due to a northerly current which set the vessel on the rocks at Cape Grosso, about seven and a half miles north-west of Cape Matapan, which it was intended to pass at a distance of 2–7 miles. The court considers that having regard to the weather conditions the master committed errors of judgement in failing to make any allowance for a current which might have been expected and in not reducing speed earlier than he contemplated doing. The court has noted with satisfaction the testimony of the passengers to the skill with which he handled the vessel immediately upon and after the casualty, and to the excellent discipline displayed by all.'

Otranto's first season of cruising was brought abruptly to an end, and it was September 18 1926 before she sailed on her second voyage to Brisbane. However, in less than two years she was involved in yet another collision. Once again she was on a cruise, but this time in the colder waters of the North Sea. On August 11 1928 she was at Immingham embarking 550 first class passengers for a 13-day cruise to the Norwegian fjords, the last of the summer season. Among the passengers were Admiral Sir Colin Keppel, Sir Lionel Earle, a government minister, as well as both British and American holidaymakers.

Otranto sailed at 6.30 pm that day, and less than two hours later, at 8.15 pm, she was in collision with the 8,000-grt Japanese cargo vessel *Kitano Maru*. The *Otranto* appears to have struck the smaller vessel a glancing blow to the forepeak on the port bow, the force of which swung the *Kitano Maru* round so that there was a second, albeit only slight, collision. Sir Lionel Earle gave this description of events. 'When the vessels crashed there was a terrific impact, and glass and china was thrown from the tables of the dining saloon. Passengers went to the portholes to see what had happened, and they saw the other ship alongside. Almost immediately the boats clashed again, but the second impact was not as severe as the first.'

Another passenger described his memories. 'I had gone up on deck some time after 8 o'clock, after dinner, when I heard a sudden severe blast. I saw the *Kitano Maru* apparently rushing to the front of our ship. Our ship, it seemed to me, was almost at a standstill, and the other vessel came on and struck our bows. The impact sent her round, and then she came back again and struck our cabins on the side; there was the sound of heavy crashings and the breaking of glass.'

The Japanese steamer was badly damaged at the point of impact in her port bow, and her forward hold was flooded. She was kept afloat, in spite of the damage, by her own pumps, and with the aid of tugs was taken back into the safety of the Humber. The damage to *Otranto* turned out to be buckling to her stem and, as it was not too severe, she was able to return to Immingham under her own steam. She arrived in the port at 5 am the next mornning and her passengers were disembarked and put on special trains for London—their cruise was over. On the Monday following the collision *Otranto* left Immingham for Southampton to go into drydock again for repairs to her bow. A court of inquiry held some time later ruled that both ships were to blame for the collision but, following an appeal, this decision was overturned and the blame was placed solely on the *Kitano Maru*.

In 1933 *Otranto* inaugurated a call at Palma on her outward voyage to Australia, enabling holidaymakers to spend some time on the island of Majorca before returning to London on the next homeward-bound Orient ship. In 1935, with the entry into service of *Orion*, the Orient Line converted all third class accommodation on their ships to tourist class. This meant that on board *Otranto* the passenger capacity in that class was halved to 522, and a great many other improvements were also made. In May 1937 she was present at the Coronation Naval Review in the Solent. The whole ship was opened as one-class with fares from 10 to 70 guineas for the occasion. Passengers embarked at Southampton on May 19 and disembarked on May 21, although for an additional guinea they could continue to Tilbury, arriving early on the morning of May 22.

By now the clouds of war were gathering over Europe, and *Otranto* sailed from London in mid-July 1939, arriving in Sydney towards the end of August. She was in Sydney when war broke out and she was requisitioned as a troopship, returning to England with the first Australian contingent of troops. In November 1939 she departed for Australia again, sailing from Sydney in early January 1940 as part of a large troop convoy which included *Orcades, Orion* and *Orford*. The Australian troops were disembarked in Egypt, where they were met by Mr Anthony Eden and General Wavell. Proceeding to Marseilles in company with *Orford, Otranto* left the port shortly before the former vessel was

Although in the years before the Second World War her career was marred by two serious collisions, Otranto *served the Orient Line for over 30 years* (P&O).

Above *May 1937,* Otranto *dressed overall for the Coronation Naval Review* (Maritime Photo Library).

Below *November 1940:* Otranto *in the Clyde during her service as a troopship* (Imperial War Museum).

attacked and set on fire. She then took part in the evacuation of troops from the French Atlantic ports, and subsequently she made a series of trooping voyages to the Middle East and Bombay via the Cape route.

In September 1942, while she was returning home independently from one of these voyages, she was involved in a dramatic rescue at sea. She was between Durban and Freetown in a position 2°N 8'E when a red sail was sighted low on the horizon off the starboard beam. On careful examination by powerful telescope Captain Hawker decided it was a ship's lifeboat. The distance was closed with a view to effecting a rescue if the captain was satisfied that there were no submarines in the vicinity. The gun crews were placed at action stations and the lifeboat was circled at full speed. The ship eventually stopped close to the boat and the occupants were instructed through loud-hailers to bring her alongside. This they did and they were embarked through the starboard gunport door. *Otranto* then proceeded at full speed, sinking the lifeboat by gunfire. Those rescued turned out to be the captain of the Blue Star liner *Tuscan Star*, his chief engineer, and several other members of the crew. Also aboard were the British Consul General from Brazil and several women and small children. Their ship had been torpedoed three days earlier, and they had been adrift with little hope of rescue. After being given suitable attention and food by the ship's staff they soon recovered and proceeded to the UK aboard *Otranto*.

In November 1942 *Otranto* took part in the North African landings, and during 'Operation Torch' she landed the commandos and US Rangers who played a prominent role in the capture of forts commanding the approaches to Algiers. She eventually entered the port and during her short stay there fought off frequent air attacks. Homeward bound from this operation she had a narrow escape from being torpedoed by a U-boat off Gibraltar. A quick alteration of helm alone saved the ship, for the torpedo then passed by harmlessly, close under her stern.

Soon after this, in February 1943, *Otranto* was specially fitted for the purpose of landing assault troops on enemy territory. This necessitated dispensing with the ship's lifeboats and replacing them with specially constructed assault craft. A central control station was also installed with loudspeakers to various parts of the ship to facilitate the embarking of troops in the assault craft. Iron ladders were constructed on the shell plating abreast of the gunport doors for the men to enter the landing craft while wearing full equipment. *Otranto* then sailed for Gare Loch where the 55th Canadian Landing Craft Flotilla were embarked as crews for the assault craft. During the week at Gare Loch stores were taken on board and the flotilla crews exercised in their boats.

On March 6 1943, the masters of *Otranto* and several other troopships similarly fitted, met Lord Louis Mountbatten, Chief of Combined Operations, for briefings. On March 9, *Otranto* sailed for Liverpool and embarked 4,575 troops for West and South Africa. Shortly after this she left in convoy for the Middle East, and on April 14 that year she arrived at Durban where her troops disembarked. She then embarked 3,800 troops of the South African Defence Force for the Middle East, and on May 6 1943 she anchored in Suez Bay.

After landing her troops she lay at anchor for a month, during which time the landing craft crews were sent to Lake Timsah in the Suez Canal for training with the men detailed for the intended landing. The troopships were divided into four parties and *Otranto* was assigned to group 'N', which also included HMS *Keren*, (Ex-BISN *Kenya*) and SS *Strathnaver*. The ships put to sea on several occasions during the month and practised the manoeuvres which would have to be carried out in the dark and without signals on 'D' day. Dummy runs were also carried out on beaches which resembled the proposed landing sites, and a high standard of speed and efficiency was achieved in lowering the landing craft and getting them away.

On June 10 1943 the squadron embarked the assault troops then proceeded down the Red Sea and up the Gulf of Aqaba where they anchored

March 1948: Otranto *in Grand Harbour, Malta, only three months before she was discharged from government service* (Michael Cassar).

close inshore. The beach at the head of the gulf had been prepared to withstand an attack, and a full scale 'dress rehearsal' was carried out. The squadron then returned to Suez, where those in command perfected plans for the real thing. On July 5 1943 'Force A' left Port Said to carry out 'Operation Husky', the object of which was to capture the south-east portion of Sicily, which would afford a stepping stone for the invasion of the Italian mainland. The force split into four groups, with HMS *Keren, Strathnaver* and *Otranto* in group one. They were to make up the port column of the convoy, their task being to capture the strip of coast off Marzamemi, about four miles north of Cape Passaro. The three ships carried over 7,000 troops composed mainly of the Hampshire Regiment and the Devon and Dorset Regiment.

The convoy skirted the coast of North Africa until just east of Malta when it altered course for the Sicilian coast. On the afternoon of July 9 fleet minesweepers and LCIs joined the convoy, and at sunset a strong wind and choppy sea developed. At 1 am the next morning the release position was reached and the landing craft were loaded with troops and lowered, which was difficult in the choppy sea. The ships were about seven miles from the coast, and at 1.15 am the flotillas of landing craft left for the shore. During the next hour the air seemed to be full of large troop-carrying aircraft as they flew inland to drop air-borne divisions, and the powerful searchlight on Cape Passaro kept sweeping its beam over the big troopships, but no shots were fired from the gun batteries. At exactly 2.45 am, after what seemed like an age, the whole shoreline appeared to be lit up by gunfire and the explosion of land mines, and those on board eagerly awaited the pre-arranged Very lights which would inform them that the beaches had been captured. At daybreak

A lovely aerial view of Otranto *in the Channel during the 1950s* (Skyfotos Ltd).

there were still a large number of troops left on board waiting to disembark, and HMS *Keren* signalled that she was closing inshore to test the shore batteries and that *Otranto* and *Strathnaver* were to follow. However, the batteries had been silenced and the ships anchored about half a mile off Marzamemi Beach where the landing was completed. After this *Otranto* and the other two troop transports left as an escorted convoy for an anchorage off Malta, the operation having been completely successful.

Otranto played her part in the Italian landings, and she was present at Salerno, but after this the operational work of the big ships came to an end, smaller craft being more suitable for the Normandy beaches. Like other Orient vessels she returned to trooping for the remainder of the war, her voyages taking her principally to India. In November 1945 she repatriated British troops from the Middle East, and in the New Year of 1946 from India. On February 12 1947 *Otranto* was in collision with the 7,000-ton cargo ship *Samrich* off Gravesend, but she suffered only very minor damage.

In June 1948 *Otranto* was discharged from her government service, during which she had steamed 335,655 miles and carried 145,448 personnel. She went to Liverpool where the conversion back to passenger liner was carried out by Cammell Laird & Co Ltd. The refit was scheduled to last for a year at a cost of £1¼ million, half of which was paid for by the Orient Line and half by the Ministry of Transport. On Saturday March 19 1949, she was being refloated in the drydock when she took a sudden 30-degree list. It brought her very near to disaster, as described by a docks policeman, 'I thought the vessel was going to fall on the dock shed, but she quivered and stayed still. The masts just missed the cranes on the dock.'

Fortunately crew members on board got busy with the pumps and slowly she righted herself, then with the assistance of tugs she was taken alongside Gladstone Dock where the final stages of the refit were completed. *Otranto* was now a 'one-class tourist' ship with accommodation for 1,412 passengers, who would be mainly emigrants to Australia. A swimming pool had been added on 'C' deck aft, and the former first class reading and writing room had become a children's playroom. There were identical menus in both dining saloons; those passengers accommodated on 'C', 'D', 'E' and 'F' decks took their meals in the forward saloon, while those on 'G' and 'H' decks used the after saloon. During the refit the crew's accommodation was much improved, and they were given a mess room, recreation room and a smoking room. Leading hands were also given their own mess room and sitting room.

The newly overhauled and refurbished liner left Liverpool for Tilbury on June 25 1949, with representatives of the Press invited on board for the trip. She sailed on the first voyage to Australia in her new role on July 14 1949, with a full complement of passengers whose fares ranged from £65 to £135. However, she had less than eight years' service left ahead of her.

Otranto maintained a 26-day schedule to Fremantle until May 1957, the routine being broken only in August 1950 when she was diverted to Jakarta to evacuate Dutch civilians. On May 13 1957 she arrived at Tilbury from Australia at the end of her last voyage on Orient Line service. She had been sold to the British Iron and Steel Corporation at Faslane, Scotland. She had had a full career and will be remembered with affection by many people in England and Australia.

Technical data

Gross tonnage: 20,026
Net tonnage: 12,031
Length overall: 657 ft 10 in (200.55 m)
Breadth: 75 ft 2 in (22.92 m)
Depth: 47 ft (14.32 m)
Main engines: Twin screw, two sets of Parsons single-reduction geared turbines, 20,000 shp, 20 knots
Boilers: Oil-fired, steam pressure 215 psi
Passengers: First class 572, Third class 1,114; 1935, First class 572, Tourist class 522; 1949, 1,412 Tourist class only

Orford 1928

Just two years after the entry into service of *Otranto*, the fourth ship of the post-war rebuilding programme was launched at Vickers' yard in Barrow-in-Furness. On Tuesday September 27 1927 Lady Ryrie, wife of the Australian High Commissioner, pulled the small lever to release a bottle of wine which crashed against the bow of the ship, and the great hull began to move slowly down the slipway towards her initial plunge. The event was favoured with hot, sunny weather, which was a welcome change from the storms which had plagued the north-west in the days prior to the launch. She had been named *Orford* after the headland in Suffolk and the village which lies south of Aldeburgh.

At 19,941 grt, the new ship was slightly smaller than her immediate predecessor, although like *Otranto* she too was powered by Parsons single-reduction geared turbines driving twin screws, which gave her a service speed of 20 knots. She had accommodation for 520 first class passengers on 'C', 'D', 'E' and 'F' decks, and 1,162 third class passengers in 232 cabins on 'G' deck and 89 on 'H' deck. Her layout was very similar to the other Orient Line vessels of the 1920s. 'A' deck was a games area, and the first class public rooms were on 'B' and 'C' decks. In addition, on 'C' deck a swimming pool was installed in place of the hold immediately abaft of the verandah café on 'B' deck. The third class public rooms were on 'D', 'E' and 'F' decks aft of the first class accommodation.

Sir Alan G. Anderson represented the managers of the Orient Line at the launching ceremony, and some of the statistics he quoted in his speech make interesting reading. He said that as they had so few ships they must in self-protection go for quality, and he continued, 'There are only 25 passenger steamers considerably larger than *Orford* and her sisters, and of these only ten are faster than *Orford*.'

By the spring of 1928 *Orford* had completed her trials and was ready to sail on April 13 on her maiden voyage, a 28-day cruise from Southampton to the Mediterranean, with fares starting at 50 guineas per person. Her second cruise was a three-week trip to the Mediterranean, and the third a two-week voyage to the Atlantic Isles. She then started a series of 13-day cruises to the Norwegian fjords in conjunction with *Otranto*, until the latter collided with the Japanese ship *Kitanu Maru* and was withdrawn for repairs. Finally, on October 13 1928 she left Tilbury for Australia, where her arrival in Sydney was a great public event, coinciding as it did with the start of the construction of the arch of Sydney Harbour Bridge. Dances and receptions were arranged and *Orford*'s officers attended one event on board the cruiser HMAS *Australia*.

In the summer of 1929 *Orford* once again cruised from Britain, and on Saturday August 17 she left Immingham for a 14-day cruise to the northern capitals and Norwegian fjords. Among her 500 passengers were a number of dis-

Above Orford *leaves Barrow in the spring of 1928* (Vickers Shipbuilding & Engineering Ltd).

Left Orford *at Tilbury Docks* (P&O).

Above right Orford *as she sails under Sydney Harbour Bridge during the opening ceremony in March 1932* (P&O).

tinguished personalities, including two former aides to King George V, and an ex-Under-Secretary of State who had been a member of Mr Stanley Baldwin's government, recently defeated at the polls. The liner's first port of call was Copenhagen, where she arrived on the morning of August 19. When she entered the harbour there was a fresh wind blowing with a strong tide running and, as she manoeuvred to her berth, she went aground. Fortunately she had grounded so gently that few of those on board were aware of the mishap. She remained fast for an hour and a half before, with the assistance of a salvage tug and the rising tide, she was refloated and brought alongside her berth. Luckily there was no damage and her itinerary was not affected.

She arrived back in Tilbury at the end of the cruise on August 31, and then sailed round to Southampton, for, along with *Orontes*, she had been chartered by the Royal Aero Club to act as one of the two official ships at that year's Schneider Trophy races around the Solent. She anchored off Cowes on Thursday September 5 1929, in preparation for the start of the event the following day. This was the last great international seaplane race and was won by H. R. D. Waghorn in his Supermarine S6, at 328.63 mph. In a positive way it laid the foundations for the

Left *Emperor Haile Selassie* (right) *on board* Orford *in June 1936* (P&O).

Below Orford *at sea* (P&O).

winning of the Battle of Britain 11 years later. That evening the Secretary of State for Air, Lord Thompson, hosted a celebration dinner on board *Orford*. Later that month, on September 29 1929, she resumed her regular sailings to Australia.

Four years after she entered service *Orford* was once again in Sydney. This time her visit coincided with the opening of the Harbour Bridge on March 19 1932, and she was the flagship of all the merchantmen present at the pomp and ceremony of the occasion. In fact *Orford* was the second ship to pass under the famous bridge, although the event was marred by bad luck as her master was taken ill shortly before she sailed, and the company's marine superintendent in the port had to take command.

In 1935 her third class accommodation was converted so that she could carry 515 passengers in the new tourist class, and the number of berths for first class passengers was reduced to 468.

In October 1935 political events, which were starting to cast shadows over Europe, also influenced *Orford*'s career. On October 3, Italian troops invaded Ethiopia at the start of Mussolini's attempt to create a new 'Roman Empire'. By February of 1936 the Italians had routed the ill-equipped Ethiopian army, and on May 1 that year the Emperor Haile Selassie fled from Addis Ababa for Djibouti, where he boarded a British warship which took him to Gibraltar and safety. From Gibraltar the Emperor was to come to England, and he embarked on *Orford* on May 31 1936 and set sail for London. The ship arrived in Tilbury at 8 am on Thursday June 4 and, at the Emperor's own request, there was no official reception, just a few members of the Ethiopian Legation to meet him. However, a special saloon was attached to the boat train to Fenchurch Street, in which Haile Selassie travelled into central London to start his five years in exile while the Italians occupied his country.

The next three years passed without any incidents, and at 6.20 pm on June 24 1939, *Orford*, commanded by Captain Charles Fox, left Tilbury for a two-week cruise to the Atlantic Isles, returning to Southampton on the morning of July 7. At 5 pm the next day she left at the start of a series of three cruises which took her to Port Monaco, Naples and other Mediterranean ports. *Orford*'s final peacetime voyage was the last of these cruises, which she began at 5.15 pm on August 5 1939 when she left Southampton, returning on the morning of August 26, six days before German troops poured over the Polish border, thereby starting the Second World War.

Orford was requisitioned by the government soon after her return, and three days later on August 29 she sailed for Alexandria with government passengers. She left that port on September 18 1939 and returned to the Solent where she lay at anchor in the Cowes Roads from October 2 to November 24, when she went into Southampton Docks to prepare for a voyage to Australia. She left Southampton on November 28 1939 with a limited number of passengers and under the command of Captain N. Savage, who was to be her master for the rest of her career. Sailing via the Mediterranean she arrived in Sydney on New Year's Eve and remained in the port for seven days, while she embarked Australian troops for the Middle East. She sailed on January 7 1940 in a large convoy, other Orient Line ships being *Orcades, Orion* and *Otranto*. On her arrival in Suez Bay on February 14, Mr Anthony Eden, General Wavell and other senior officers boarded *Orford* to welcome the first Australian contingent to the Middle East. However, there were some difficulties with the Egyptian authorities, who objected to the Australians being camped in their country. The problem was solved by sending *Orford* up the Suez Canal to Kantara on the east bank, just north of Lake Ballah, where they were disembarked directly onto the railway station there. Orders were then received for *Orford* in company with *Otranto* to proceed to Toulon. At Toulon the two ships lay at the inner buoys in the harbour for some appreciable time and they were loaned to the French Admiralty as troop transports.

From this time on all arrangements were chaotic, a situation which ultimately led to the loss of *Orford*. In March the two Orient ships were sent, without passengers, to the port of Tamatave on the east coast of Madagascar. On arrival it was found that the port could not accommodate two 20,000-ton liners, so *Otranto* entered the harbour while *Orford* anchored in Diego Suarez Bay until there was room at Tamatave. Eventually she was able to get a berth and 3,500 native troops, mainly labour battalions, together with 200 French officers, officials and their families, were embarked. Captain Savage had great difficulty in getting any sailing orders, and he was merely told to proceed to Mombasa and load cotton. From there, having received no orders, she sailed for Port Said, but on her arrival the British authorities knew nothing about her and still the French had no orders, but thought she ought to go back to Toulon. As the Mediterranean was then closed to British shipping both Captain Savage and *Otranto*'s master made strong representations to obtain an escort and eventually a French submarine, with a maximum speed of 13 knots, was detailed to undertake the task. As they approached Malta the submarine ordered them into Grand Harbour, but no sooner had they made fast, than the British naval authorities ordered them out. So the two ships then proceeded without an escort at their best speed to Toulon, where they were allotted berths, but again, before the ships were properly moored they were ordered to go immediately to Marseilles. When the two vessels arrived at the port they were able to go alongside and disembark the troops. *Otranto* was left at her reasonably safe berth but *Orford* was sent to an anchorage in the Estaque Roads on the north coast of the city. This was the third week in May 1940, when the German army was rapidly overrunning France and the Low Countries.

Captain Savage was not happy at having to anchor his ship in such an exposed position, and he protested strongly to the French naval authorities that she was well outside the protection of the guns of the port, but no notice was taken of him. By June 1 1940 the evacuation of Allied forces from France was well under way, but at Marseilles *Orford* lay idle, 'awaiting orders'. The events of that day are perhaps best told in the words of her master, Captain Savage. 'On Saturday June 1 1940, at approximately 2.30 pm, while lying at anchor in the Estaque Roads, Marseilles, I heard what I thought might have been the air raid alarm being sounded at the factory at Estaque, and went up on to the bridge to see. The ship was attacked by six German bombers and, having only one antiquated 12-pounder anti-aircraft gun, they just made target practice of us. I observed a plane which dropped a bomb close to the breakwater. I sounded off action stations, closed watertight doors, put the engines on stand-by, and then saw two planes approaching from ahead. They dived low over the ship and dropped two bombs which struck the ship on the fiddley above the café and smoke-room. The anti-aircraft gun was brought into action as soon as it was possible to train on the enemy and I am convinced that this prevented them from returning and dropping more bombs. The bombs which dropped penetrated the ship somewhere by the engine room and galley, and in a matter of minutes the ship was ablaze fore and aft. When I asked for power on the fire-main and windlass, I could not get it. I then rang the engines to move ahead, the engineers could not do so and replied on the telegraph "finished with engines". I then sounded the abandon ship signal and all hands that could went to their boat stations.'

At the time that the crew were abandoning ship the fire was raging to such an extent that it was impossible to move on 'B' and 'C' decks and the after end of 'D' deck. A local fire float had come alongside, and after it had been pumping water for four hours, the Admiral of the port decided that *Orford* must be beached. With no power available the anchor cable had to be cut through, and when this was done two tugs started to tow the crippled ship towards the beach. While the tow was under way the forward funnel collapsed and the bonnet looped itself onto the starboard davits. Once *Orford* was firmly aground in a small cove, well clear of the port limits and traffic, the French Admiral ordered a naval party to dynamite holes in number four and six holds, to make doubly sure she would not move.

Fourteen of *Orford*'s crew had been killed and 25 injured in the attack. It had been particularly difficult to evacuate the wounded, who had been carried down the gangway into launches and boats alongside. All the crew who were fit to travel, with the exception of the Captain and Chief Engineer, were sent across to Cherbourg by what was probably one of the last trains to make that run, as the Germans were advancing on Paris. Captain Savage stayed behind in Marseilles and, together with a Lloyd's surveyor, he examined the gutted wreck after it had cooled sufficiently; inevitably it was declared a total loss. Together the two men rescued the ship's bell which was handed over to the company's agents ashore. The surveyor, Mr Douglas Ray, took several photographs of the wreck, but sadly these were lost in the blitz on London. It soon became apparent to Captain Savage that he could do nothing more, and he decided to return to England while he still could. On June 13 1940, three days after Italy declared war, he set off by train, car and on foot to Bordeaux where he managed to obtain a lift on the British collier SS *Witch*, only 24 hours before the port was occupied by the Germans. As the small coaster made its way up the Irish Sea he saw the *Otranto* and *Ormonde* making their way south to assist in the evacuation.

The hulk that was once *Oford* lay for the duration of the war where it had been beached. It was not until 1947 that it was refloated and broken up at Savona in Italy. In May 1954, when Mr Ford Geddes was returning home in *Orsova, Orford*'s bell was handed over to him by the Orient Line agents at Marseilles in a small ceremony held on board.

Orford was the first Orient liner to be lost during the Second World War, and the final word on the subject should be given by her last master, Captain Savage, 'I always feel very sad when I think of *Orford*—that lovely proud ship slaughtered while doing a job which seemed to me quite unnecessary.'

Technical data

Gross tonnage: 19,941
Net tonnage: 12,027
Length overall: 657 ft 10 in (200.55 m)
Breadth: 75 ft (22.86 m)
Depth: 43 ft (13.11 m)
Main engines: Twin screw, two sets of Parsons single-reduction geared turbines, 20,000 shp, 20 knots
Boilers: Oil-fired, steam pressure 215 psi
Passengers: First class 520, Third class 1,162; 1935, First class 468, Tourist class 515

Orontes 1929

The last of the five 20,000-tonners to be built for the Orient Line during the 1920s was the second *Orontes*. She was constructed by Vickers Ltd at Barrow-in-Furness, and was launched on the afternoon of Tuesday February 27 1929. It was a cold winter's day at Barrow, with heavy snow falling when Lady Anderson, wife of Sir Alan G. Anderson, Chairman of the Orient Line, sent the huge ship down the slipway to the Walney Channel. Work to complete the fitting out was finished without a hitch, and the new vessel had completed her trials by mid-September that year.

Orontes' hull design differed from that of her four sisters in that she had a raked stem, which at the time was a novel idea, and at 20,186 grt she was the largest of the five ships. She had accommodation for 500 first and 1,123 third class passengers. Internally her design was similar to the previous vessels of the 1920s, with first class passengers being accommodated on 'A' down to 'F' decks, amidships, and third class passengers on 'D' to 'H' decks. Special features of the first class section were the large number of single-berth cabins and the lift between passenger decks. The lounge, situated on 'B' deck, was planned on palatial lines both in its area and height. The dark mahogany fluted columns, with their silver caps and bases, formed a pleasing and effective contrast to the Borneo cedar panelling of the walls. The ceiling, except for its cornice and beams, was plain plaster, an excellent foil to the more elaborate decoration of the walls. Glazed doors at the after end of the lounge gave access to the dancing space, which could be converted into an enclosed ballroom by means of hinged screens. The café, also on 'B' deck, was a very fine room, the general style being reminiscent of the 17th-century English Renaissance. The high centre part had bronze grilles for light and ventilation and there were access doors both to the dancing space and adjacent smoking room. The latter was just aft of the café, and had an air of English comfort about it. It was panelled in zebra-wood set in Australian black bean, and the ceiling, with its decorative beams and cornices, was of plaster. On 'C' deck, which was the first class promenade, the first class cabins were mainly single-berth, and at the after end of the deckhouse there was an open-air swimming bath.

Dining saloons for both classes were on 'F' deck, the first class saloon being designed in an English Renaissance style. It was decorated in soft tones of ivory, and the raised centre part or 'well' was of enriched plaster and had modelled and perforated bronze panels depicting the world's famous navigators. Forward of the saloon, on the same deck, was the main entrance foyer which was designed *en suite* with the saloon. The reading and writing room was entered from the foyer, and it was decorated in tones of parchment and blue, with large panels of Chinese lacquer of a golden-yellow hue.

Particular attention was paid to the comfort of the third class passengers, whose cabins were situated on 'G' and 'H' decks. A large number of

Right Orontes *was launched on February 27 1929. She is seen here leaving Barrow in September of that year* (Vickers Shipbuilding & Engineering Ltd).

Below Orontes *at Southampton* (Southampton City Museums).

them were arranged as two-berths, and were situated adjacent to the side of the ship with portholes. The third class public rooms consisted of a lounge, smoking room and dining saloon. This latter room was handsomely panelled in oak, and the layout of its furniture allowed for quick service to the diners. The lounge on 'E' deck was panelled in birch, and incorporated a library and writing room.

Orontes completed her trials on the Clyde and arrived in Southampton in early September 1929. She had been chartered, along with the *Orford*, by the Royal Aero Club as one of the official ships at the Schneider Trophy races to be held on September 5. Both vessels were stationed on the starting and finishing line off Ryde Pier in the Solent. On the following weekend *Orontes* made a shakedown cruise with a large number of Orient Line guests on board. She left Southampton on the evening of Friday September 13, and the following morning she reached Mounts Bay near Penzance where she turned around. That same evening she anchored in Plymouth Sound overnight, before returning to Southampton on Sunday September 15 1929. From there she sailed to Tilbury in preparation for her maiden voyage to Brisbane, and ten days later she took her place in the Australian mail service. In 1933 she made a six-week cruise to the West Indies, and in the following year she suffered her first mishap when she ran aground, fortunately without damage, on the Gallipoli coast while on a cruise around the Greek Islands.

Five years later, in the fateful summer of 1939, *Orontes* was still maintaining her service to Australia and left Brisbane for home on July 3, arriving in Tilbury at 8 am on August 24. She had been scheduled to sail again for Australia on September 25, and the outbreak of war earlier that month did little to disrupt this, for in fact she left for Brisbane a day early. She had escaped being requisitioned and sailed with a full passenger list for the voyage. *Orontes* arrived back in Tilbury at the end of December that year with very few passengers but with a very valuable cargo of foodstuffs. Two weeks later, in mid-January 1940, she left for Australia once again, and after embarking her passengers in Southampton she sailed via Suez for more peaceful waters. She arrived back in Tilbury on April 16 1940, to find that the 'Phoney War' was well and truly over, and she was requisitioned by the government. During the next four weeks, while she lay at Tilbury, she was refitted to accommodate 3,226 troops: 308 men were billeted in hammocks in what was the third class dining saloon, and a further 1,762 were accommodated in messes on 'F' 'G' and 'H' decks, again in hammocks.

Orontes left Tilbury as a requisitioned liner on May 18 1940 for Australia, and in the area off the Kent coast known as the Downs she experienced the first recorded attack on one of the company's ships, when she was dive-bombed by an enemy plane; although there were some near misses, no damage was caused. She continued her passage via Cape Town and on the voyage home she carried Australian service personnel to Singapore. Her decks, including the boat deck, were packed with Australian-built Wirraway and Hudson aircraft, and she was escorted by HMAS *Perth*. Calls were made at Colombo and Bombay and a number of mixed service personnel embarked for the UK. *Orontes* finally arrived back in Liverpool on September 9 1940, after which she made one voyage to Suez via South Africa and on her return she then sailed for Halifax, Nova Scotia. She arrived in the Clyde on the last day of February 1941 and there then followed a succession of trooping voyages in convoy via Cape Town to the Middle East and Colombo, with the occasional diversion to Canada and the United States.

In December 1942 *Orontes* took part in the assault on North Africa, landing her troops at Oran. Subsequently, in July 1943, she played her role in the offensive against Sicily and the mainland of Italy. In the attack on Sicily she landed her troops at the Avola beach in the first wave of the operation, which involved disembarking close on 4,000 men in under two hours. Soon afterwards the successful progress of the landing was confirmed when a Union Jack, autographed by the ship's officers from *Orontes*,

Above *May 1940: an artist's impression of* Orontes *under aerial attack off the Kent coast* (P&O).

Below Orontes *at the Sicilian landings, July 1943* (P&O).

was seen flying above the captured town of Avola. Shortly after *Orontes* left the anchorage she was attacked by a Junkers 88 and, although straddled by five bombs, she miraculously escaped damage. Indeed, her own gunners hit an attacking aircraft, bringing it down in flames.

On her next voyage, under US control, she was involved in the first attack on the Italian mainland, landing her troops in the thick of the action on the Salerno beach. This incursion was fiercely resisted by the enemy, and *Orontes* was subjected to repeated attacks by aircraft and submarines. Once again she was lucky to escape casualties among those on board. She remained under American control, reinforcing the Italian fronts, until the end of 1943. Following these months of active service, *Orontes* resumed long trooping voyages to Bombay in preparation for an anticipated assault on Japan. In June 1945 she visited Australia again, for the first time in five years, and she was also the first Orient liner to call there since *Orcades* in March 1942. After the collapse of Japan, *Orontes* conveyed French troops from Marseilles to Saigon, to reimpose their country's rule on this colonial territory which had been effectively occupied by the Japanese since September 1940. It was also the start of over 30 years of upheaval in that part of Asia. *Orontes* returned home to Southampton on Saturday March 9 1946 and was immediately quarantined as a smallpox victim was on board. Some days later she disembarked her 4,500 troops and released PoWs. From the outbreak of war to the surrender of Japan she had steamed some 371,409 miles and had carried 139,167 troops, civilians and PoWs. Her mileage exceeded by nearly 36,000 the distance travelled by any other single Orient liner.

Orontes was released by the Ministry of Transport in April 1947, and she went into Southampton Docks where she was reconditioned by Messrs J. I. Thorneycroft & Co Ltd. The conversion took a year and cost just over £1 million. She was the third ship of the pre-war fleet to return to the Australian service, as *Orion* and *Ormonde* were already back on the route. *Orontes* now carried 502 first class and 618 'tourist B class' passengers, thus allowing more room for improved crew accommodation. On 'H' deck the 304 tourist berths could be dismantled to provide extra cargo space. By early June 1948 she was back in Tilbury preparing to sail once more for Australia, and on June 15 representatives of the Press were invited on board for an inspection with Mr F. I. Geddes. In a speech to those assembled he said, 'By pre-war standards *Orontes* is no longer a new ship, but the old standards have changed and, if the passengers who wish to travel are to be carried, we have to alter our ideas and ships must be made to have a longer useful life than they had before the war. On the other hand, passengers will not thank us if we provide an out-of-date ship for them to travel in, and I hope you will feel that epithet does not apply to this ship and that she is worthy to take her place by the side of her younger sisters. Among the major improvements that have been carried out has been the provision of hot and cold running water in all the cabins in both classes with, of course, the exception of the portable accommodation on 'H' deck. We have, in addition, installed a sprinkler fire protection system throughout the ship. The passenger and crew accommodation have also been completely re-designed and we hope that you will feel, as a result of your inspection this morning, that our guess of what the public wants has been correct.' *Orontes* sailed for Sydney the next day, and for the next five years she ran without incident.

In the summer of 1953 she was converted to a tourist 'one-class' ship, with an increase of 250 in her passenger accommodation, and on August 29 that year she made her first voyage to Australia in this role, most of the berths being taken by emigrants on assisted passages. Three years later, in August 1956, *Orontes*' homeward passage from Fremantle to London was diverted from the Suez route to go instead via Cape Town. In England the Ministry of Transport was requisitioning ships for military service, as the Suez crisis was imminent. It was June 1957 before *Orontes* used the Suez Canal again, and it was the first time since the controversial crisis that an Orient liner had used the waterway. Her north-

Orontes *at Cape Town during the Suez crisis* (Robert Pabst).

Orontes *at Tilbury Docks, March 1958, with* Orsova *in the background* (P&O).

February 26 1962: Orontes *leaves the Thames for shipbreakers in Valencia, Spain* (A. Duncan).

bound transit passed without incident, and soon traffic through the highly politicized canal was back to normal again. In August the following year *Orontes* had a minor collision in the Thames with the *Empire Baltic* belonging to the Transport Ferry Service.

Although *Orontes* was over 30 years old she was still a popular ship, and she continued to run cruises from Sydney. In May 1960, on one of these cruises, she called at Hayman Island off the north-east coast of Queensland in Australia. There she had the honour to play host to Queen Salote's sister and to her brother, who was Prime Minister of Tonga. A party was held on board, but the Queen herself could not attend because of ill-health. On April 14 1961, when *Orontes* was homeward bound from Australia, she anchored for the day off Tobruk. It was the 20th anniversary of the siege, when Tobruk's defenders beat back a determined attack by the German 5th Light Division. Captain R. J. Brittain and the Staff Commander took floral tributes to the men who died in the siege. Later that year, on November 5 1961, *Orontes* was once again returning to London from Australia, and during the voyage she made her usual routine call at Marseilles. As she was berthing alongside, a mooring rope snapped and the liner was swung against the quayside, tearing a hole some 12 ft square just above the waterline at the stern. She was finally brought alongside and the overland passengers were disembarked. After temporary repairs were carried out, *Orontes* was able to continue her journey to Tilbury, where she arrived a week later.

The end was near for the old ship, and on December 12 1961 it was announced that she was to be broken up. She did not make any more sailings to Australia, and in January 1962 it was reported that she had been sold to Italian shipbreakers for £301,000. However, this sale was not completed and in the following month it was confirmed that *Orontes* had finally been purchased by J. F. Ordas of Madrid and that she was to be broken up at Valencia in Spain. In the event, with a depressed market, she fetched a lower price of £282,000, and she left her home port of Tilbury on February 26 1962, arriving in Valencia seven days later on March 5. She was the Orient Line's last link with the 1920s and the pre-war age.

Technical data

Gross tonnage: 20,186
Net tonnage: 12,010
Length overall: 663 ft 10 in (202.38 m)
Breadth: 75 ft (22.86 m)
Depth: 47 ft (14.32 m)
Main engines: Twin screw, two sets of Parsons single-reduction geared turbines, 20,000 shp, 20 knots
Boilers: Oil-fired, steam pressure 215 psi
Passengers: First class 500, Third class 1,123; 1935, First class 463, Tourist class 518; 1948, First class 502, Tourist class 618; 1953, 1,370 Tourist class only

Orion 1935

Of all the passenger ships built for the Orient Line between the wars, *Orion* was the best known, and her good reputation lasted throughout her career. There is no doubt that she is a landmark in British shipbuilding history, and there was something about her appearance which suggested that she was a ship of the future, something which set her apart from other liners. In the early 1930s it was unusual for large liners to be fitted with a single funnel, and even more so for them to have only one mast. This departure from common practice and the refusal to accept precedent for convention's sake showed great courage on behalf of the managers of the line, but this progressive policy had always distinguished the Orient Line from others.

Orion's launch was, apart from that of the Atlantic giant *Queen Mary*, the most publicized ceremony of the 1930s. The construction contract had been awarded to Vickers Armstrong Ltd, and she became yard number 697 at the Barrow-in-Furness shipyard. *Orion* was launched on December 7 1934, only three months after the *Queen Mary*, and, to a world still recovering from the Great Depression, it signalled the return of some normality to the shipbuilding industry.

The launching of *Orion* was unique, the ceremony being carried out by HRH the Duke of Gloucester, who was at the time many thousands of miles away in Brisbane. The proceedings were in fact carried out by radio, and, transmitting from Government House in the city, the Duke made the following speech: 'Before performing this act of magic which will cause this beautiful ship to take the water so many miles away, I send a greeting to my countrymen in Barrow-in-Furness who are so fortunate as to be present at her launching. I am acquainted with her elder sisters, from two of whom, *Orama* and *Oronsay*, I received messages of greeting on my way to Australia, and as a sponsor I offer to the youngest daughter of the family my congratulations on her birthday, and I wish her many happy returns on her voyages between England and Australia. I name you *Orion*. Good fortune attend you always and those whom you bear across the world to their brothers overseas.' The Duke then operated a switch in Brisbane which, by radio signals, released the ship, which slowly began her journey down the slipway to the channel.

Orion's story began in 1932, when the order for the ship was about to be placed. Colin Skelton Anderson, who was then a junior partner in Anderson, Green & Co, managers of the Orient Line, was a man of vision whose interest in the arts convinced him that, in a world which was becoming more and more design-conscious, there was a great need for improvement in his own erstwhile conservative business of shipping. With some trepidation he approached his seniors and laid before them a contemporary formula for the vessel's decor and, to his surprise, they approved. But he was told that he must take full responsibility himself, which included finding an architect imbued with the same ideas as his. After a lengthy search Colin Anderson discovered a

young man of about his own age by the name of Brian O'Rorke whose imaginative ideas matched his own. It proved to be the start of a long and happy association, for after *Orion* they were responsible for the interior design of every Orient vessel, including a part of *Oriana*, which was too vast for one architect to design all the public spaces on his own. Work on the *Orion* went on apace and the two men plunged into the formidable task of breaking down the long-standing taboos governing almost all the features of a ship's interior and exterior appearance. They determined to accept the lines of the ship instead of trying to conceal them. They produced a ship interior which looked like a ship interior instead of a rather ill-proportioned series of grand hotel lounges. It was farewell to the wonderful vista, the grand stairway and the extravagant use of precious space that had been the fashion for so long. The vessel was allowed to impose her own symmetry so strongly that she created her own style.

Orion was probably the first ship on which a designer exercised any real influence. The eye trained to see things economically disposed and well-balanced saw that many time-hallowed shipyard fittings could be improved. These designs, dating back to days when conditions at sea were very different, were found to be capable of re-design, with no loss of efficiency and a great gain in appearance. It soon became clear that virtually none of the thousands of utensils and furnishings which would automatically have been ordered for the old kind of interior would look right in the new. The problem was not merely the design of an architectural setting, but its complete equipment. Designers had to be found who could produce suitable china for the dining saloons, new glassware, new handles for doors, cupboards, windows and furniture; brasswork was banished and plastic adopted in its place. New door curtains, bedspreads, table linen, blankets, bathmats and letterheadings were needed, as were new stewards' uniforms, deck chairs and cutlery. This was by no means all, but it shows the enormousness of the venture and that the new policy could not be achieved by half measures.

With a gross tonnage of 23,371, *Orion* had eight passenger decks, ranging from the sun deck to 'G' deck. Originally she carried 486 first class and 653 tourist class passengers. Most of the first class public rooms were on 'B' deck. The lounge, situated forward, was remarkable, not for its magnificence, but for its restraint. The plain ceiling was supported by a number of smooth white columns and was illuminated by concealed lights. The floor of jarrah and Australian myrtle was partly covered with hand-tufted rugs. The tables were plain and light in colour, and the comfortable chairs were covered in light-blue textile. The galleries which led from the lounge to the library further aft were not merely passages, for along their outer sides were many alcoves with writing desks. Armchairs and sofas with occasional tables allowed passengers to relax without being disturbed by others passing through. The library was a fine, airy room with

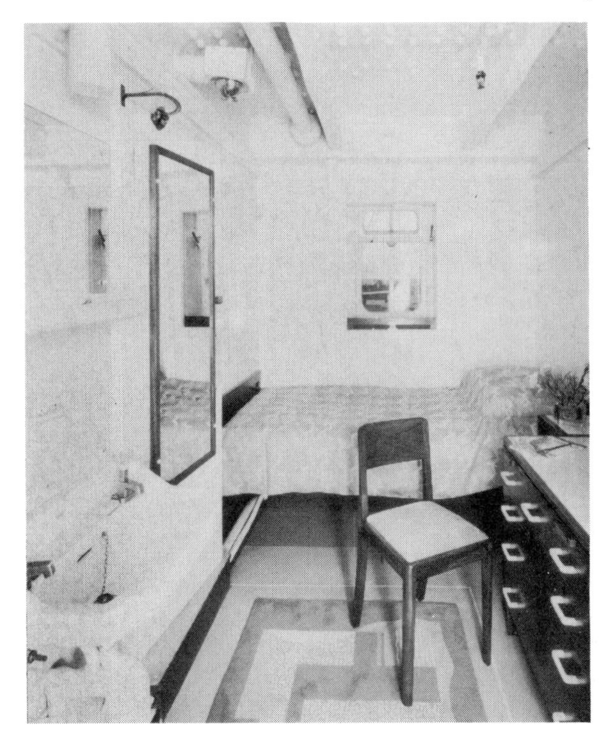

Above left *The launch of* Orion *on December 7 1934 at Barrow-in-Furness* (P&O).

Above right *A first class cabin on 'D' deck* (P&O).

Right *The first class lounge on board* Orion, *remarkable not for its magnificence, but for its restraint* (P&O).

Above *The engine room starting platform* (Vickers).

Left Orion *in Southampton Water; a flying boat comes in for a closer look* (Vickers).

Right Orion *belches black smoke as she docks at Southampton* (Vickers).

sycamore furniture. The after gallery had sliding windows which could be opened so that the room became part of the dancing space aft. Farthest aft on this deck was the café, which, together with the verandah outside, overlooked the swimming pool on 'C' deck.

Forward on 'C' deck was the children's playroom and playdeck. All the first class cabins on this deck were furnished in Australian silky oak, among them 14 two-berth special staterooms containing two full-size beds and luxury furniture. Other staterooms were situated on 'D' and 'E' decks. Dining saloons for both classes were situated on 'F' deck, the first class saloon being just aft of the main entrance foyer, and panelled in weathered sycamore. The central space was lit by concealed lights in a shallow dome. Two of the walls were made up of mirrors, one of which was a representation of Orion the Giant and his constellation. The whole saloon was air-conditioned, which was itself unusual in a large passenger liner. The tourist dining saloon was similar in many ways, but one wall was made entirely of glass and separated the room from the tourist lounge. Stairs led up to the tourist class café on 'E' deck, which was decorated in fawn and blue, with a huge photomontage on the forward bulkhead. The café was surrounded by a promenade space for the tourist class passengers, whose cabins were of almost as high a standard as those provided in the first class section. Every cabin was furnished with a washbasin, wardrobe and a chest of drawers. Apart from the first class dining saloon, which was air-conditioned, the ventilation was of the punkah-louvre type and, as was usual in Orient Line ships, it worked very efficiently. Every precaution was taken against fire, and *Orion* was the first British liner to be fitted with the Grinell sprinkler system, in addition to the extensive use of fire-resistant paint.

Down below, *Orion* was powered by two sets of Parsons single-reduction geared turbines, designed to run at 1,715 rpm and to develop a total shaft horsepower of 24,000, giving the ship a service speed of 21 knots. The steam for the main engines was supplied by six Babcock and Wilcox boilers, four large and two small, fitted with superheaters and burning oil fuel.

So the scene was set for this lovely ship to sail on her maiden voyage, a shakedown cruise in the Mediterranean with accommodation for first class passengers only, the tourist class area not being ready. She sailed from Southampton on August 14 1935, and most of the cruise passed off without incident. On September 3, 19 days after

she left, *Orion* arrived in Lisbon, her last port of call before returning to Tilbury. She left the port at 5 pm the following day and at 3.20 am on September 5 ran into thick fog which caused her to reduce speed. Forty minutes later she received a distress call from the Cunard White Star liner *Doric*, which had been involved in a collision with the French coaster *Formigney* outside Lisbon. *Orion* turned back and went to the scene at full speed, arriving two and a half hours later, at 6.30 am. For the next two hours she and P&O's *Viceroy of India* embarked *Doric*'s passengers, of whom *Orion* took on board 486 and 42 crew. They were all in good spirits and one girl passenger was heard to call up from a lifeboat, 'Is there any dancing tonight?' By 9 am, with the embarkation completed, *Orion* got under way once again and set course for Tilbury where she arrived on September 9, with all her stores running very short. Nineteen days later, with the final fitting out of her tourist class accommodation complete, she set sail on her maiden voyage to Australia where she received a great welcome. She made three round voyages to Australia before spending the summer of 1936 cruising from the UK. In the autumn of that year she resumed her Australian voyages, before cruising once again from Tilbury. The first cruise of 1937 was in July to the northern capitals, and later that year in September she set sail for Australia again.

On January 28 1939, less than four years after her maiden cruise, *Orion* left London for her final pre-war voyage to Brisbane. Politically things did not seem too bad in Europe; Hitler made a speech widely regarded by observers as

Left Orion *at Southampton preparing for her maiden cruise* (Vickers).

Right *An imposing view of the bow of* Orion (Southampton City Museums).

conciliatory in which he claimed that 'Germany has no territorial claims on England and France, except the return of her colonies'. *Orion* arrived in Brisbane on March 13 1939 and was back in Tilbury at 6.30 am on May 4. By this time the situation in Europe had deteriorated and Hitler was putting pressure on Poland for control over Danzig and the Polish Corridor. For *Orion* a series of three cruises to the fjords and the northern capitals lay ahead. She left Tilbury on June 30 for Immingham where she embarked passengers, leaving for the cruise at 5.30 am the following day. Among the places on her itinerary were Stockholm, Copenhagen and Oslo. The second cruise started from Immingham on July 15, and the third, a 20-day voyage, started on July 29. Her first port of call was Kirkwall in the Orkney Isles and the second Reykjavik in Iceland, after which she left for the Norwegian fjords. Passengers were disembarked in Immingham at noon on August 18, and the following morning *Orion* arrived in Tilbury. She had been scheduled to sail for Brisbane once more on September 9, but by now war was only weeks away.

Only eight days after she arrived in London *Orion* was requisitioned by the government and stores for three months were taken on board. Only minor alterations were made after which she had accommodation for 500 first and second class passengers and 440 troops. On August 28 she sailed for Gourock, arriving in the Clyde three days later. When war was finally declared *Orion* was embarking troops, and she left Gourock for Egypt on September 5 at the head of the first troop convoy to sail. Embarkation had been chaotic, the troops being fitted aboard the

Orion *departing Southampton in the 1930s* (Southampton City Museums).

various ships by agreement between the masters concerned. *Orion* was carrying about 2,500 troops and 38 nurses. Also in the convoy were the *Orcades* and *Orford* and they arrived at Alexandria safely where the troops disembarked. *Orion* made her way back to Tilbury unescorted after calling at Plymouth for orders, but when she arrived in London on September 29 there was some confusion as the managers were not expecting her. It was not until the master telephoned them from the pier that they knew the ship was in port, and when they contacted the Ministry of War Transport they discovered that *Orion* had been taken off hire.

A month later, on October 22, *Orion* was once again on hire to the government as a requisitioned liner, and she sailed for Sydney carrying a full complement of civilian passengers, mainly Australians who had been stranded in England after war had broken out. She arrived in Sydney in early December and was taken straight into dockyard hands to be fitted out as a troopship with accommodation for 1,504 officers and men. On January 2 1940, as soon as the conversion work was completed, *Orion* sailed from Sydney with Australian troops on board. She arrived in Wellington four days later and embarked New Zealand service personnel, sailing the same day and rendezvousing with other troopships, including *Orcades*. The whole convoy then set course for Egypt, where the troops were disembarked. By February 27 *Orion* was back in Tilbury, but it was to be her last visit to the port for four years as soon afterwards the east coast ports came to be in the front line.

For over two months *Orion* lay at Tilbury

until, on April 9, Germany invaded Denmark and Norway. The invasion caught the Norwegians by surprise, and plans were made to land British and Allied troops at Narvik, Andalsnes and Namsos to render assistance. On April 11 1940 *Orion* left Tilbury for Leith where it had been intended that she would embark troops and sail for Namsos escorted by the cruisers *Galatea* and *Arethusa*. However, it was decided that manoeuvring *Orion* in narrow, steep-sided fjords, possibly under air attack, would be courting disaster, and the troops were embarked in cruisers instead and *Orion* became the depot ship at Leith. During her stay there she made one trooping voyage to Scapa Flow and back. By the end of May that year she was once again employed as a troop transport and she sailed for Durban, arriving back in Liverpool on July 17. Less than three weeks later she sailed for Bombay via Cape Town with just over 2,000 troops and 244 first class passengers. From there she went to Suez, Durban and then on to Sydney, where she was once again taken in hand by the Cockatoo Docks & Engineering Company and fitted out to accommodate 4,435 troops. The bulk of these were to have hammocks on 'G' and 'H' decks.

On November 14 1940 *Orion* sailed again from Sydney with Australian troops, this time bound for Haifa where they were disembarked one month later. She then left once more for Liverpool, and having to sail by way of Cape Town did not arrive until early February 1941. There then followed another voyage to South Africa and the Middle East with troops, and on the return journey she went to Halifax, Nova Scotia, via Trinidad. The Canadian troops brought over were disembarked in Avonmouth on August 14 1941 and the following day she sailed in convoy, once again bound for Suez. On Tuesday September 2, at 11 pm, in a position 4°12'W, 10°36'S, the whole convoy had just resumed a zigzag course. The battleship HMS *Revenge* was directly ahead of *Orion* when, 29 minutes later, her steering failed and she swung to starboard. The officer of the watch on board *Revenge* ordered 'full astern both engines', and this put her directly into *Orion*'s path. At exactly 11.33 pm *Orion* collided with *Revenge*'s stern, causing considerable damage to *Orion*'s bows. However, she was able to proceed under her own steam, and the convoy reached Cape Town on September 11. Temporary repairs were carried out in the port and a board of inquiry was held on board *Revenge*. The officer of the watch on *Revenge* was held entirely responsible for the collision and was subsequently dismissed his ship.

The convoy left Cape Town on Sunday September 14, and both *Orion* and HMS *Revenge* were once again stationkeeping with each other. However, they arrived at Suez safely on October 1 where the troops were disembarked. There then remained the problem of where full repairs to *Orion*'s bow could be carried out, and it was decided to send her to Keppel Harbour in Singapore. She sailed for the Far East via Bombay, and arrived in Singapore on November 6 1941, the day on which the Japanese Southern Army, based in French Indo-China, was ordered to prepare for attacks on Malaya, the Philippines and the East Indies.

Orion was taken into drydock and her ship's company were able to enjoy the last few days of peace in Malaya and the Far East. On December 7 1941 this peace was shattered when the Japanese army invaded Malaya, landing at Kota Bharu on the north-east coast and advancing from ports in Thailand. The Japanese were a formidable foe and they advanced rapidly in Malaya, using a series of 'pincer movements', always threatening to surround the hard-pressed British forces who were forced into a continual series of retreats in order to stave off disaster.

On Singapore island life went on fairly normally, and several members of the crew were discharged ashore. One unfortunate steward fell down a manhole ashore and was admitted to the Singapore General Hospital. An able seaman was sentenced by a civil court to three months' imprisonment for desertion. They were just two of the half-dozen unfortunate individuals who eventually ended up as prisoners-of-war in Japanese hands, some of them not surviving the ordeal. By the end of December 1941 the

Japanese army had broken through the British defences on the Slim River, and Kuala Lumpur was directly threatened. Civil labour at the docks had been severely disrupted by Japanese bombing raids, but fortunately on December 31 *Orion* was ready for sea. She had embarked wounded troops and civilian evacuees and sailed into the dangerous waters surrounding the island. The voyage passed without any incidents, although on January 5 1942, the day before she arrived in Fremantle, a baby girl, Margaret K. Johnson, was born on board. Her mother was the wife of a mining engineer from Kuala Lumpur, and her father had stayed behind in Malaya. *Orion* finally returned home to Liverpool via Melbourne, Sydney and Auckland and through the Panama Canal to Halifax, arriving in the Clyde in March 1942.

In April 1942 *Orion* left the UK for another trooping voyage to the Middle East by way of Freetown, Cape Town, Durban and Tanga in East Africa, and she was back in Liverpool in early October that year. Her next voyage was as part of the 'Operation Torch' convoy, during which she carried 5,300 troops to Algiers. While she was in the port she came under heavy air attack, and on her next voyage to bring reinforcements to North Africa, she was again attacked unsuccessfully by aircraft in the Mediterranean. In August 1943, after more trooping voyages to South Africa and the Middle East, *Orion* arrived in New York to embark troops for the Clyde. The general policy regarding troopships during the war was to fill them with as many men as possible, since this was a time when the delivery of maximum numbers of 'bodies' without too much detriment to their health was the main consideration. *Orion*'s two voyages to the United States were a prime example of this policy. Over 7,000 US troops were embarked and *Orion* sailed on September 3, arriving in the Clyde ten days later. She then returned to New York where she embarked another 7,000 troops, landing them at Greenock on November 1 1943. These lifts of

Orion *in black livery during the Second World War. The warship in the foreground is HMS* Orion. *The venue is Grand Harbour, Malta, December 1943* (Imperial War Museum).

such large numbers of troops were never repeated, for the practice was quite rightly regarded as being too dangerous and unhealthy.

In mid-November 1943 *Orion* was back on the route to Suez, this time sailing through the Mediterranean for the first time since early 1940. She had on board 5,000 troops who were destined eventually for Persia and Iraq. The voyage passed without incident until the convoy passed Oran, when the alarm bells sounded. The whole convoy was then subjected to a very intense air attack by about 30 aircraft, and one vessel in the convoy, the BI ship *Rohna*, was hit and subsequently sank with a heavy loss of life to the US troops on board. The convoy was attacked again off Crete, and after some very near misses *Orion* came through with only superficial damage to her superstructure, arriving in Port Said on December 3. On the return voyage *Orion* called into Grand Harbour where she met her namesake, the cruiser HMS *Orion*. During her stay in the port she suffered damage to her port propeller and rudder when she hit a submerged object.

In the early part of 1944 *Orion* underwent a refit in Liverpool and made another voyage to New York before returning to the Mediterranean where, in May and June, she made a series of trooping voyages between Port Said and Taranto to reinforce the Allied offensive in Italy. In the latter half of that year she was once again 'East of Suez', carrying troops to Bombay. She stayed on this route until the end of the war, and in October 1945 she arrived at Southampton with ex-internees and PoWs from Hong Kong. In the following month on November 11 she received adverse publicity when she sailed from Southampton carrying repatriated Australian servicemen. Four hundred officers and warrant officers had walked off the ship, complaining about the 'overcrowded conditions' on board. Two days later *Orion* herself was back in Southampton with engine trouble and all the troops were disembarked; *Orion* then left for Barrow where repairs were carried out. The 'walk off' incident was the subject of a question in Parliament, and it seems that the government, in an attempt to get as many men home for Christmas as possible, had in fact accommodated officers in tier berths rather than cabins: it was a genuine attempt to assist men to get home in the face of enormous pressures on passenger shipping.

Orion sailed once again for Bombay when the repairs were completed, but the continuing press publicity about bad conditions aboard dogged her. She arrived back in Liverpool on Sunday April 7 1946 at the end of her final voyage on government service. She had had an extremely full wartime career, and in the six years and eight months since she was first requisitioned she had carried over 175,000 troops, prisoners and civilians, and had steamed some 380,000 miles.

On May 1 1946 *Orion* was sent back to Vickers Armstrong's yards at Barrow-in-Furness. She was the first Orient liner to be handed back to the company by the government, and it was thought that she would be ready for service towards the end of 1946. However, this was wildly optimistic because, like most liners, she had been requisitioned at short notice on the outbreak of war and during the course of her voyages she had been gradually stripped of her fittings at various ports so as not to hold up movements of the troops. It was a period of great urgency and all these fittings, which normally would have been carefully stored, were torn down and hurled ashore. So in most respects whole new purchases had to be made, and with the shortages prevailing in the immediate post-war years there were inevitable delays.

However, by February 1947 re-conditioning was completed, and although a fair proportion of her accommodation, including all the bathroom cabins, had been refitted in their pre-war condition, much of it was modified to meet the needs of the wider social range of post-war travellers. The first class accommodation was increased to carry 550 and the tourist class to carry 700 passengers. This was done in spite of the fact that space which had accommodated about 200 passengers in pre-war days was given over to provide better quarters for the crew. New features included a restaurant for first class

passengers on the after end of the boat deck, where an elaborate menu was offered. Above this was a new games deck with a wind deflector across its forward end, the idea of which was to create calm conditions while preserving the panoramic views. The whole refit cost some £500,000.

Orion made her first post-war sailing from Tilbury on Tuesday February 25 1947, and during her second round voyage to Australia her return to Tilbury was delayed by engine problems. By the summer of 1951 things had returned to normal at last and on June 29 *Orion* began a 13-day cruise to the Norwegian fjords. It was the first post-war cruise to north European ports by a British liner and fares ranged from £39 to £65. In July 1953 it was announced that *Orion* would make an experimental voyage from Australia to the Pacific coast of North America in the following year. So on September 17 1954 she left Sydney for Vancouver and San Francisco on her first venture into the Pacific since her sailing from Singapore in the dark days of January 1942.

However, during 1958 she was converted to cater for 342 cabin class passengers and 722 in tourist class, now being described as 'two-class tourist'. By this time she was heavily dependent on emigrants to Australia, and frequently on her return voyages she made calls at Singapore and Penang. From 1961 she was run effectively as a 'one-class tourist' ship, but by now her days were numbered. She was 25 years old and the arduous war service had taken its toll.

On November 20 1962 P&O-Orient Lines announced that *Orion* was to be withdrawn from service within 18 months and that her future was 'under discussion'. She left Tilbury on her final Australian voyage on February 28 1963, and left Sydney for the last time on April 8 that year. On May 15 she steamed slowly up the Thames, her 84-ft paying-off pennant flying bravely from the masthead. It had already been announced in

Above left Orion *at Cape Town during the Middle East crisis of 1956* (Robert Pabst).

Above *A magnificent aerial view of* Orion *in the Straits of Dover during the 1950s* (Skyfotos Ltd).

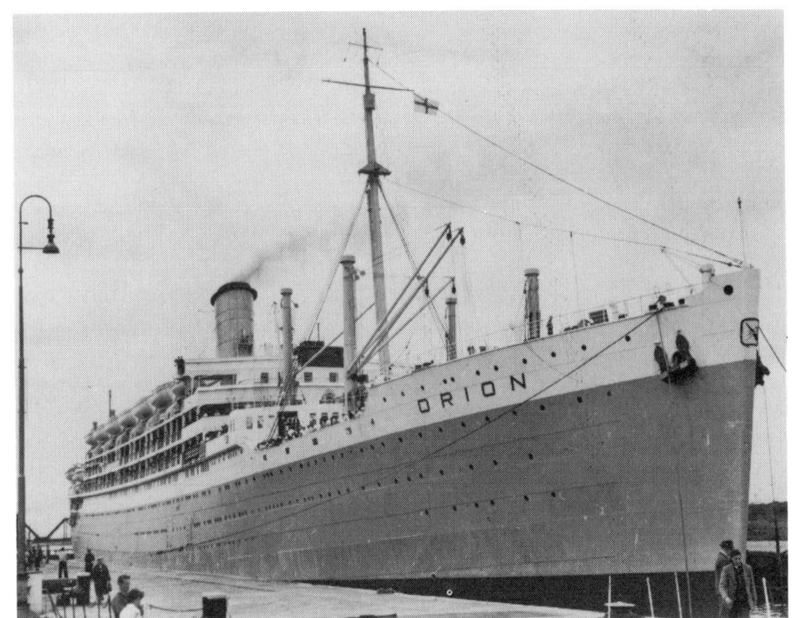

Right Orion *at Tilbury, August 13 1960* (P&O).

January 1963 that she was to be chartered by Firma Otto Friedrich Bahnke, well-known West German hoteliers, from May to September 1963 for service as a hotel ship in Hamburg during the International Horticultural Exhibition in the city. She sailed from Tilbury for Hamburg on May 21 and, under the terms of the charter, P&O-Orient Lines provided 40 deck and engineering staff to maintain the ship's services while she was alongside, but all the catering was undertaken by the charterers. She was berthed at the Overseas Landing Stage at Hamburg where she provided accommodation for 1,150 visitors, as well as opening her restaurant to 'non-residents'. On the last day of September the charter came to an end, and she was sold to Jos Boles & Son SA of Tamise, Belgium. On October 7 1963 *Orion* arrived in Antwerp for the final indignity—the breakers' yard.

Technical data

Gross tonnage: 23,371
Net tonnage: 14,032
Length overall: 665 ft (202.7 m)
Breadth: 84 ft 6 in (25.75 m)
Depth: 33 ft 7 in (10.24 m)
Main engines: Twin screw, two sets of Parsons single-reduction geared turbines, 24,000 shp, 21 knots
Boilers: Oil-fired, steam pressure 450 psi
Passengers: First class 486, Tourist class 653; 1961, 1,697 Tourist class only

Orcades 1937

Just two months before the *Orion* was launched, on October 11 1935, the managers of the Orient Line announced that they had placed a further contract with Vickers Armstrong Ltd of Barrow to build a sister ship. As it happened, the new vessel was to have a hull design identical to that of P&O's *Strathallan*, and even her career mirrored that of the P&O ship. Both liners were sunk within weeks of each other, and were the victims of enemy submarines.

In December 1935 it was announced that the new Orient Liner was to be called *Orcades*, the classical title given to the Orkney Islands, and a name which had only been used once before by the company for the ex-German ship *Prinz Ludwig*. The keel for the new vessel was laid in early 1936, and there were so many ships under construction at the time that the slipway had to be modified for the *Orcades*. The launch was scheduled for December 1936, and although it was a much more low-key affair than *Orion*'s it broke new ground, as a running commentary of the proceedings was broadcast on the BBC's northern radio programme. The ceremony took place on Tuesday December 1 1936, with Mrs I. C. Geddes, the wife of the chairman of the managers, acting as sponsor. There were strong north-westerly winds blowing that day and, as the great ship plunged into the choppy waters of the Walney Channel, it was very difficult to control her. Because of the weather conditions it was decided to take *Orcades* into the deep-water berth in the channel above Ramsden Dock instead of into the dock itself, and while she was being towed there she hit a disused wooden pier, demolishing some 20 ft of it. Much more serious, however, was the fact that she was aground for about an hour before the tugs were able to free her. Fortunately, after this mishap everything went well and work was commenced to prepare the ship for her service with the Orient Line.

The *Orcades* had a gross tonnage of 23,456, and her appearance internally and externally was very similar to that of *Orion*, both ships having a corn-coloured hull. Some modifications, however, were introduced in *Orcades*' design. Internally, the first class public rooms were rearranged and those of the tourist class enlarged. Externally, the single funnel was heightened by 9 ft in order to ensure better dispersal of funnel smuts. Another improvement was the reduction in the number of uprights which supported the promenade deck. She could accommodate 463 first class passengers in 303 single- and two-berth cabins, and in the tourist class 605 passengers in 270 cabins, the total of 1,068 being less than the passenger capacity of the *Orion*. First class passengers had the run of the games or 'A' deck, and most of their public rooms were on the promenade or 'B' deck amidships. Right forward and overlooking the forecastle was the library with the foyer and lounge. Moving aft one passed through the dance space into the verandah café which overlooked the swimming pool down below on the lower promenade or 'C' deck. This deck was 51 ft

Wednesday, December 2, 1936 THE DAILY MIRROR Page 3

GALE DRIVEN SEAS RAVAGE COAST OF BRITAIN

GIANT seas driven by a seventy-mile-an-hour gale ravaged many parts of the coast of Britain yesterday. Three houses were washed into the sea near Lowestoft.

At Abergele, North Wales, holes were torn under the main Chester-Holyhead railway track between Abergele and Kinmel Bay. Houses near the sea had to be barricaded with sandbags at the doors and windows. Hundreds of acres of land were flooded and the sea defence walls were in danger of crumpling.

Railway employees were rushed to keep constant watch for twenty-four hours upon the railway track, others patrolled the sea-walls which stand between the sea and the track for four miles.

Lashed by the fiercest gale in living memory, the huge waves swamped the men as they fought desperately to repair in the few seconds between each wave the holes at the side of the line.

Large foundation stones were carried away by the rushing seas as if they were ping pong balls.

Old bathing huts used as chalets at Ebbfleet were battered to pieces; a petrol filling station adjoining the main road was threatened with inundation, the seas having reached the back door.

Water from the Humber washed into Nelson-street adjoining the Corporation pier at Hull. Barges at their moorings appeared to be resting on the walls and ships in the two-miles-wide river looked as if they were sailing on the road level.

The River Hull overflowed its banks and water poured into the cellars of houses in Wincolme.

Houses Washed Away

Three recently vacated houses at Pakefield, near Lowestoft, were washed into the sea by a high tide, while the occupiers of other cottages threatened on the cliff edge hurriedly removed their furniture.

A seventy-mile-an-hour north-westerly gale swept the London barge Lady Gwynfred, which was aground at East Runton, out to sea and back again to within a quarter of a mile of Cromer, where she may now become a total wreck.

Several hundred acres of riverside land and several miles of towpath on the upper reaches of the Thames were under water early last evening.

When the tide reached its highest point it was 1ft. above the danger level at the House of Commons. In some places it overflowed on to the terrace.

THE JETTY HAD THE WORST OF IT

NEW LINER IN MISHAP

The new Orient liner Orcades being towed to the fitting-out station after her launch at Barrow-in-Furness yesterday.

A strong wind was blowing, and on the way she struck the end of a disused railway jetty, damaging it as seen in the picture below.

She did not herself suffer any harm.

KILLED ON FATHER CHRISTMAS TRIP

ONE woman was killed and another injured yesterday when their car, laden with Christmas toys, was smashed in a collision near Walthamstow, London.

Miss Lilian Bennett, aged sixty-six, of Park View-gardens, Hendon, was killed, and Mrs. H. H. Bullock, her next-door-neighbour, was injured.

They were taking Christmas presents to young relatives.

MAYORESS'S CHAIN OF OFFICE ON COFFIN

The Mayoress of Gateshead, Mrs. J. White, who died suddenly in the town hall on Friday, was buried yesterday. Her chain of office was among the flowers on the coffin. Hundreds of women lined the three-mile route from Mrs White's home to the cemetery.

PRISON FOR MAN WHO HAD SERVED LIFE SENTENCE

BY A SPECIAL CORRESPONDENT

TO Louise Hammond Cullender love has meant the ordeal of waiting patiently as her sweetheart lay under sentence of death for murder . . . fifteen years of prison interviews with her fiancee . . . a few brief months of married happiness.

Frederick James Cullender, thirty-five, killed a warder in an attempt to escape from Rochester Borstal Institution sixteen years ago. He was then eighteen, and was sentenced to death at Maidstone Assizes with a strong recommendation to mercy.

His sentence was commuted to one of penal servitude for life, but Louise Hammond, who had played in the same Bermondsey tenement with him from the age of five, did not lose hope.

Cullender was released on licence on April 26 last year, and Louise met him at the prison gates, and the plans they had made together at last were fulfilled.

Then Cullender lost his work as a carpenter. They were starving

At the Old Bailey yesterday Louise heard her husband plead guilty to five charges of breaking and entering, carrying a weapon and possessing house-breaking implements by night.

She listened anxiously as a police officer told the Recorder, Sir Holman Gregory, that Cullender's sentence expired in 1940, and his criminal licence at death.

Sentencing Cullender to twenty-two months' hard labour, the Recorder said he was liable to penal servitude for life.

"This sentence can only mean another sixteen or seventeen months without him," Mrs. Cullender told me.

SIR H. PRESTON'S £50,000 FOR WIFE

SIR Harry Preston, the famous sportsman, who died at Brighton in August, is believed to have left all his fortune to Lady Preston.

It is estimated that when the estate is wound up it will amount to about £50,000.

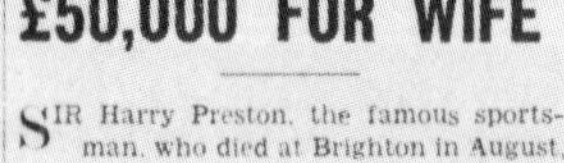

EVERY MAN TO HIS JOB

Counsel, cross-examining a defendant at Bow County Court yesterday, asked: Do you question what she said on that point?

The Defendant (a lorry driver): I'm not going to question anything here. That's not my job. That's a job for my counsel!

DEATH SENTENCE IN TIN TRUNK MURDER

Andrew Anderson Bagley, alias William Smith, aged sixty-two, a builder's labourer, was at Leeds Assizes yesterday found guilty of the murder of Irene Hart, his daughter's sixteen-year-old stepchild. He was sentenced to death.

The girl's body was found in a tin trunk in the loft at her home in Rotherham where Bagley also lived.

During the hearing one of the jurymen was twice taken ill and had to leave the box.

Eventually the Crown and the defence agreed to the case going on with eleven jurors only, and the sick man was excused.

above the waterline, and the distance seven and a half times around it equalled one mile. At the forward end of 'C' deck was the children's playroom with the de luxe cabins aft, and a tavern overlooking the pool. Most of the first class cabins were on 'D' and 'E' decks, and on 'F' deck there were the main entrance foyer and the dining saloon. The tourist class accommodation was aft on 'D' down to 'H' decks. They had a café and dance space on 'E' deck, with the dining saloon and lounge on 'F' deck. With fewer passengers and larger rooms, the *Orcades*' standard of comfort was a distinct improvement upon the *Orion*'s.

Work on the new ship was completed in early July 1937, and on the 7th of that month she left Barrow for drydocking in Cammell Laird's number seven drydock for two days where her underwater hull was cleaned and painted. This was followed by trials on the Clyde, during which she achieved a speed of 22.3 knots. On completion of her trials a number of guests were

Left The Daily Mirror, *Wednesday December 2 1936, shows* Orcades *aground on the day of her launch* (Syndication International Ltd).

Above right and right Orcades, *a lovely ship with a profile very similar to that of* Orion (Vickers).

Above Orcades *at Southampton* (Vickers).

Below Orcades *at sea during the 1930s* (South African Defence Force).

embarked for the passage to Tilbury, where she arrived during the afternoon of Thursday July 15 1937. It was at Tilbury that the new vessel was handed over to the Orient Line, and a few days later, on July 20, representatives of the Press were invited on board to give her some publicity.

Just five days after the Press visit *Orcades* left Tilbury for Southampton, where she embarked passengers and sailed on her maiden cruise to the Mediterranean. As she sailed down Southampton Water on the evening of Saturday August 21 1937, she was closely followed by the P&O liner *Moldavia*. *Orcades* looked resplendent with her corn-coloured hull, single mast and single buff funnel, alongside the black paint of the rather outdated-looking P&O ship. The three-week cruise took *Orcades* to Capri, Kotlor, Dubrovnik, Istanbul and Palermo, before returning to London early in the morning of September 14 that year to prepare for the next voyage, which was to Brisbane. *Orcades* made three round voyages to Australia before undertaking several cruises to the Mediterranean and the northern capitals in the summer of 1938. She made only two more line voyages to Australia, leaving Tilbury on the second of these on December 31 1938 and arriving back in the port at 8 am on April 6 1939. She was then scheduled to make a series of four cruises, the first three to the Mediterranean, each cruise being of three weeks' duration, and carrying first class passengers only, who had access to all the public rooms. Fares for these cruises were to have been from 40 to 207 guineas. The final cruise was from Immingham to the northern capitals, again with only first class passengers and with fares ranging from 22 to 229 guineas. Her programme then was to sail for Brisbane on October 7 1939 on what would have been her sixth line voyage for the company.

In the event only the first cruise, on April 20 that year, to Malta, Port Said, Cyprus, Athens and Gibraltar, went ahead and she arrived back at Southampton at 8 am on May 12 with engine trouble. Initially only the second cruise was cancelled, but in fact *Orcades* had carried her last peacetime passengers, for she went up to Barrow for an overhaul and when she emerged it was as a troopship. She arrived in the Ramsden Dock on the morning of Thursday May 18 1939, just over 24 hours after leaving Southampton and, as she was assisted by the tugs *Ramsden* and *Yorkgarth*, a large crowd of spectators saw her 'home' for the last time.

As *Orcades* lay at Barrow during the late spring and summer of 1939, the political situation in Europe darkened as the Second World War loomed closer. She left Vickers' yard at 12.17 pm on August 15 1939, partially fitted out for the transport of troops, and, in fact, on the front of her official log 'Mediterranean Cruising' was struck through and replaced by the word 'Troopship'. The following day she arrived at Southampton and lay in the port until the end of that month awaiting the inevitable declaration of war. At 8.10 am on August 30 she left Southampton for the Clyde where she arrived the following afternoon and anchored off Greenock. There she joined her older sister *Orion* and other liners which had been pressed into service as troop transports. Over the next four days she embarked 26 British officers and 961 troops as well as 15 Egyptian army officers and 49 civilian passengers all travelling on government service. She left the Clyde at 5.23 pm on September 5 1939 in a fast convoy in which the *Orion* was commodore ship, arriving in Alexandria 11 days later on September 16, where the troops and passengers disembarked. During her return passage to the UK, on September 25, she was involved in a slight collision with a small cargo ship, the SS *Makalla*, in Gibraltar Bay. There was little damage to either vessel and *Orcades* arrived back in the Solent at 8 am on October 1 1939, and anchored in Cowes Roads for the rest of that month. On October 23 1939 Captain Charles Fox took over command of the ship and eight days later, on November 1, *Orcades* left the Solent for Tilbury, where she arrived the following day.

Orcades' next voyage took her out to Australia where she embarked Australian troops for the Middle East, and over the next 12 months she ran between the UK, Australia and the Suez Canal via Cape Town, the Mediterranean being closed to Allied shipping. At 7.36 am on October 30 1941

Left Orcades *arriving at Southampton on August 16 1939, after leaving Barrow the previous day. She had been partially fitted out as a troopship* (Southampton City Museums).

Right Orcades *enters Cape Town harbour in 1940, still in Orient Line colours* (University of Cape Town).

Orcades left the Mersey carrying troops, most of whom assumed they were destined for North Africa. However, they headed out into the Atlantic and halfway across the US Navy took over the convoy escort with an aircraft carrier and several other ships. Although the United States was not officially at war, it was relieving the hard-pressed Royal Navy of many Atlantic escorts. According to one soldier on board *Orcades*, Mr Len Baynes, 'We said "Good old Roosevelt", and felt much safer.' *Orcades* arrived in Halifax, Nova Scotia, on the evening of November 8 1941 and her troops disembarked, after which they were taken by the US troop transport *West Point* (ex-*America*) to Singapore, just in time to be captured by the Japanese.

From Halifax *Orcades* returned to Liverpool where she remained until December 6 that year, when she too sailed for the dangerous waters of the Far East. She left Freetown on Christmas Day and arrived in Cape Town on January 5 1942. From there she sailed to Aden and then to Suez where she embarked 'Black Force', a mixed brigade of the 1st Australian Corps. From there she set course east, calling at Colombo on February 9 1942. She was originally to have landed the Australians at Singapore, but with the surrender of the island less than a week away, she was diverted to the Dutch port of Oosthaven (now Telukbetung) on the southern tip of Sumatra. She arrived in the port at 10.35 am on February 15 1942, the day Singapore fell. The Australian troops were about to disembark when the news came that the Japanese were advancing in strength down the railway from Palembang. Sumatra was as good as lost, so early next morning *Orcades* weighed anchor and left for Batavia (now Jakarta) in Java where she arrived six hours later. There the Australians were able to land in a vain attempt to stop the Japanese advance. While she was anchored off Batavia she embarked a number of Headquarters personnel, nurses, civilian evacuees and survivors of the ill-fated ships HMS *Repulse* and *Prince of Wales*, all of whom had escaped from Singapore.

Orcades left Batavia shortly before midnight on February 21 1942, only six days before a powerful Japanese invasion force landed just a few miles away from the town. She was in fact the last ship of any size to leave the port, sailing into what were now extremely dangerous waters where the Japanese Navy reigned supreme. On February 27 *Orcades* arrived in Colombo where her motley assortment of passengers disembarked. From Colombo she sailed to Adelaide and Sydney in March 1942, before going on to Wellington and then Canada via the Panama Canal. She was the last Orient liner to call into

Australian ports for a number of years. She finally arrived off Greenock on May 11 1942, six months after she had left Liverpool on a very eventful and dangerous voyage.

When *Orcades* left Britain on her next voyage to the Middle East it was to be her last, for on the return passage in October 1942 she fell victim to a U-boat. In late August that year four German submarines had left Germany for the sea lanes off Cape Town. It was called 'Operation Polar Bear' and the submarines were under orders not to engage in action before October 8 1942. By that time *Orcades* was in Cape Town and she had embarked some 1,300 passengers, including women, children, religious groups, wounded servicemen and survivors from sunken merchant ships. On October 7 and 8 four merchant ships were sunk off Cape Town and Captain Fox protested strongly about having to pass through the same area alone and under orders to steam at somewhat less than her full speed. His protests were obviously ignored for, at 4 pm on October 9, *Orcades* left Cape Town bound for Freetown and home.

Soon after leaving the port Captain Fox was very uneasy when they came across wreckage from a recent sinking, but he had to obey orders and they steamed on. All the passengers were ordered to lifeboat drill and to carry their lifebelts with them all the time. As an extra precaution the lifeboats were lowered to the embarkation deck ready for any emergencies. That night the weather deteriorated, turning wet and cold, and the sea became rougher with a heavy swell which caused the ship to pitch slightly. That night Captain Fox felt very anxious about the situation and he had little sleep, visiting the bridge several times.

Next morning the passengers breakfasted early, there was another boat drill and the accommodation was inspected by the Staff Commander. The routines were completed at about 11 am and Captain Fox was sitting in his cabin dozing when a loud explosion shook the ship. *Orcades* had been hit by a torpedo from *U 172*, one of those engaged in 'Operation Polar Bear', and a few minutes later two more missiles hit the ship in quick succession.

The story now is best taken up by Mrs Susan Whitley, who as 13-year-old Susan Kennaway was a passenger aboard *Orcades* with her mother and three sisters. The family had been separated during the evacuation from Singapore in January 1942, and Mr Kennaway, who was serving with the Army in Malaya, was captured by the Japanese. Eventually Mrs Kennaway and her four daughters had been reunited in Rhodesia and were returning home to England. 'I remember walking round the deck after breakfast the next morning and thinking the sea looked choppy, just a grey day with a fine drizzly rain, a few white horses here and there, but not really rough. At 11 o'clock I went along to the saloon and had just taken a book out of the ship's library, a glass-fronted book case opened every day at that hour, and was writing my diary at one of the tables when the first torpedo hit the ship. Suddenly there was an awful crash, the ship shuddered, the glass in the windows smashed and all the tables fell over. It was the worst moment of all, my knees felt weak and we were all rather scared, I think. Bells started to ring and people were shouting orders. I stayed close to my 18-year-old sister, Elizabeth—luckily we were all four together in the saloon—and my mother arrived a few minutes later having looked for us all over the place. Voices called out "to the lifeboats" and we went to our places on deck. It was horribly cold and still raining. My eldest sister, Anne, had only a thin blouse on, so said she would go down to the cabin to get our coats. It was a terrible five minutes waiting for her to come up: two more torpedoes hit the ship while she was down there. However, up she came with four coats and a pair of eyelash curlers, the only thing she managed to grab. My diary and pen were the only things I regretted having lost.

'After standing there for a while, the order came to abandon ship and we were told to get into the lifeboats—which we did—about 50 of us. We were immediately lowered down, but stuck midway for some time, as a boat filled with frightened Lascars had got under ours and couldn't get away from the side of the ship—it was the only sign of panic I saw the whole time. Once we touched the water I was sick and I didn't stop being sick in the bottom of the boat the whole day. The sea, which had looked choppy from the deck earlier, now surrounded us like huge grey mountains. The seamen at the oars pulled together and we would rise up to the top of the waves and then plunge down the other side.

'The rest of the day had an eerie quality about it; after all the noise on board the ship nobody spoke much in the lifeboat. We could see another lifeboat for a while and then it drifted away. Occasionally we had a glimpse of the *Orcades* too; she was some way off, looking grey and still in those now rough seas and incredibly sad. The unusually large number of religious groups on board the *Orcades* was considered an ill omen by some of the seamen and I heard muttering among them. Ship's biscuits were given out by the crew, many of whom had been torpedoed before; they knew exactly what to do and I felt safe in their hands. A few hours later we sighted a ship and hoisted a yellow flag—yellow is seen from a distance—and the ship answered us and stopped. It was a Polish cargo ship, the *Narvik,* on its way to America.'

Meanwhile, on board *Orcades*, within seconds of the first torpedo hitting the ship, Captain Fox was on the bridge and assessing the damage. The missile had struck the port quarter, damaging the propeller on that side and the steering gear. It had also claimed the lives of two greasers working in the port shaft tunnel. The second and third torpedoes had hit the ship on the port side abaft number two and three holds and the cargo of oranges had been scattered over the sea. Fortunately there was no damage to the boiler and engine rooms and the ship remained on an even keel, and Captain Fox was determined to get his ship back to Cape Town if possible. Although the ship's speed was reduced to 6 knots there was every possibility she could be saved, but first he wisely decided to put all the passengers and crew who were not required off in the ship's lifeboats, knowing that his SOS signals had been acknowledged. Sadly, during this operation one of the boats was upset while it was being lowered and the occupants were flung into the water with the loss of 38 lives, including the chief steward and the ship's nursing sister. As the boats disappeared into the misty rain, Captain Fox and his crew of 51 volunteers set course for Cape Town.

At 2.15 pm, two hours after *Orcades* had set out for safety, the *Narvik* was spotted and Captain Fox, unaware that she was taking on survivors, flashed a warning that submarines

A dramatic view of Orcades *shortly after she had been hit by a torpedo in October 1942. The photograph was taken from one of the ship's lifeboats and must have been the last one ever taken of the ship* (Susan Whitley).

were in the vicinity. All those remaining on board were warned to stay close to the upper decks, and the chief engineer kept his men as close to the escape ladders as he could. For over three hours *Orcades* steamed along at 6 knots and hopes were rising that the ship might be saved. Then at 4.30 pm there were three shattering explosions in quick succession—it seemed that *U 172* was determined to finish her off. These last three torpedoes hit *Orcades* in the starboard side amidships and no merchant ship could survive six torpedo hits. No sooner had the sound of the explosions subsided than the *Orcades* began to heel over to starboard. Captain Fox was the last to leave the ship after ensuring all his crew were away and destroying the code books. When he jumped overboard the ship had a 30-degree list and she was turning over quickly. He heard the sounds of fittings and bulkheads breaking up down below and his last memory was of the Red Ensign still flying. As he swam on his back away from the ship, *Orcades* was lying right over on her side with both the mast and funnel touching the water. Slowly the once proud ship sank lower and lower until she disappeared beneath the waves, still on her side.

Captain Fox managed to reach the safety of a raft and after rescuing two crew members from the sea, one of whom was unconscious, he and the other two were picked up by a lifeboat. Fortunately the 9,000-ton *Narvik,* a liberty-built ship, was still searching for survivors, and by 2.00 am on October 11 she had taken everybody on board and was heading for Cape Town.

The story can be taken up again by Mrs Whitley. 'We got alongside in the early evening and soon they started to pick us up by what we called the scrambles. A criss-cross of ropes hung halfway down the side of the ship, another rope was thrown down and tied round our middles and, as the boat went down and then up with the waves, at the top point of a wave we made a wild jump for the scrambles, climbing up them and at the same time being hauled up by the rope. One by one we went up this way.

'It's impossible to say how grateful we were to the crew of that ship. They risked their lives and ship by stopping for us. We were 300 miles from port, no help at hand and the U-boat was still in the area. The ship really carried a crew of 47 and they picked up 1,700 of us. Our lifeboats were tied to the stern of the ship but broke away during the night. My mother, sisters and I slept in the narrow passage of the crew's quarters for the first night, we had very little to eat, but didn't want it anyway. Food ran out very quickly and when a Royal Navy destroyer arrived to escort us back to Cape Town, they shot some more tea over. The second night my 15-year-old sister, Pippa, and I slept top to toe in one of the few bunks. I have never been so uncomfortable in my life—her feet smelt terrible and I don't suppose I smelt too fresh either. Sleeping figures everywhere occupied all available space on deck with the more fortunate ones on the floor of the cabins and in the passages.

Captain Charles Fox CBE, the last master of Orcades (South African Defence Force).

'Day was breaking over Table Bay as we arrived back in Cape Town escorted by two destroyers. The sea was calm by then and the sun was rising to a bright morning. Table Mountain stood out clearly against the sky with the white houses of Cape Town spread out below it. As we entered harbour, a padre held a service on deck, the engines had stopped, and when we glided silently into port, hundreds of weary men stood crammed on deck in silence as the lone voice of the padre offered up prayers. I have always treasured that memory.'

The *U 172* had a short but deadly career. Between the summer of 1942 and her demise in December 1943, when she was sunk by the US Air Force, she sank 22 Allied ships. The gallant *Narvik* survived the war and she remained in the service of the Polish Steamship Company until February 1972 when she went to Spanish shipbreakers. Her master in October 1942, Captain Stanislaus Zawada, was decorated for his brave action, as was Captain Fox, who was awarded the CBE and Lloyd's War Medal for the way in which he handled his ship. After the war Captain Zawada went to live in Australia, and it was only fitting that the Orient Line had the honour of taking him there.

Technical data

Gross tonnage: 23,456
Net tonnage: 14,029
Length overall: 664 ft 11 in (202.68 m)
Breadth: 83 ft 10 in (25.60 m)
Depth: 47 ft 6 in (14.48 m)
Main engines: Twin screw, two sets of Parsons single-reduction geared turbines, 24,000 shp, 21 knots
Boilers: Oil-fired, steam pressure 450 psi.
Passengers: First class 463, Tourist class 605

Orcades 1948

When the Second World War ended in August 1945 the Orient Line had lost exactly half its fleet, which in August 1939 had consisted of eight ships totalling some 161,858 gross tons. Six years later, with only four ships totalling 78,476 gross tons remaining, and after the loss of the company's latest and best ship, it was clear that urgent new building was needed. The first ship in the post-war programme had actually been ordered in March 1945, when the end of the war was in sight. Once again the contract went to Vickers Armstrong Ltd at Barrow-in-Furness and the keel was laid on September 17 that year. In January 1946 it was announced that the new liner would be named *Orcades,* after her predecessor which had been lost in 1942. It had been hoped that the new *Orcades* would be in service by the spring of 1947 and under normal circumstances this would have been so. However, in the aftermath of the war there were long delays in the delivery of materials and a shortage of skilled labour, and it became clear that this time the work would take longer. During the building at Barrow there was a lot of interest shown in the method of construction as large welded pre-fabricated bulkheads were placed in position. Nowadays welded hulls are the norm, but in 1946 they were unusual. It was a method of construction which had been perfected in the United States, where ships had been built by this method almost on a production-line basis.

The *Orcades* was finally launched on Tuesday October 14 1947, two years after her keel was laid, with the ceremony being performed by Lady Morshead, the wife of Sir Leslie J. Morshead, the Sydney manager of the Orient Line. Four hours after taking to the water, *Orcades* was alongside her fitting out berth, where she remained for many months. That same day it was announced that the keel of yet another new vessel for the Orient Line was to be laid down in the berth vacated by *Orcades.* It was more than a year after her launch before fitting out was completed on *Orcades,* and she left Barrow on November 1 1948 bound for the Gladstone drydock at Liverpool. Once the task of cleaning and painting the underwater hull was completed, she left the Mersey and anchored off Greenock at 9 pm on November 11. Trials commenced the following morning, culminating in her runs over the measured mile off Arran on Saturday November 13. During the full power trials she attained a speed of 24.74 knots, and she kept up a good speed between the Clyde and Tilbury, arriving off the Nore Light at 8 am on Monday November 15 1948.

Orcades was very similar in appearance to her predecessor, the main distinguishing features being her single funnel and single tripod mast built in a style resembling a naval control tower. Her navigating bridge was further aft than those in the older ships and there were no old-fashioned cowl ventilators. There were eight continuous decks designated 'A' to 'H' inclusive, intended for the use of passengers, and the design of the accommodation had received very special

ORCADES

attention. Her 770 first class passengers were given single- and two-berth cabins on 'C', 'D' and 'E' decks, and also on 'F' deck forward of the foyer. Several of the cabins had private bathrooms attached and 12 inboard cabins on 'E' and 19 on 'D' deck were air-conditioned. A large dining saloon for first class passengers was amidships on 'F' deck, aft of the foyer, and adjacent to this room were two annexes which could be used by children, or by passengers who wished to give private parties. The saloon could seat 418 people at one sitting, and for added comfort it was air-conditioned.

From the main foyer two wide staircases led up as far as 'B' deck, and opening off the after end of the entrance on 'B' deck was the first class lounge, which was also air-conditioned. Abreast the port and starboard machinery casings and leading from the lounge were the galleries and these led to the dance space which was arranged with sliding and folding side-screens so that the whole deck could be opened up if conditions permitted. This space could also be arranged as a cinema. Still proceeding aft, wide entrances on both sides of the ship brought one to the café, the after end of which overlooked the swimming pool below. Large promenades were arranged on both port and starboard sides of 'B' deck, but the main open-air spaces for first class passengers were on 'A' or the boat deck. Here one could find a novel feature in the special glass-fronted sun deck. This was arranged with longitudinal folding and sliding screens with overhead sun-canopies extending from the forward end of the deck along each side to the main bridge house. In this draught-proof sun-trap an enclosed sports deck was provided, but any feeling of being closed in was avoided by the glazing and the height of the side-screens.

The remainder of 'A' deck was devoted to open-air sports, except at the after end where a small first class restaurant and lounge with their kitchens were placed. The restaurant was air-conditioned and intended for passengers who wished to take their meals in more relaxed surroundings than was possible in the main saloon. On top of the restaurant and lounge was a sports deck fitted with a windscreen across the forward end. From the forward entrance on 'C' deck the shop, hairdressing salons and the library were arranged on the centre line of the ship and they were also accessible on the after end from a

Above left *The launch of* Orcades *on October 14 1947* (Vickers).

Left Orcades *on her trials in November 1948* (Vickers).

Right *The wall decoration in the first class lounge* (P&O).

wide stairway leading from 'E' to 'C' deck. Towards the after end of 'C' deck was the tavern, arranged with sliding and folding screens across the whole side of the room, which allowed the space to be opened up to the first class swimming pool. Two passenger lifts served all the forward first class entrances and also led down to the passengers' baggage rooms on 'G' deck. A separate stairway gave access from below to the first class children's playroom and games deck at the forward end of 'B' deck.

The 742 tourist passengers were accommodated on 'F', 'G' and 'H' decks, mainly in two- and four-berth attractively furnished cabins. Dining facilities were provided in a spacious saloon on 'F' deck which was capable of seating 394 passengers. Immediately aft of the saloon was the tourist lounge, narrowed in width by the provision of outside promenades. Leading up from the saloon was a wide staircase to 'E' deck where the tourist smoke room was situated over the lounge, and aft of the smoke room was the dance space, promenade and children's playroom, while a large café for tourist passengers was provided on 'D' deck. Intercommunicating stairs were arranged between all tourist entrances, and a lift was provided between 'D' and 'C' decks. Accommodation for the 608 crew members received special consideration with spacious messing, smoking and recreation rooms being provided. All officers and engineers were accommodated in single cabins, while POs and leading hands were given two-berth cabins.

Orcades was propelled by twin screws, each driven by a set of Parsons double-reduction geared turbines, designed for a maximum shp of 42,500. The boilers burned oil fuel under forced draught and provided superheated steam at 590 psi. The ship had cost £3,250,000 to build.

When *Orcades* left Tilbury for Australia on December 14 1948, she was commanded by Captain Charles Fox, who had been the last master of the previous *Orcades*. Fares for the first class accommodation ranged from £110 to £425 in a special suite and, in the tourist class, from £59 to £89. She was fully booked when she sailed and her passengers included 149 emigrants sponsored by the Australian government. Among the VIPs on board were Mr I. C. Geddes, Sir Alan Anderson and Mr Robert Menzies, who was then leader of the Federal Opposition. He had just made a six-month tour of Europe and the USA, where he had seen the Iron Curtain, and the Soviet belligerence over Berlin and the blockade. Also on board was Peter Dawson, the Australian tenor, and Miss Cecilia O'Rorke, sister of the vessel's interior designer. Among the crew were 24 members from the old *Orcades*, including Captain Fox, and the new liner was also carrying the chronometer from her namesake, the only instrument salvaged when the ship was sunk in 1942.

The maiden voyage was an outstanding success, despite a great deal of press publicity about a 'mystery wind current which makes deck quoits an embarrassing adventure for women passengers not wearing slacks'. *Orcades* arrived in Sydney at 6 am on January 14 1949 to a rousing welcome. Dozens of small craft met the liner near Watson's Bay and provided an impromptu escort to the Harbour Bridge. As she passed Rose Bay on her way up harbour, a floral harp, the badge of the ship, was delivered to the ship's sponsor, Lady Morshead, at her home. An accompanying card read, 'To Lady Morshead, from her godchild, on her maiden voyage.' Then, as *Orcades* berthed at Wharf 13 Pyrmont, 5,000 people turned out to cheer her in. Two weeks later, when she left the port for the return voyage with 1,050 passengers on board, over 7,000 people packed the docks to say goodbye. She arrived back in London in March 1949. The whole voyage had been a resounding success, and during the passage she cut ten days off the pre-war schedule, having arrived in Melbourne 26 days after leaving London.

In January 1951, Captain Charles Fox, who was now Commodore of the Orient Line, retired. He had commanded *Orcades* for her first two years of service and was succeeded by Captain I. E. G. Goldsworthy. In the summer of that year *Orcades* made a series of cruises from Tilbury, and on the first two of these she called at

Above Orcades *at Southampton's Western Docks* (Skyfotos Ltd).

Below Orcades *at Southampton after her 'Welsh Hat' steampipe was fitted* (Southampton City Museums).

A magnificent bow view of Orcades *at Sydney* (P&O).

Orcades *afloat in No 7 drydock, Southampton, in the late 1950s* (Southampton City Museums).

Barcelona, becoming the first Orient liner to visit any Spanish port since the start of the Civil War in that country in 1936. In the early hours of Wednesday May 7 1952, while leaving Melbourne, *Orcades* ran aground on a sandbank at the edge of the south channel in Port Phillip Bay. Tugs were quickly on the scene, but strong north-westerly winds lashed the ship, countering efforts to free her. However, later that day she was pulled clear and an examination of her plates revealed no damage. She was then able to continue her voyage to London, much to the relief of her 1,215 passengers. In the early 1950s the very distinctive black 'Welsh Hat' steampipe was added to her funnel in an attempt to solve the problem of funnel smuts.

In June 1953 *Orcades* took part in the Coronation Review off Spithead when she led the fleet of liners carrying government guests at the event. This was perhaps her greatest moment, for by the mid-1950s the post-war travel boom was subsiding, foreign competition was becoming serious, and *Orcades* had to move with the times. Cruising had been re-introduced in the UK, and in 1952 *Orcades* made a cruise from Sydney, the first since before the war. In 1954 she followed the lead set by *Oronsay* and made a trans-Pacific voyage. By the summer of 1957 these Pacific voyages from Australia had become a regular feature of their itinerary. It was during one of these world voyages in July 1957, that an outbreak of Asian 'flu occurred on the ship.

Fortunately it was a mild strain and nobody was seriously ill, but a total of 92 cases was reported among passengers and crew. The outbreak began shortly after *Orcades* left Panama, and by the time she was in mid-Atlantic 40 first class cabins had been turned into hospital wards.

In August 1957 *Orcades* had a troublesome voyage to Australia. At Aden she was involved in a collision with the French ship *Picardie*, which occurred while *Orcades* was manoeuvring to leave the port with the help of tugs. The strong wind caused her to drift and she bumped the French vessel. Then, in the Arabian Sea, the severe south-west monsoon created very uncomfortable conditions on board, and between Aden and Colombo two passengers died from heat exhaustion. Later that year *Orcades* rescued a sick seaman from the British freighter *Glenmoor* in very heavy seas, 300 miles off the Australian coast. She was able to land him at Fremantle on Boxing Day, where he was given urgent hospital treatment.

By the end of the 1950s air travel was making its impact on the ocean liner, the seller's market was well and truly over for the shipping companies, and new ideas were needed to entice passengers to travel by sea. The liners were called upon to show all their talents, as people now travelled by sea through choice rather than necessity. Entertainment became a major feature of a voyage; permanent staff and hostesses replaced the old passengers' sports committees, and orchestras were carried. *Orcades* lacked one major facility for the real comfort of passengers in tropical climes, and that was air-conditioning.

In the middle of the winter season in early January 1959, *Orcades* was the first of the Orient liners to be fitted throughout with air-conditioning. The work was carried out by Harland & Wolff at Belfast and was completed in ten weeks. At one stage there were 1,500 men working round the clock in order to finish the work in time, and the refit cost the company £1 million. It was a job for any British yard to be proud of, for the tender had been rejected by a German company, who said the time allowed was too short. During the refit the deck numbering was altered. 'A' deck became the 'Stadium' deck, 'B' deck became the 'Verandah' deck and 'C' deck became the new 'A' deck, the decks below this being altered accordingly. The dining saloons were designated restaurants and a new swimming pool was fitted, all in preparation for attracting 'tourists' who may otherwise have chosen to fly to their destinations. When the work was completed *Orcades* steamed across to Liverpool to pick up guests and 600 pressmen and travel agents, who would all be expected to report favourably on the 'new look'. No longer would passengers have to sleep on camp beds on deck trying desperately to catch any hint of a breeze in the Red Sea.

On September 21 1962 *Orcades* was transferred to P&O ownership, and just over 18 months later the inevitable happened; the ship became 'one-class tourist' carrying 1,635 passengers. She took on P&O's white livery, and poker machines made their appearance in the Tartan Bar, which was renamed the Casino. The 'Grill Room' became a cinema and the former tourist class lounge a nightclub, remaining open until the small hours. All this was a far cry from the silent ship which more or less 'closed down' at midnight as far as passenger entertainment was concerned.

By 1970 *Orcades* was regularly employed in cruising from both Australia and the UK with positioning voyages between Southampton and Sydney. In June 1970 she was nearing the end of one of these voyages and was between Fremantle and Sydney when she was battered by heavy seas which damaged her steering gear. The ship was turned into the wind, and engine room staff worked to restore the steering, after the compartment had flooded. After five hours she had sufficient steering power to return to Fremantle where she arrived the following day.

By now *Orcades*' career was drawing to a close. She made her last voyage from Sydney on March 16 1972, and on April 26 it was announced that she was to be withdrawn from service. During the voyage to Southampton, when *Orcades* was in the southern Indian Ocean, she made a 640-mile mercy dash to aid an injured

ORCADES
LONDON

ORCADES

Above left Orcades *on the day of her arrival at Kaohsiung, February 2 1973* (James L. Shaw).

Left Orcades *shortly after her arrival at Kaohsiung* (James L. Shaw).

Above Orcades *was broken up during 1973: her stern section is rapidly disappearing* (James L. Shaw).

Swedish seaman from the Norwegian ore carrier *Berge Istra*. The two ships rendezvoused in mid-ocean and the injured man, who had been hurt in an engine-room accident, was transferred in a lifeboat. These were the years when De Lessep's waterway, the Suez Canal, was closed and so the injured man was landed at Durban, the next port of call.

Orcades' last few months of service were spent cruising from Southampton, and at the end of the season, on October 13 1972, she was decommissioned at Southampton after 24 years of service. *Orcades* lay in the port for eight weeks before, on December 8 1972, she sailed from there for the last time, bound for Taiwan. She was handed over to Mitsui & Company's shipbreakers at Kaohsiung on February 6 1973, and by the end of that year she had ceased to exist.

Technical data

Gross tonnage: 28,472
Net tonnage: 11,140
Length overall: 708 ft 7 in (215.99 m)
Breadth: 90 ft 5 in (27.58 m)
Depth: 31 ft (9.45 m)
Main engines: Twin screw, two sets of Parsons double-reduction geared turbines, 42,500 shp, 22 knots
Boilers: Oil-fired, steam pressure 590 psi
Passengers: First class 770, Tourist class 742; 1964, 1,635 tourist class only

Oronsay 1951

The second ship to be built as part of the post-1945 reconstruction programme was the third *Oronsay*. Once again the company went to Vickers Armstrong Ltd for the ship, and she was laid down in early 1949, in the berth which had been vacated by the *Orcades* just over two months earlier. At 28,136 gross tons, the new vessel would be slightly smaller than *Orcades*, but her design was to be very similar. She had accommodation for 688 first and 833 'tourist B' passengers, with the emphasis on tourist class to cater for the post-war flood of emigrants to Australia.

Oronsay was launched on Friday June 30 1950 by Mrs A. I. Anderson, wife of the chairman of the managers. The ceremony took place just before noon and coincided with President Truman's authorization for US troops to go into action in Korea, signalling the start of the Korean War. Four months later, at 9 pm on Saturday October 28, *Oronsay* was lying at her fitting-out berth in Buccleuch Dock, when flames were seen coming from No 2 hold. The Barrow and Vickers fire brigades were soon on the scene, but it was found that the outbreak had got a firm hold and it was necessary to sound the general alarm. This brought 23 other brigades into operation from an area between Workington, Kirkby Lonsdale and Blackpool. They were assisted by two tugs and a firefloat. The fire had started accidentally in the hold's insulating cork during welding operations, and had smouldered unnoticed for some hours before spreading rapidly. The fumes given off by the burning cork were so bad that firemen had to wear breathing apparatus and even so two of them were overcome. The blaze spread to No 1 hold, and so No 3 hold was flooded to prevent any spread in that direction. Early on the morning of Sunday October 29 there was an additional danger when the vessel developed a list to port approaching 20 degrees because of the great weight of water which had been pumped into her. The list was away from the dock and at one time it was feared she might capsize. This was prevented by lowering the level of water in the dock, flooding *Oronsay*'s starboard tanks and burning holes in the hull to release the water. At one stage conditions were so difficult for firemen fighting the fire that they could only work in relays of five minutes each. It was Tuesday October 31 before the fire was finally extinguished, and until proper investigations could be made it was thought that the damage was severe.

The Orient Line had already announced that *Oronsay*'s maiden voyage was to be on March 14 1951 and passenger bookings had been taken for this date, but any further requests for passages on the ship were now turned down. Fortunately, by November 1 it was ascertained that the damage was not as extensive as feared and the work on fitting out was resumed. That same day a Home Office forensic scientist determined that the cause of the fire was accidental, which was a great relief to all concerned. Later that month *Oronsay*'s maiden voyage was set for May 16 1951 and the passenger lists were re-opened.

What had at first appeared to be a disaster had only delayed the vessel's completion by eight weeks.

Oronsay left Barrow's Ramsden Dock at 10.30 am on Saturday April 29 and headed north for the Clyde, where she was to start her trials the next day. By 6 pm on Monday April 30 her speed trials were completed and she anchored off Gourock to embark a number of guests, and four hours later she left for the Thames, arriving in Tilbury at 9 am on Thursday May 3 1951.

Oronsay's first class accommodation was amidships on seven decks, from the sun deck down to 'F' deck. The sun deck was an area of some 3,400 sq ft, aft of the funnel and directly above the cinema. Below this was 'A' deck with the lookout and games stadium forward; aft of this on the starboard side was the library and 295 feet of games deck. Right aft on this deck was the cinema which was used by both classes. The main public rooms were on 'B' or the promenade deck, and once again Brian O'Rorke was responsible for all the interior architecture. Forward was the children's playroom and open deck, and the forward foyer. Aft of this was the main lounge, with the main foyer dividing it from the port and starboard galleries, which were, in effect, corridor lounges. Aft of the galleries were the ballroom and 'Verandah Bar', which overlooked the swimming pool on the deck below. 'A' deck was given over largely to suites and cabins, with the 'Tavern' and swimming pool situated aft of them. 'C' and 'D' decks were occupied mainly by cabin accommodation and on 'F' deck there were more cabins. The first class restaurant was sited aft of these and was air-conditioned, as were some of the suites on 'C' deck. Tourist class passengers were accommodated aft on 'C' to 'H' decks, with a swimming pool on 'B' deck. The children's playroom and ballroom were on 'D' deck, with the lounge on 'E' deck and the restaurant and another lounge on 'F' deck.

Oronsay was a twin-screw ship powered by double-reduction steam turbines which developed 42,500 shp and gave her a service speed of 22 knots. She had in fact cost £4,228,000 to build, which indicated the enormous increase in costs to the owners since the end of the war.

As *Oronsay* lay at Tilbury waiting to sail on her

Oronsay *at sea shortly after completing her trials* (Vickers Shipbuilding & Engineering Ltd).

Above *A fine aerial view of* Oronsay *in the Channel* (Skyfotos Ltd).

Left Oronsay *in King George V drydock, Southampton, after her familiar 'Welsh Hat' steampipe was fitted* (Southampton City Museums).

maiden voyage, some 400 workmen were busily engaged in completing the furnishings and fittings on board, and their work was not finished until May 15 1951, the day before she left the port. Fortunately the stewards were then able to prepare the cabins for passengers, who were embarked early on the morning of her departure. She had a full complement of passengers for the maiden voyage, and as the sailing was in the quietest season, a few first class passengers were able to book for Gibraltar and Naples. The demand for tourist berths was unaffected, the majority of these passengers being subsidized by the Australian government, and there were still long lists of people waiting to emigrate. *Oronsay* sailed on schedule on May 16 1951, commanded by Captain T. L. Shurrock, and she was given a rousing welcome in all the Australian ports.

In October 1951, on the homeward leg of her second voyage, she embarked 61 servicemen's wives and 106 children at Port Said. The Egyptian government had recently abrogated the Anglo-Egyptian Treaty of 1936, and this was the first act in a series of events which finally led to the crisis of 1956. Recognizing that this move would lead to increased tensions in the Suez Canal zone the government decided to evacuate families of servicemen from the area. *Oronsay* arrived in Southampton on Saturday November 3 1951, where members of the WVS were on hand to assist with the evacuees.

In the summer of 1952 *Oronsay* made her first cruise from Tilbury, a 13-day voyage into the Mediterranean. Tourist class fares were from £37 and in the first class they started at £66. A year later plans were in hand to extend the voyages of Orient liners from Sydney into the Pacific, and to the west coast of North America, in an attempt to attract US tourists. The first of these experimental voyages was made by *Oronsay* and she sailed as normal from London to Sydney on November 26 1953. She left Sydney on January 1 1954 and called at Auckland, Suva, Honolulu, Vancouver and San Francisco, returning to Sydney by the same ports and arriving back in Tilbury via Suez at the end of March 1954. At the company's AGM a few weeks later, Mr A. I. Anderson paid tribute to Captain Hawker and his ship's company for the good start they had made with the 'dollar-earning cruises', which were specifically designed to attract US passengers to Australia and the South Pacific. Also during 1954, *Oronsay* was given a 'Welsh Hat' extension to her funnel, a feature which would always identify her and the other post-war sisters, *Orcades* and *Orsova*, immediately.

Just over two years later, on September 1 1956, as the Suez crisis came to a head and British and French troops were building up in Cyprus, *Oronsay* was routed home from Australia via Cape Town. This, of course, delayed her arrival in London, which was further disrupted by fog in the Thames estuary. However, she eventually arrived in Tilbury on September 27. By the end of 1957 she was sailing via Suez again, although her schedules would be disrupted once again when war broke out in the Middle East ten years later.

In October 1958 an incident took place which could have had serious consequences. *Oronsay* was outward-bound between Aden and Colombo when, at 5.45 am on October 22 1958, both of the ship's surgeons were awoken by a strong smell of burning and saw dense smoke in No 2 ward of the hospital. They rushed to the scene and found that a convector heater had ignited clothing which had fallen onto it, but fortunately they were able to extinguish the flames quickly. The only patient at the time was one of the officers who was suffering from fever, and in a dazed condition he had left the heater on and fallen asleep. All the passengers were evacuated from the cabins above on 'D' deck, but happily they were soon able to return and the patient was found wandering in the vicinity.

In early September 1959 *Oronsay* was sent up to Gladstone Dock in Liverpool for an extensive refit which included the installation of air-conditioning throughout the passenger and crew accommodation. The whole refit was dogged by industrial disputes, which did the Port of Liverpool no good at all, particularly when one considers the demise of the port today. All together, within the space of a few weeks, there were six stoppages of work on the liner. Little wonder that no other ships were sent for refits at Liverpool by the company. During *Oronsay*'s refit the nomenclature of the decks was altered, 'A' deck became the 'Stadium' deck and 'B' deck became the 'Verandah' deck. 'C' deck became 'A' deck and so on down to 'H', which became 'F' deck. The work was finally completed in November 1959, and later that month she sailed for Australia, experiencing some very severe weather which forced her to seek shelter in Algeciras Bay where the *Braemar Castle* had run aground.

In April 1964 *Oronsay* was transferred to P&O ownership and she was the first Orient liner to adopt P&O's white hull in place of her corn colour, although she retained Orient's green boot topping. Three years later, in July 1967, while

Left *A bow view of* Oronsay *at Sydney* (P&O).

Below Oronsay *at Sydney* (P&O).

Below right Oronsay *at Cape Town* (Robert Pabst).

Oronsay was homeward bound from the Pacific, there was a fire in one of her lower holds aft. There were no casualties, but 43 tourist class cabins were damaged and the passengers were moved into the first class section. She spent several days in Hong Kong while thorough inspections were carried out, before resuming her voyage home via Cape Town, as the Suez Canal was again closed owing to the war in the Middle East. On her way home she called at Bombay, and when she sailed it was the last homeward sailing of a P&O-Orient liner from that port.

In January 1970 *Oronsay* was once again in the news. She had been at Port Everglades on December 29 1969, *en route* to the Pacific, when a crew member and passenger were landed who soon afterwards developed symptoms of typhoid. Nine days later *Oronsay* was quarantined at Vancouver and the number of confirmed cases of the disease on board had risen to 32. All during January 1970 *Oronsay* was held in Vancouver, and at one stage there were 100 doctors, technicians and clerical staff working full time to isolate the typhoid carrier. In the event the individual concerned was a Goanese member of the crew who had been living in an area where the disease was prevalent. The ship was eventually released on Wednesday February 4 1970, by which time 69 passengers had been sent to hospital. Three hundred and ninety of the passengers cancelled their passages and found other transport, while the remainder stayed with the ship to Australia. All together the whole incident cost the company £500,000.

By the end of 1972 *Oronsay* was operating as an 'open-class' ship, carrying 1,400 passengers and just over 600 crew members. By now she was cruising year round, especially from Australia, in and around the Pacific. By February 1974 she was the sole survivor of the post-war trio built during the 1950s, but her career was also drawing to a close. On April 2 1975 P&O announced that *Oronsay* was to be withdrawn

ORONSAY

ORONSAY

Left Oronsay *in the 1970s; by now she was flying the P&O houseflag* (J.K. Byass).

Below left Oronsay *meets P&O's* Canberra (P&O).

Right Oronsay *at the Kaohsiung breakers' yard of the Nan Feng Steel Company in November/December 1975. In the foreground is Mr P.T. Chang, the general manager of Nan Feng, and his daughter* (James L. Shaw).

from service in September that year and that she would carry her last passengers between Sydney and Hong Kong before going to the shipbreakers.

Oronsay made her last cruise from Southampton on July 22 1975; it was for 12 days, calling at Gibraltar, Casablanca, Tenerife, Madeira and Corunna, returning to Southampton on August 3. The cruise was an extra one in her itinerary in place of a three-week refit, and the fares were cut slightly because of the late announcement. Despite the short notice, *Oronsay*'s farewell cruise from the UK was fully booked. She left Southampton and England for the last time on August 4 1975, commanded by Captain 'Jack' Lefrevre. She was given a glorious send-off from the port as she sailed, dressed overall and flying her paying-off pennant. A Royal Marine band played her away from the dockside and the ship's musicians struck up 'Scotland the Brave' and other appropriate tunes to remind all those present of her Scottish name. Across the Atlantic, when she sailed from Port Everglades at midnight, it was to the accompanying din of car horns and klaxons. Her departures from Los Angeles, where Captain John Terry took command, and San Francisco were quieter. In Honolulu a pipe band made up of expatriate Scotsmen, Australians, New Zealanders and Americans bade her farewell. As *Oronsay* sailed a single piper played a lament.

Finally she left Sydney on her last cruise to Hong Kong via Brisbane. She had on board 700 passengers, all of them determined to give the old ship a good send-off. At sea, every night was a gala night, but the last one before docking in Hong Kong was a special *Oronsay* night with the gala ball lasting into the small hours of Sunday September 28, ending with a farewell song to the ship by her officers. Two days later her European crew flew home and, on October 4 1975, the Goanese crew left for India. *Oronsay* departed her berth at Ocean Terminal for Kellett Bank, where the operation of de-storing was completed. The remaining officers and crew left the ship on October 5 that year, and four days later she was sold to the Nan Feng Steel Enterprise Company of Kaohsiung, Taiwan, to be broken up.

She had called at 150 ports during her 25-year career and had completed 64 line voyages and 37 cruises.

Technical data

Gross tonnage: 28,136
Net tonnage: 11,130
Length overall: 708 ft 7 in (215.99 m)
Breadth: 93 ft 5 in (28.49 m)
Depth: 31 ft (9.45 m)
Main engines: Twin screw, two sets of Parsons double-reduction geared turbines, 42,500 shp, 22 knots
Boilers: Oil-fired, steam pressure 590 psi
Passengers: First class 688, Tourist class 833; 1960s, 1,400 tourist class only

Orsova 1954

The *Orsova* of 1954 was the last of the post-war trio of mail liners built for the Orient Line as part of their rebuilding programme. 1954 had started with an air disaster when a BOAC Comet, flying from Rome to London on the final stage from Singapore, disintegrated ten miles south of Elba with the loss of all those on board. BOAC was also in difficulties with the Britannia aircraft, so because of this and the Elba Comet disaster, British aviation had been very badly hit. It therefore seemed that the airliner would not provide any serious competition for the brand new *Orsova*, particularly on the long route to Australia. But within 20 years the whole situation would change, and the Boeing 747 cruising at 550 mph and carrying 404 passengers would put *Orsova* and many other liners prematurely into the shipbreakers' yards of Taiwan.

The contract for building the new ship went once again to Vickers Armstrong Ltd at Barrow, and work started early in 1952. It soon became clear that this latest vessel would have a new and unusual profile, as she was to be the first ship of any importance to do away with the conventional mast, the funnel instead being rigged to carry wireless aerials and halyards. This was necessary because the engines were to be placed further forward than usual and, had a single mast been retained, it would have had to have been repositioned, thus reducing the space available for the games deck forward of the bridge. Either the funnel and mast had to be placed close together or merged into one unit, and so the latter course was chosen. The funnel itself was unusual in that the 'Welsh Hat' steampipe was built into it, to serve the functional purpose of dealing with smoke and smuts. Those who might lament the disappearance of a formal mast and a traditional funnel could hardly cavil at the clean clipper-like lines of her stem and stern, for the added curve of her bow not only gave her additional grace, but provided for more deck space and improved sea-keeping qualities.

Orsova was launched shortly after noon on Thursday May 14 1953, and the ceremony was performed by Lady Anderson, wife of Sir Colin Anderson, chairman of the managers. One of the biggest ever crowds turned out to see the launch, regardless of the fact that it was a dull, grey and damp day. Among the guests assembled at Barrow were a group of players from the touring Australian cricket team, including Ritchie Benaud. Just over two hours after *Orsova*'s launch, the P&O Company launched the *Arcadia* on the Clyde. The two ships together represented the largest amount of tonnage launched in Britain on any one day. Even at this stage the shipbuilders and shipowners were deeply conscious of the competition posed by the airlines, as all the speeches followed the theme of how sea and air services could be complementary rather that competitive. Just ten months after the launch, on March 8 1954, *Orsova* ran her trials on the Clyde, attaining a speed of 26.08 knots, and soon after this she arrived in Tilbury to prepare for her maiden voyage.

At 29,091 gross tons *Orsova* was slightly larger than her two post-war predecessors. She carried 685 first and 800 tourist passengers and was built for long voyages. Her interior, on traditional British lines by Brian O'Rorke, was aimed at maximum deck and public room space, and the comfortable cabins were correspondingly modest in size and facilities. There were eight main decks available for passengers, designated by letters from 'A' downwards. Rising up around the funnel from 'A' deck were the three bridge decks, which accommodated the captain's rooms, the cabins for the navigating and other officers, the chartroom, wheelhouse and compass platform. 'A' deck itself had three distinct games areas for first class passengers as well as the library and table tennis room. At the after end was the restaurant, where the decor was a mixture of simplicity and sophistication. The patterned carpet was in dusky pink, the walls in lime with scrapbook decorations arranged by Miss Barbara Jones. At night 'star' lights, set into a dark ceiling, shone directly onto tables without glare and the carpet concealed a small dance floor for special occasions.

The main feature of 'B' deck was the wide promenade which surrounded the public rooms. At the forward end was the children's playroom, which had as much access as possible to the open air by the use of large sliding doors onto the playdeck with its paddling pool and sand-pit. Other 'necessities of life' for the younger passengers included miniature furniture, a slide, a climbing frame and see-saw. The first class lounge had large full-height windows along each side, with wide, soft-cushioned window seats. The room was simple in its general scheme, with doors and other woodwork in English ash and the walls and ceilings painted. The main decoration was a whole wall painted as an 'eye deceiver'—appearing to be rough boards, perhaps the size of a boathouse, hung with objects one would expect to find in such a place, an old lamp, ropes, boathooks and flags, all designed by Mr Humphrey Spender. Aft of this room were two galleries, which were long sitting rooms linking the lounge with 'The Square'. The port-side gallery was decorated in red and the starboard-side gallery was in green, which must have been a help to passengers who could not remember which side of the ship was which. 'The Square', situated aft of the galleries, was used as the cinema, and for dancing and other large social occasions. Right aft on 'B' deck was the 'Verandah Bar', a large room with wide windows opening out onto the sheltered 'Verandah' deck. At each side were big bays raised a little and separated from the rest of the room by railings, so that they were almost verandahs themselves.

'C' deck was given over to first class cabins, with the 'Tavern' and swimming pool at the after end. 'D' deck was taken up almost entirely by first class cabins, and included 'the flat' and the special staterooms. The flat was a self-contained, air-conditioned living unit, made up of a sitting room, a double bedroom, a pantry and a bathroom. 'E' deck amidships was once again given over to first class cabins, a number of which were occupied by ship's staff. The first class dining saloon was amidships on 'F' deck and it covered a large area. As most passengers preferred not to sit in the middle of the room, ingenuity was used to avoid this. A centre 'room within a room' was made by the use of panelled screens. The panelling and chairs of this centre room were of dark mansonia and rosewood, so that they contrasted with the outer areas which were decorated in lighter colours with chairs and slatted panelling in pinkish beechwood. The effect, looking past the screens from the centre, was that of looking out onto bright verandahs. The 'set piece' decoration was a mural, 'A Vision of London' by Ceri Richards.

The tourist class passengers were accommodated on 'C' down to 'H' decks, and careful planning again raised the already high level of comfort found in Orient liners. The large open space at the after end of 'C' deck was the tourist games area with a swimming pool. On 'D' deck there was the tourist dance space which also doubled as a cinema, and aft of this was the 'Verandah Bar', curved to resemble the stern of the ship. The main feature was the large semi-circular range of windows looking out aft. Café

ORSOVA
LONDON

Left Orsova *on the stocks at Barrow-in-Furness* (P&O).

Right *Final preparations are made for the launching ceremony in May 1953* (P&O).

Left Orsova *is towed to the fitting-out basin, May 14 1953* (P&O).

tables were arranged against the windows to make the best of an unrivalled view. The tourist library was on 'E' deck and aft of this was the children's playroom which followed the same pattern as that in the first class, with hinged screens which could shut out bad weather, or admit fine weather in the tropical sections of the voyage. The large tourist dining saloon was on 'F' deck, but to avoid making passengers feel they were sitting in too large a space, an ingenious arrangement of glazed screens was introduced which appeared to divide the room, but at the same time retained an airy and spacious effect. Immediately aft of the dining saloon was the tourist lounge; a comfortable room with its settees and easy chairs, it was partially panelled and was separated from the stair landing by a low balustrade. In warm weather, doors in the ship's side could be opened, giving a lovely view over the sea and at the same time providing a welcome breeze. The tourist class cabins were situated on 'F', 'G' and 'H' decks, those on 'H' deck being four- and six-berth cabins.

Orsova carried a crew of approximately 620 officers, petty officers, leading hands and ratings. All the officers had single-berth cabins, the navigators being berthed on the bridge decks and all engineer officers having cabins on 'E' deck with an air-conditioned sitting room and mess close by. Petty officers and leading hands were berthed in single- and two-berth cabins, many of which were air-conditioned. Most of the ratings had cabins forward on 'F' and 'G' decks. The vessel was propelled by twin screws, each driven by a set of Parsons geared turbines, designed for an shp of 42,500. Steam was supplied by three Foster Wheeler water-tube boilers at a pressure of 500 psi and a temperature of 850°F, providing for a service speed of 22.5 knots.

Orsova sailed from Tilbury on her maiden voyage to Australia on March 17 1954, and she still had a number of workmen on board completing the fitting-out of the first class 'Verandah Bar'. The company offered first class passengers a 10 per cent rebate on their fares for the inconvenience, but as the work was finished before the vessel reached Port Said many passengers declined to accept it, declaring themselves perfectly satisfied with the accommodation. Once into the Mediterranean, the ship met fairly rough seas, but fortunately the rolling was reduced by the stabilizers and she reached Naples on Monday March 22 1954. She arrived in the Australian ports in the following month and she returned home by the same route.

In the spring of the following year *Orsova* made her first voyage into the Pacific, and on April 12 1955 it was announced that she had broken a speed record for merchant ships which had stood for 30 years. She covered the 2,100 miles between San Francisco and Honolulu in 3 days 17 hours, nearly three hours less than the previous record time—but speed records at sea were now becoming irrelevant as the world entered the 'jet age'. It was Wednesday July 13 1955 before *Orsova* arrived back in Tilbury again after her first world voyage. In the following year, in the early hours of May 24 1956, *Orsova* ran aground in Port Phillip Bay outside Melbourne. Fortunately she was on a sandy reef, and at 1.15 pm that day, when the tide was high, she was refloated with the aid of three tugs. There was no damage and she was able to continue her voyage.

In the New Year of 1960 *Orsova* was temporarily taken out of service and sent for a ten-week refit at Vickers Armstrong (Shipbuilders), Walker-on-Tyne, on the east coast. The work undertaken there completed the air-conditioning of the post-war Orient Line ships, and in addition to this and other improvements, the decks were renamed. 'A' deck became the 'Stadium' deck and 'B' deck became the 'Verandah' deck. 'C' deck then became 'A', and this was carried on downwards so that 'H' deck became 'F' deck. The first class restaurant on 'A' deck became 'The Grill' on the 'Stadium' deck, and the two dining saloons were re-designated as restaurants. It was

Above right *Still in her Orient Line livery,* Orsova *enters Tilbury Docks* (Skyfotos Ltd).

Right Orsova *is towed through the locks into Tilbury Docks* (P&O).

ORSOVA

Left *A dramatic bow view of* Orsova *at Sydney. It shows her 'Welsh Hat' funnel to its best advantage* (P&O).
Right and below right Orsova *at Cape Town* (Robert Pabst).

while *Orsova* was in dock that the P&O merged their fleet and the Orient ships, following the acquisition of minority shareholdings in the Orient SNCo. The new operating company became known as P&O-Orient Lines (Passenger Services) Ltd, and initially there were no outward signs of the new organization, but it was the first step towards the Orient Line's loss of its separate identity. *Orsova* left the Tyne at 2 pm on Saturday March 12 1960, and she arrived at Tilbury two days later. Four months later, while in the Pacific, she embarked over 500 passengers at Los Angeles—the largest number of passengers ever to leave the city for Europe. *Orsova* conveyed them via Panama and Bermuda to Southampton, along with a further 460 passengers who had embarked at San Francisco and Vancouver. By 1964 the Orient Line's corn-coloured hull had given way to P&O's white hull, marking the end of the colours which had been a tradition on Orient ships since the *Orion* of 1935.

During the 1960s *Orsova* called regularly at Southampton, usually at the end of her long Pacific voyages, and during the summer she cruised from the port. On March 31 1965 *Orsova* was registered under the ownership of the P&O company and she, together with *Oriana*, lost her Orient Line identity. In June 1967 the Six-Day War in the Middle East between Egypt and Israel broke out, and the Suez Canal was closed to shipping. Sailing via Cape Town added to the cost of the voyages to Australia, and in February 1971 the huge increases in the price of oil, together with the overwhelming competition from the airlines, sounded the death-knell for many of the great liners, among them the *Orsova*.

In early February 1971 *Orsova* received unwelcome publicity when two of her crew members appeared in a Sydney court charged with the attempted murder of the Master-at-Arms on board. The incident, it appeared, had happened about a mile outside territorial waters when the offenders tried to throw the Master-at-Arms overboard.

Just a year later, in February 1972, when *Orsova* was in the Pacific *en route* from Los Angeles to Honolulu, she made a 150-mile mercy dash to assist a sick officer aboard a US tug, the *Tecumseh*. The man, who had suffered a thrombosis in his right leg, was transferred to *Orsova*'s hospital where he was able to receive treatment which undoubtedly saved his life.

Later that year, in November 1972, while on a cruise from Southampton, over 300 passengers and crew were taken ill with a mild form of dysentery. When the ship returned to Southampton crew members were asked to undergo tests in an attempt to find a carrier of the disease. Two hundred and twelve of the Goanese

ORSOVA

ORSOVA

stewards on board refused to take the test and they were dismissed. *Orsova* had arrived back in Southampton on November 26 1972 and immediately went in for a three-week refit. However, the dispute over medical tests had still not been resolved when she was preparing to sail on her next cruise, a 16-day 'West African-Christmas Cruise', starting on December 17 that year. In the event the ship was so short of skilled kitchen staff that passenger numbers were cut to 650, all sailing first class, and these included 120 tourist class passengers who were transferred to the first class section. Despite its being a 'first-class only' cruise there were a number of complaints about conditions on board, and as a result all the passengers were offered a refund of their fares.

Orsova *at the scrapyard in Kaohsiung during 1974. She is rapidly disappearing as the cutting torches slice her in half* (P&O).

In the early summer of 1973 it was announced that P&O's *Canberra* was to be withdrawn from service and that *Orsova* would take over her 1974 cruise programme. It seemed that *Orsova* was to have her life extended, and the reason for the decision was apparently that *Canberra* was not regarded as suitable for cruising. Then suddenly, in August 1973, the position was reversed; *Orsova* was to be withdrawn from service on November 25 1973 with *Canberra* now taking over her cruising programme. It was difficult to see the reason for this sudden reversal of thinking, but the company explained that there had been a sudden upsurge in demand for open class cruising in the UK market and the cost of converting *Orsova* from her first and tourist class configuration would have been too great.

Orsova's final months were spent cruising from Southampton, and on November 25 1973 she completed her final commercial voyage when she entered Southampton for the last time. Just 20 days later, on December 14 that year, she left Southampton for the scrapyards of Taiwan. She had on board a skeleton crew of 72, and in the interests of economy she steamed slowly out to the Far East via Cape Town, reporting her position by radio every seven days. She arrived off Kaohsiung on February 15 1974 and was sold to the Nan Feng Steel Enterprise Co to be broken up. She was another one of the many liners which went to a premature grave in the scrapyards during the early 1970s.

Technical data

Gross tonnage: 29,091
Net tonnage: 11,940
Length overall: 722 ft 6 in (220.24 m)
Breadth: 90 ft 6 in (27.60 m)
Depth: 39 ft 10 in (12.19 m)
Main engines: Twin screw, six sets of Parsons double-reduction geared turbines, 42,500 shp, 22 knots
Boilers: Oil-fired, steam pressure 630 psi
Passengers: First class 685, Tourist class 800

Oriana 1960—The Last of the Line

In 1954, when the Orient Line extended its voyages across the Pacific Ocean to call at Hawaii and the west coast of North America, it also extended the traditional voyages way beyond Sydney to create a whole new service. The potential of these new routes was enormous and, as all of them meant much longer journeys, the next priority was to shorten the sailing times by means of greater speeds. If two new ships of a similar size to *Oronsay* or *Orsova* were built, it was doubtful whether they could achieve the speeds required and, with the increases in building costs, it would have been impossible to make them pay. So the technical requirement for the new service entailed a much larger and faster ship, but at the same time one which could negotiate the Suez Canal. The outcome of these plans was the biggest and fastest, but, sadly, the last great passenger ship to be built for the Orient Line.

It was perhaps natural that the new ship should be built by Vickers Armstrong at Barrow, where a good relationship had been built up between the management and that of the Orient Line. So it came as no surprise when Vickers received the tender in 1956, and the keel of yard number 1061 was laid on September 18 1957. It was fitting that the new vessel should be named *Oriana*. For over 70 years the names of Orient liners had started with the letters 'Or', and as *Gloriana* was the name given by Elizabethan poets to Queen Elizabeth I, it seemed a particularly suitable name in the second Elizabethan era, when *Oriana* was the largest ship ever to be built in that part of the kingdom ruled over by the first Queen Elizabeth. *Oriana*'s badge was designed by Mr Milner Gray RDI, to symbolize the link between the first and second Elizabethan eras. The double 'E' monogram represented the two queens, with the surrounding 'O' for Orient, and the whole capped with a formalized interpretation of an Elizabethan eight-arched pearl crown. The largest example of this badge was placed on her bows.

As the 1950s drew to a close, work was proceeding well at Barrow and the launch date was set for November 1959. But prior to this a major policy change was announced by the Orient Line, who had decided that Southampton was to be *Oriana*'s terminal port instead of London. Although it meant a considerable loss of trade for London, the decision was a wise and logical one, for by turning round at Southampton the extra journey up the Channel would be saved and the voyage time cut by a day. Moreover, Southampton, which had long been Britain's leading passenger port, was better able to handle the increased number of passengers which *Oriana* would carry. She was to be over 41,000 gross tons, with accommodation for 2,184 passengers and a speed of 27 knots.

On August 27 1959 it was announced that HRH Princess Alexandra would launch *Oriana*, and the announcement itself provided yet another link with history for it was made from Government House, Brisbane, during Her Royal Highness' tour of Australia. *Orion* had been

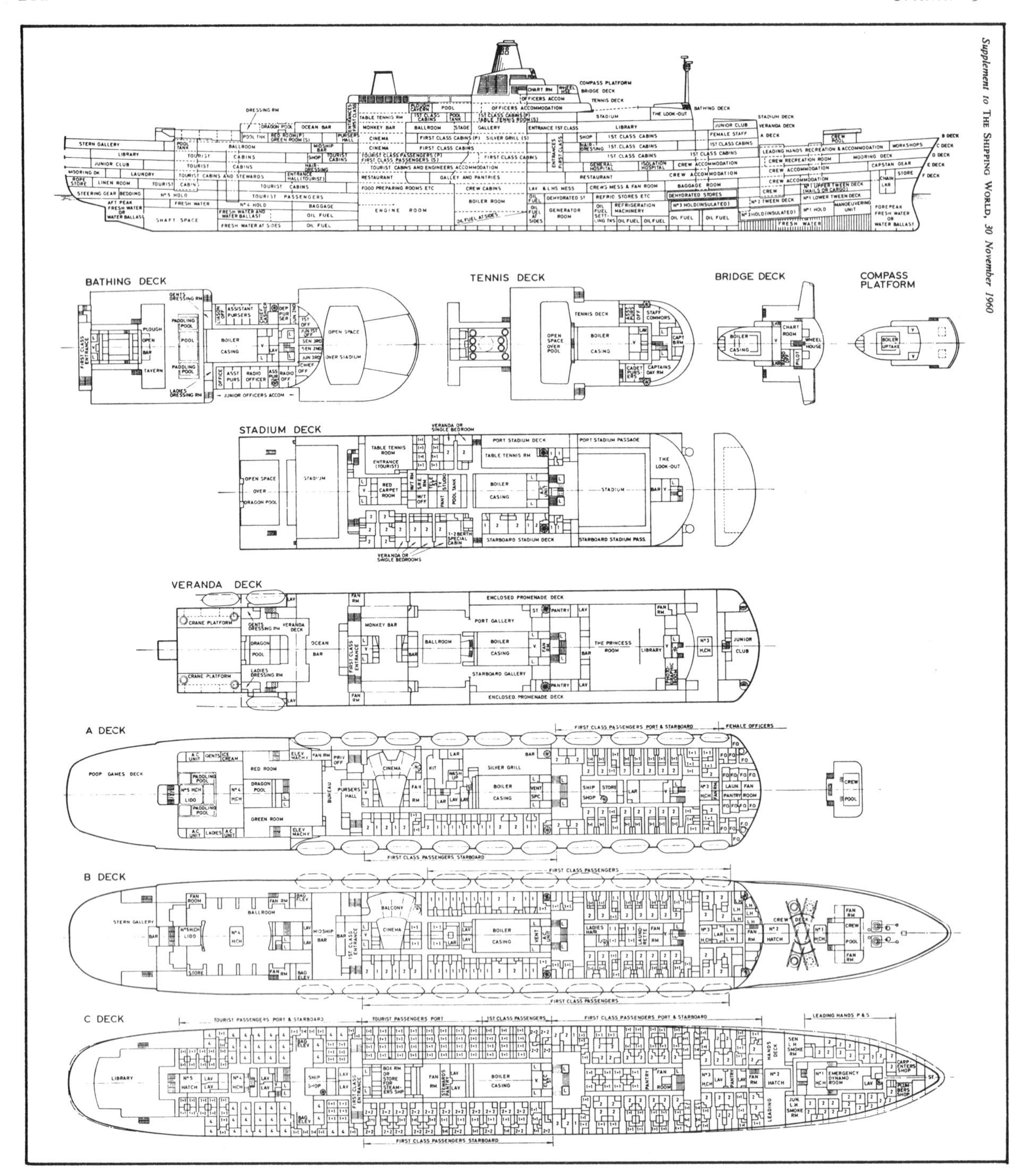

Supplement to THE SHIPPING WORLD, *30 November 1960*

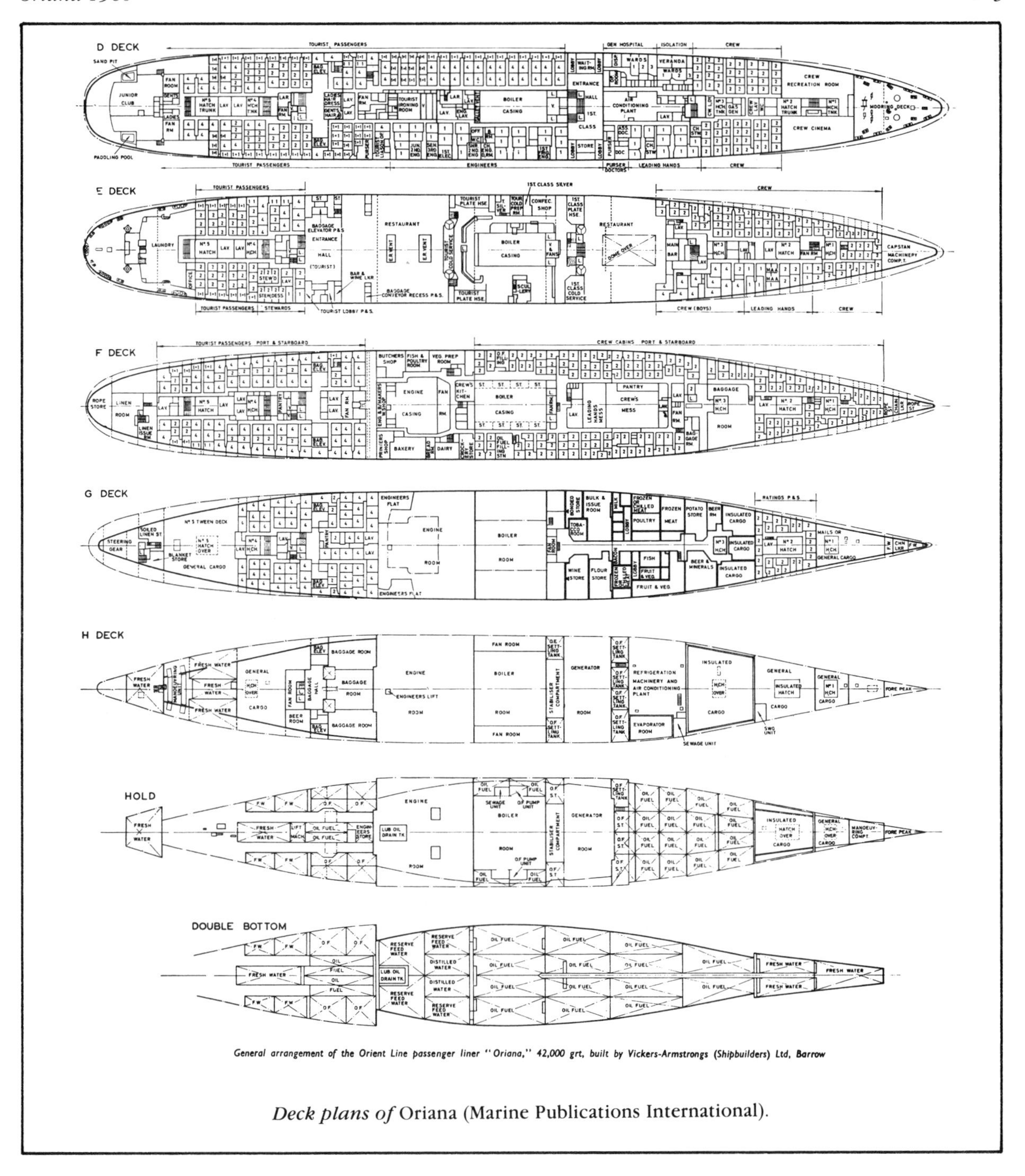

General arrangement of the Orient Line passenger liner "Oriana," 42,000 grt, built by Vickers-Armstrongs (Shipbuilders) Ltd, Barrow

Deck plans of Oriana (Marine Publications International).

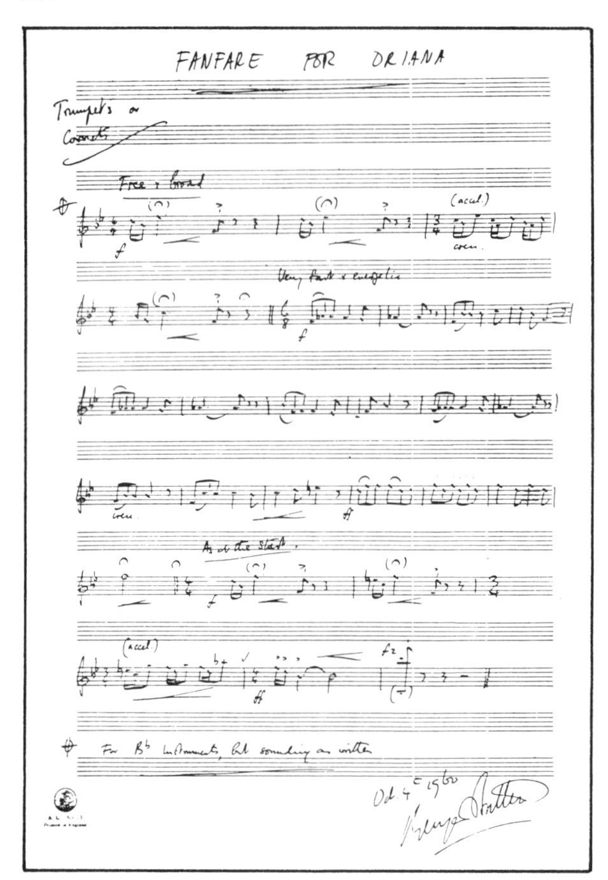

launched from Brisbane by Princess Alexandra's uncle, the Duke of Gloucester, and the ship was now in Brisbane on August 27 1959 for Queensland's centenary celebrations. *Oriana* would be the first passenger liner launched by Princess Alexandra, although at the age of nine, in June 1945, she had sponsored the oil tanker *British Soldier* on the Clyde, and in 1957 the frigate HMS *Jaguar*.

Just over two years after her keel was laid, *Oriana* was ready to be launched. The ceremony took place on Tuesday November 3 1959, and it was one of the first of Princess Alexandra's public engagements following her triumphant tour of Australia. The Princess travelled up to Barrow by train overnight, and arrived at the town's railway station at 11 am. She was then driven to Vickers' shipyard where she was welcomed by the chairman, Lord Knollys, and Sir Austin Anderson. With half an hour still to go before the launch, the Princess went to the joiners' shop where she was able to see how *Oriana*'s completed cabins would look. At 11.40 am she inspected the Barrow Sea Cadets and Red Cross Cadets before being shown the launching mechanism under the ship. Then, on the hour exactly, to the accompaniment of a fanfare and the national anthem, the Princess sent the great ship into the waters of the Walney Channel. *Oriana* had been christened with three bottles of wine—one Australian, one Californian and one bottle of Château Talbot, a claret which was drunk in the first Elizabethan era, thus symbolizing the ties between the three countries.

At the lunch which followed the launching ceremony, Princess Alexandra spoke of the doubts that had existed at one stage as to whether *Oriana* would take to the water on time, a reference to a tugmen's strike which had just been settled. But in a more positive vein she told the assembled dignitaries of the link that the ship would forge between Britain and Australia and how any step that brought Australia a week closer could only be a good one. Sir Austin Anderson said, 'All who served the Orient Company, afloat and ashore, were honoured at having a "Royal Godmother" for their latest ship.' So the last Orient Line vessel was towed to her fitting-out berth in Buccleuch Dock, where she would remain for a year before she was completed.

Although it cannot be said that *Oriana* was a beautiful ship, she had a profile which was unique and immediately recognizable the world over. Perhaps her most unusual features were the small 'flower pot' shaped funnels, the after one of which was a dummy and served as a housing for the engine room exhaust fans. However, it was not by accident that she had such an unusual design. Sixteen different hull models had been tested in Vickers Armstrong's experimental tank at St Albans, and the one which was finally selected included the bulbous bow, which at the time was exceptional among large passenger ships. The building of her superstructure too was far from conventional. Over 1,000 tons of aluminium were used for this task, with the whole of the structure above the strength deck being constructed of this material. The general principle followed in the welding of the aluminium superstructure was to align the plate edges with stiffeners wherever possible, the stiffeners thus providing permanent backing bars for the butt welds. Almost 350,000 sq ft of aluminium plating together with 20 miles of special extruded aluminium sections were used, some of the panels being 30 ft square, but weighing only 35 cwt.

Far left *'Fanfare for* Oriana*' by Benjamin Britten* (P&O).

Above left *Tuesday November 3 1959;* Oriana *takes to the water. She was christened by HRH Princess Alexandra* (Vickers).

Right Oriana *in the fitting-out basin at Barrow* (P&O).

Down below in the main machinery spaces, things were more conventional. *Oriana* was powered by a two-shaft arrangement of double-reduction geared turbines of Pametreda design. They developed 65,000 shp and maintained a service speed of 27.5 knots. Steam was supplied by four Foster Wheeler ESD boilers. The boilers were mounted athwartships forward and aft of a central firing aisle with the forced-draught fans located in the boiler room wings. Immediately forward of the boiler room was the stabilizer compartment and forward of that was the main generator room in which there were four Allen turbo-generators. From this room a ladderway in an oiltight passage led up to the refrigeration and air-conditioning plant. In the engine room the superheated steam at 700 psi and 900°F powered two sets of machinery, each consisting of high, intermediate and low pressure turbines. The turbines drove the four-bladed twin screws of 20 ft diameter through double-reduction gearing.

Below the waterline the most interesting features were the tranverse propulsion units. Berthing a ship is always a difficult operation and, although moving a ship sideways was not a new idea, *Oriana* was the first large vessel to adopt the principle as a major auxiliary installation. Each unit comprised an electrically-driven impeller carried in a horizontal streamlined casing with geared drive at right angles to the impeller shaft. The impeller casing with its drive was mounted in a cylindrical tube fitted athwartships some distance below the waterline. The operating principle was like that of a jet engine, with water drawn in through the shell opening on one side of the ship and expelled through the opposite side. Direction was reversed by simply reversing the impeller motor. The shell openings for the impellers were provided with steel doors to reduce resistance when they were not in use. Four separate units were employed, two forward and two aft, and each unit was under separate remote control from the consoles on the navigating bridge. This gave an instantaneous response when checking any undesirable rotation of the vessel, thus reducing delays which can occur when instructions are passed to tugs or on-shore operators.

The age-old problem of funnel smuts was given special attention, and the bridge design produced fore and aft passages each side of the funnel.

Above left Oriana*'s after funnel which was a dummy and served as a housing for engine-room exhausts* (Author's collection).

Left Oriana *was not a beautiful ship, but she had a profile which was unique and immediately recognizable the world over* (Southampton City Museums).

Right *The engine-room control platform* (P&O).

This page: above left *The promenade deck ('B') port side.* **Above** *'Tennis' deck, showing forward funnel.* **Left** *Enclosed deck, 'B' deck, port side.* **Below left** *Looking aft from the 'Bathing' deck.* **Below** *'Tennis' deck, port side looking forward* (All author's collection).

Top right *The 'Princess Room', a drawing room with a section screened off as a library. It was the first class lounge prior to 1973* (P&O).

Right *The 'Starboard Gallery', 'Verandah' deck, decorated with early Australasian prints* (Author's collection).

Bottom right *The 'Monkey Bar', 'Verandah' deck. The main features were the drawings 'Monkeys and Foliage' by Madeleine Pearson* (Author's collection).

These passages had open ends just below the centre of the funnel. Wind from forward entered the passages and passed quickly aft striking the vertical walls at the closed ends of the passages. The air was then forced up to join the smoke coming away from the top of the funnel, and both were thus taken upwards and aft away from the ship's decks.

When Orient Line started planning *Oriana* they appointed the Design Research Unit, of which Professor Misha Black and Mr Milner Gray were partners, to co-ordinate the design of the public rooms, a total area of some 110,000 sq ft, which with staircases and entrances was spread over 11 decks.

Oriana's accommodation was designed for 688 first class and 1,496 tourist class passengers. She was fully air-conditioned and set new standards of passenger comfort. The 11 passenger decks ranged from the 'Tennis' deck amidships, down to 'G' deck which housed tourist class cabins. The first class accommodation was originally in the midships section, and the uppermost of their public rooms was the 'Plough Tavern' on the 'Bathing' deck. This room with a bar opened onto the swimming pool and open deck with sliding folding screens and large windows. All the other wall surfaces were in cedar, with all corners rounded to a generous radius. The engraved glass panels which lined the bulkheads of the passages to the 'Plough Tavern' were from 'The Plough' public house, Notting Hill Gate, London, demolished in 1957.

On the 'Stadium' deck, below the 'Bathing' deck, were the 'Lookout' and the 'Red Carpet Room'. The former was an observation room with fine views aft, but unfortunately the views forward were obstructed by the first class children's nursery. The bulkheads were panelled in cherrywood veneer and blue plastic-faced panels containing the ship's crest. The Red Carpet Room was a small room for special functions. Its walls were panelled in olive ash relieved by an incised and gilded design, the floor was covered with a 'Red Diablo' carpet and the focal point of the room was a painting entitled 'Sunflower', by Edward Middleditch. The main

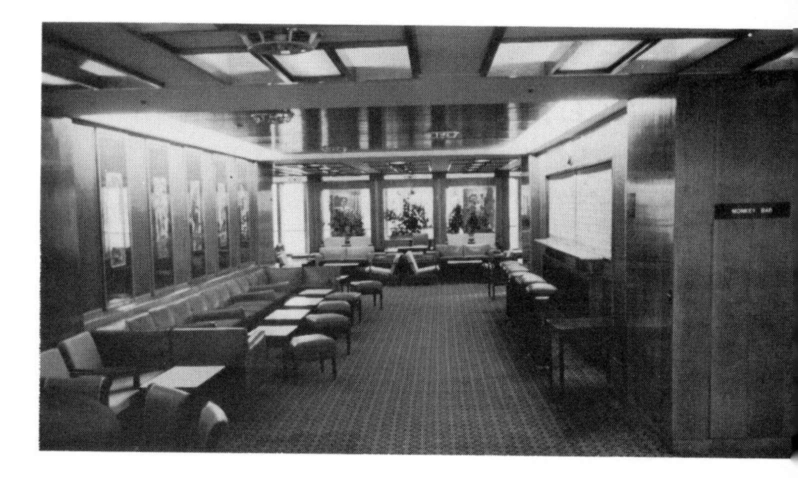

first class public rooms were on the 'Verandah' deck, the chief one, forward, being the 'Princess Room'. This was the most used 'drawing room' on the ship with a section screened off as a library. In the main foyer aft of the 'Princess Room' was a large portrait of Princess Alexandra by Judy Cassab, an Australian artist. Aft of this foyer were the port and starboard galleries; these were used as lounges, with the walls panelled in elm and the floors carpeted in a special design in lavender greys and lime green. Both galleries were decorated with early Australasian prints. Aft again were the ballroom and 'Monkey Bar', and to give continuity both of them were carpeted in the same design as the galleries. The main features of the 'Monkey Bar' were the drawings 'Monkeys and Foliage' by Madeleine Pearson, and side areas which were separated from the main bar by glass panels and planted with semi-tropical foliage.

On 'A' deck beneath the port gallery was the 'Silver Grill', an exclusive restaurant with bar and portable dance floor. The main dining room was the 'Elizabethan Restaurant', which seated 360 and was divided by rosewood screens into a large central area with smaller bays either side. The lighting in the room could be adjusted to suit its varied uses. The first class cabins were on the 'Stadium' deck down to 'C' deck, and all of them had a bathroom or shower and toilet. An unusual feature was the 'court cabin', where inside cabins were arranged round a courtyard with large windows, giving them all some natural daylight.

The tourist class public rooms were almost as luxurious as the first class, the uppermost being the 'Ocean Bar', just aft of the 'Monkey Bar' on the 'Verandah' deck. This room opened with sliding folding doors onto the 'Dragon Pool'. Below this on 'A' deck were the 'Red' and 'Green' Rooms, cul-de-sacs off the main bureau, being small carpeted lounges with writing facilities. Aft of these rooms was the Lido area with deep and shallow swimming pools. The main ballroom area was the 'Carnival Room' on 'B' deck, and, like the adjoining 'Midship Bar', this was decorated in a harlequin design, 'Masque of *Oriana*'. Right aft on 'B' deck was the 'Stern

Left *The portrait of HRH Princess Alexandra by Judy Cassab. The portrait was in the foyer on the 'Verandah' deck aft of the Princess Room* (P&O).

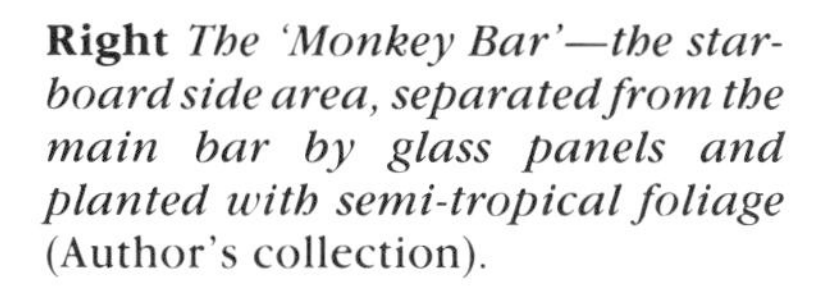

Right *The 'Monkey Bar'—the starboard side area, separated from the main bar by glass panels and planted with semi-tropical foliage* (Author's collection).

Right *The 'Ocean Bar', 'Verandah' deck* (Author's collection).

Right *The 'Elizabethan Restaurant', divided by rosewood screens into a large central area with smaller bays either side* (P&O).

Gallery' with a fine view through large windows. At the after end of 'C' deck was the library and writing room, which was furnished as a lounge with a number of writing desks, and an engraved glass panel forming a screen to the end of the room. Beneath this on 'E' deck was the 'Drake Restaurant', which seated 784 passengers. There was also a purpose-built cinema on 'A' and 'B' decks which served both classes.

Cabins for the crew set new standards in accommodation. For the first time in a British passenger ship, every adult member of the crew had either a single- or a two-berth cabin, all air-conditioned and fitted with wash basins. The built-in cabin furniture was made of pale African mahogany with plastic top surfaces. Floor coverings were plastic-type tiles with a rug beside the bunks. The crew recreation room and cinema was forward on 'D' deck and the mess rooms were on 'F' deck beneath the 'Elizabethan Restaurant'. The captain's and staff captain's accommodation was forward on the 'Tennis' deck, and most of the other officers were accommodated directly beneath on the 'Bathing' deck.

By the latter half of 1960 work on the great new ship was nearing completion and she was almost ready to leave Barrow-in-Furness for dry-docking and trials. Shortly before the liner sailed, Her Majesty the Queen and HRH the Duke of

Left *The 'Stern Gallery', 'B' deck aft* (Author's collection).

Above right and right *The library and writing room, 'C' deck aft* (Author's collection).

Right *The leading hands' smoke room, which was situated forward on 'C' deck* (P&O).

Left *Her Majesty the Queen visits* Oriana *at Barrow on October 21 1960* (P&O).

Below Oriana *in drydock at Falmouth after leaving the builders and before she ran her trials* (P&O).

Edinburgh, accompanied by Lord Mountbatten, visited her while they were at Vickers' yards for the launching of HMS *Dreadnought*. Although it was the Navy's day, Her Majesty spent nearly an hour touring *Oriana* after she had completed the launch of the submarine.

In fact, *Oriana* had originally been scheduled to sail the following day, October 22, but this had been postponed owing to industrial troubles at Vickers' yard. There had been a dispute with the contractors responsible for fitting out the public rooms, which resulted in them being paid off by the company who then took on the work themselves; a plumbers' strike and supply problems had also caused delays. So the new sailing date was set for November 3 when, at 6.30 am, she would leave the fitting-out basin. However, there was a further 24-hour delay when severe gales swept the north-west coast of England. So finally, at 6.50 am on Friday November 4, *Oriana* left the basin at Buccleuch Dock. Her 97 ft beam went faultlessly through the Buccleuch Bridge and with only a foot to spare on either side she went through the dock opening and into the Walney Channel, assisted by three Liverpool tugs. On board were 200 Vickers' men who were to travel with her to complete the finishing touches. Thousands of sightseers turned out to see her slip into the Walney Channel and Morecambe Bay as she headed south for Falmouth.

Early the next morning she arrived off the Carrick Roads ready to be docked in the Queen Elizabeth Drydock. Despite the early hour hundreds of sightseers turned out again and *Oriana* looked resplendent in her traditional Orient Line livery of corn-coloured hull, green boot topping, white upperworks and buff-coloured funnels. Once in the drydock she towered impressively over the ship in the next drydock, but not everyone was impressed. One old sailer was heard to say that she had too top-heavy an appearance to be graceful, and another commented that she looked like a 'floating block of flats'.

After having her underwater hull painted, *Oriana* left Falmouth for the Clyde where, on Sunday November 12, during her trials and while developing an overload power of 82,500 shp, she attained a speed of 30.64 knots in a force 7 gale. During astern manoeuvring trials the ship was brought to a stop from 28 knots ahead and then attained a speed of 15 knots astern in a time of five minutes.

Two days after completing her trials, *Oriana* arrived at her home port of Southampton, early on Tuesday November 15 1960. Her reception was quiet, but displayed on the new passenger terminal at 105-106 berth was a large notice saying, 'Good Luck to the *Oriana*'. The front of the terminal was dressed with bunting, as were the tugs which brought her alongside. Ten days later she left the port for a five-day shakedown cruise to Lisbon. For this trip she embarked just over 800 passengers, members of the Association of British Travel Agents, who were holding their tenth annual convention on board. It was the first time the convention had been held outside Britain, although it was still on British territory. *Oriana* returned to Southampton on November 27, and two days later the new passenger terminal was opened by Field Marshal Lord Slim.

Oriana was due to sail on her maiden voyage to Australia on Saturday December 3 1960, and on the eve of her departure she was visited by Princess Alexandra together with her mother the Duchess of Kent. The Princess had wanted to visit 'her ship' again; indeed, after the launching ceremony in the previous year she had written to the chairman of Vickers Armstrong, Lord Knollys, 'Last Tuesday was such a wonderful experience and I do want to thank you for your kindness in asking me to launch *Oriana*. And I so hope one day I will have the opportunity of seeing her again, when she is completed.' The visit was very informal, and after touring the ship the royal guests had lunch with the master, Captain Clifford Edgecombe, his wife, and directors of the line.

The following day the great new liner embarked 2,200 passengers, and at 2.30 pm on a very cold, wet and windy day the multi-coloured streamers linking the ship and the quayside were broken as *Oriana* set sail on her maiden voyage.

Left *At sea* (Author's collection).

Right Oriana *in King George V drydock at Southampton. She still has her corn-coloured livery* (Skyfotos Ltd).

Despite the foul weather and an industrial dispute by Southampton's dock workers everything went well. Among the well-wishers on the quay was the comedian, Tony Hancock, who was saying farewell to friends. Further down, just outside Southampton's Western Docks, in Mayflower Park and on Royal Pier, hundreds of people turned out to watch *Oriana* go by as the park echoed to the sound of car horns. Those were the days when liner sailings from the port were an everyday occurrence, and indeed the Atlantic giants *Queen Mary* and *United States* were also sailing that day; but without a doubt it was *Oriana* the crowds had come to see this time.

The first few days of the maiden voyage were uncomfortable for *Oriana*'s passengers, as she encountered severe weather conditions. However, once into the Mediterranean the weather improved and on December 10 she made her first southbound transit of the Suez Canal. She arrived in Fremantle on December 23, just in time to disembark her passengers for that port in time for Christmas. Eight days later, early in the morning on New Year's Eve, she arrived in Sydney where she was given a tremendous welcome. Hundreds of small craft whistled and tooted as the gleaming new liner slid through Sydney Heads and down the harbour. Thousands of onlookers lined the vantage points as *Oriana* headed for the new Overseas Shipping Terminal at Circular Quay, where she was the first vessel to tie up at the wharf. In fact, the construction of the new terminal had been largely influenced by her building and that of P&O's *Canberra*. A long and costly dredging operation would otherwise have been necessary to accommodate these vessels within the port.

From Sydney, *Oriana* undertook a ten-day cruise before finally leaving the port for Auckland, where she received another great reception. Perhaps the warmest welcomes were in Vancouver and San Francisco, and in the latter port the city council proclaimed February 5 '*Oriana* Day'. By the end of February she was back in Sydney preparing for the voyage home to Southampton, via Suez, arriving on Friday March 24 1961. She had been away for three and a half months and had steamed some 45,000 miles, calling at 15 different ports in eleven countries. She started her second voyage on April 12, bound once again for Sydney and the west coast of the USA, returning this time via Panama.

When *Oriana* returned to Southampton on January 23 1962 from her fourth round voyage, she had been in service for just over a year and she held every speed record from 'Gibraltar

December 3 1962: the damage to Oriana's *bow after her collision with the USS* Kearsarge *(San Francisco Chronicle*/Associated Press).

through Suez to Australia and New Zealand, and across the Pacific to the USA'. She was the only liner known to have left the UK for Sydney one month and to have returned to Southampton the following month. However, by 1962 BOAC were flying their VC 10s and Boeing 707s to Australia, and consequently speed records at sea were becoming far less relevant.

In December 1962, exactly two years to a day since she left Southampton on her maiden voyage, *Oriana* was involved in a collision with the aircraft carrier USS *Kearsarge* while on a regular trans-Pacific voyage from Australia. *Oriana* had called at San Francisco and was scheduled to make a short stop at Long Beach before sailing to Honolulu and home via Australia and Suez. Halfway between San Francisco and Los Angeles she ran into a thick fog bank and speed was reduced. At 9.10 am on the morning of Monday December 3, she was just outside the breakwater at Long Beach when she collided with the *Kearsarge* which had left the harbour about 20 minutes previously. Both suffered fairly extensive damage to their bows, and fire broke out in one of *Oriana*'s paint storage lockers. Fortunately it was soon brought under control and extinguished. A hole approximately 10 ft × 25 ft was torn in the starboard bow of the *Kearsarge*, and a 16 ft gash was gouged in *Oriana*'s bow on 'B' deck. Once again the dangers of fog to mariners were all too clearly spelt out, for, despite the fact that both vessels were plotting each other's movements on their radar screens, they still collided. Fortunately, no one was injured.

One passenger told reporters how he was standing in a public room watching the ship enter port, when, 'Suddenly this huge grey ship appeared out of the fog. They crossed our bow and we hit them.' Most passengers were at breakfast at the time, and they testified that they felt nothing more than a slight jolt. Another passenger said the impact was 'so light it only caused the water in my glass to rock a bit'. The passengers went to boat stations, or at least the majority did, for one lady remembers, 'I left my cabin and saw people going upstairs with their lifebelts on, but I didn't bother.' However, generally there was praise for the crew. As one man said, 'We were in our cabin, we felt a slight jolt. Then the alarm bell sounded and we put on our lifejackets. Stewards were running everywhere telling people nothing serious was wrong but that we should go to our lifeboat stations. There was no panic, everyone was very calm.'

Fortunately there was no danger and *Oriana* was able to enter port under her own power where she docked at 10.45 am. *Kearsarge* too was able to return to port unaided and a US Navy court of inquiry was soon set up. She was one of the 'Essex' class aircraft carriers, and she had been completed in March 1946, just too late to see war service. She had a displacement of 33,000 tons and carried 28 fixed-wing aircraft and a crew of over 2,000. Perhaps her main claim to fame was that in October 1962 she picked up the astronaut, Walter Schirra, from the Pacific Ocean.

Once alongside, surveyors inspected the damage to *Oriana*. They found her bow plating displaced and second strakes extending 25 ft aft buckled and pierced; her deck plating had also buckled. She went into the Todd shipyard were work proceeded day and night to repair the damaged bow. The extended stay enabled the passengers to take advantage of extra sightseeing excursions, and *Oriana* was finally able to sail for Honolulu at 12.15 am on Friday December 7 1962. Subsequently a United States court of inquiry found that *Oriana* was to blame for the collision.

It is interesting to see part of the testimony given by Captain E. P. Rankin USN, commander of the USS *Kearsarge*, at the inquiry. After giving evidence that, following consultation with Rear Admiral Joseph Tibbetts USN, he ordered the *Kearsarge* to sail from Long Beach at 8 am on December 3, he continued, 'I ordered the inland fog signal sounded every minute. We arrived at the breakwater at 8.51 am. There was lots of traffic and we were keeping track of every vessel on radar and visually. I was on the bridge and was constantly advised by both the radar and Combat Intelligence Center. We passed the Long Beach buoy 100 yards to port at 9 am. At that time there was no ship traffic ahead of us. Our first warning of the *Oriana* indicated she would pass 600 yards ahead of us at 9.11 am if we continued on our course. We slowed to 7 knots. Visibility was about 1,000 yards. I considered this a moderate speed because we were not bothered by traffic ahead of us.

'Then we heard a fog signal, presumably from the *Oriana*, at about 9.05 or 9.06 am. It was off our starboard bow. Another radar plot was taken and the *Oriana* was picked up visually at 9.08 am. I immediately ordered engines full into reverse and left rudder. At that time *Oriana* was about 1,000 yards away. A collision did not appear imminent, it seemed likely she would pass ahead of us. Then I took another look at *Oriana* and she appeared to swing right, there were three blasts from *Oriana*'s whistle indicating she was going astern. I then realized we were on a collision course. I ordered the starboard side cleared of personnel. We were then about 500 yards apart. As the ships continued to close it looked like it would be "nip and tuck" whether *Oriana* would clear us or not. When we were 300 yards apart I noticed the wash of the *Oriana*'s reverse engines and saw her swing to the right. At 9.10 am her bow knifed into the *Kearsarge*.'

The next few years passed without any major incidents for the liner, although in May 1963 she was in the news when one of her stewards was caught attempting to smuggle gold sovereigns past the customs at Southampton. In late 1964

ORIANA

CALSHOT
SOUTHAMPTON

Left Oriana *alongside Southampton's Western Docks, now in P&O's white livery* (F.R. Sherlock).

Below left *August 11 1970:* Oriana *lies helpless with all power lost after her boiler-room fire in Southampton Water. She is surrounded by firefloats and tugs* (Southern Newspapers).

Oriana's corn-coloured hull was repainted white and in early 1965, when P&O acquired the outstanding minority shareholding in the Orient Steam Navigation Company, she was transferred to P&O registry. Since this change her name has become synonymous with P&O, and many people have forgotten her Orient Line origins.

In September 1966 she was in the news again when she was the victim of a bomb hoaxer. At that time this problem was not as common as it is today, but all the same the ship was evacuated and thoroughly searched, and luckily nothing was found. Nineteen months later, on April 7 1968, when she was making a westbound transit of the Panama Canal, her starboard propeller struck the bank, damaging both the propeller and the shaft. In fact, one of the propeller blades had been lost. Temporary repairs were carried out at Cristobal, and she finally left the port at midnight on April 8. Originally she had been scheduled to call at Nassau, Port Everglades, Bermuda and Le Havre. But with just her port propeller serviceable and her speed much reduced, visits to the latter two ports were cancelled. She arrived at Nassau at 11.30 am on April 12, but owing to adverse weather conditions she stayed only a short time before leaving for Port Everglades. She arrived there the following day and an attempt was made to cut off the damaged propeller, but this was unsuccessful and she left at 4 pm on April 14 for Southampton. Finally, on Sunday April 28 1968, five days late, she arrived back in her home port, where she went into drydock for repairs to be carried out. Her next voyage to Australia was delayed until May 15, and a cruise from Sydney scheduled for May 27 1968 was cancelled.

Two years later *Oriana* was involved in two far more serious incidents. The first of these was in June 1970, when she was on a Pacific cruise from Sydney and fire broke out in the boiler room. Fortunately it was extinguished within 45 minutes, but all precautions were taken and the passengers were mustered at boat stations. On her return to Southampton she was prepared for another voyage to Australia and New Zealand. She left 106 berth with 1,500 passengers on board at 1 pm on Tuesday August 11 1970, and one hour later, when she was off Calshot Spit in Southampton Water, the alarm bells rang. It was not a practice drill for passengers, but a genuine emergency, and again it was a fire in the boiler room. As the great ship anchored, sightseers saw thick, oily, black smoke billowing from the funnel. This time the fire was far more serious, and *Oriana* lay helpless with all power in the ship lost.

On board there was no panic among the passengers, and one American, now a well-known P&O cruise lecturer, who was travelling to Port Everglades, recalls the incident. 'We sailed promptly at 1 pm on Tuesday August 11, and I stayed on deck to photograph the other ships in port until the first sitting was called at 1.30 pm. While we were taking the first sips of onion soup the lights went out, but no one paid very much attention as there was natural sunlight streaming through the portholes. I overheard a steward say that nobody could go into the galley as there was smoke. Almost immediately the Staff Captain came over the public address saying that there was a fire in the boiler room and as a precaution we should proceed directly to our lifeboat stations. Smoke then came billowing out of the kitchen, and everyone knew that he was not kidding. There was a good deal of bustle in the passages as no one could see very well, but my cabin was not very far, and I quickly climbed to the boat deck.

'The engines had stopped and we were drifting out with the tide past Calshot. Black smoke poured across the water on the fine, sunny, warm day. I could see lots of smoke belching from the funnel when I looked up between the boats. In the distance, in the direction of Southampton Docks, I could see at least a dozen

Left *Slowly the* Oriana, *a dead ship, was towed back to her berth on August 11 1970, after the boiler-room fire* (Southern Newspapers).

Right Oriana *in drydock—an excellent view of her gallery stern* (Southampton City Museums).

boats heading our way strung across the water. Soon planes and helicopters began flying overhead. The passengers remained calm and cheerful, and only one little girl cried. Fireboats, tugs, police launches and a television vessel circled around and we were taken in tow. The Captain spoke to us at 3.30 pm telling us that the fire was out, that we could take off our lifejackets but we should remain at our stations.

'Slowly the *Oriana*, a dead ship, was towed back to her berth. I recall seeing men atop the funnel of SA *Oranje* looking down at us as we berthed just aft. TV and radio crews had mounted the gantry cranes in an effort to get first-hand stories of panic or chaos, but only those on the very lowest decks had been much affected by either the smoke or the heat. The captain told us that we would remain at Southampton for at least several days, and as soon as possible the ship would be moved into drydock for inspection and repairs. The ship became very stuffy and dirty, and it was very hard to get about in the dark. We were fed a cold supper at 7.30 pm, and at 11 pm the lights came on, but there was still no ventilation.

'When it became known next morning that *Oriana* would be immobilized for some time, I decided to transfer to the *QE2*. After two days on the waiting list, I got a berth and sailed on August 14 for New York. The *QE2*'s Commodore invited me to a before-lunch cocktail party, and when he greeted me at the door of his quarters he said, "Welcome to the *Oriana* refugee party. I suspect you will recognize a few faces here." I heard from one of the engineers at the time that the ship was almost lost, and I had this confirmed some years later. If the fireboats had not come within five minutes of when they did, *Oriana* would have burned. The ship had lost all, including emergency, power, and she was in danger of grounding in addition to being unable to fight the fire.'

The fire which lasted for 70 minutes was finally extinguished by use of the ship's multi-spray system and the efforts of her engineers, who shut down the boilers. The initial examination showed that serious damage had been sustained, and the boiler room was in a state of disorder with oily water over the floor plates and the entire space blackened with smoke. After this oily water had been pumped out and transferred to barges, access was gained around the boilers. The main boilers were designated Nos 1 and 2 forward, port and starboard, and Nos 3 and 4 aft, port and starboard. The greatest severity of the fire appeared to be in front of and under No 3 boiler, where heavy charring of boiler casings and pipework insulation was found. The fire

ORIANA

appeared to have travelled from the port side of No 3 boiler alongside the port side of No 1 boiler and across the forward end of the boiler room. All the electric cables to fans, control panels, starter boxes, bilge and transfer pumps, soot blower motors and other pumps were completely burnt out. The telegraph system and other instruments and pipework had all been heavily damaged by the effects of the fire. As well as the destruction in the boiler room, the paintwork and vinyl coverings in various cabins on 'A', 'B' and 'C' decks around the boiler uptakes were also damaged, as well as carpets and some furniture.

Meanwhile, the ship was docked and it soon became clear that she would be delayed for at least two weeks, so many of her passengers found alternative transport to continue their journeys to Australia. P&O offered a refund to them all. At first it was hoped that *Oriana* would be ready to sail on Monday August 24, but in fact it was three days later on August 27 that she left Southampton. It had been decided that she keep to her original timetable, with only her stay in Bermuda cut short, so she would have to steam hard across the Atlantic. As *Oriana* left Southampton and sailed past Ocean Terminal she was given a farewell siren salute by *QE2*. Captain Law on board *QE2* spoke to *Oriana*'s Captain Cutler over the radio, telling him that they were sorry to hear of his ship's bad luck and wishing him *bon voyage*. Fortunately she did not experience any major mechanical problems over the next few years.

By 1972 *Oriana*, like most other liners, was spending much more of her time cruising, and in August that year it was announced that for her 12 cruises in 1973 she would operate as a one-class ship. Very few alterations were required internally, but the exclusive 'Silver Grill' on 'A' deck disappeared and made way for ten extra cabins, five of these being special staterooms. Her passenger capacity was reduced to 1,700, mainly by the conversion of a large number of four-berth cabins to two-berth. The first class children's playroom at the forward end of the 'Verandah' deck fell into disuse, and the former tourist class playroom at the after end of 'D' deck catered for all the children on board. *Oriana*'s best assets as a cruise liner were her size and the spaciousness of her open decks, particularly the poop games deck at the after end of 'A' deck. Perhaps the main criticism from passengers was the difficulty in finding their way between what used to be two separate class sections on the ship. However, her first season as an open-class ship was so successful that in 1974 it was decided to drop all class barriers on what had now become 'P&O Cruises'.

During the latter half of the 1970s *Oriana* would cruise from Southampton during the summer months, and in October or November she would make a positioning voyage to Sydney via Panama and the west coast of the USA. She would then cruise from Sydney during the Australian summer before making the homeward voyage to Southampton by the same route in April the following year. By January 1976, with the withdrawal and scrapping of *Oronsay*, *Oriana* became the last representative of the Orient Line.

In May 1978 *Oriana* was making headlines in the world's Press once again. She had arrived back in Southampton from Australia on May 16, and four days later on Saturday May 20 she left the port on the first cruise of her UK summer season. It was a 20-day Caribbean cruise, calling at San Juan, Barbados, Grenada, Martinique, Antigua and, on her way home, at Ponta Delgada in the Azores. At 9.30 am on May 23, when she was some three days out of Southampton, an anonymous letter was received at P&O Cruises' office in London, stating that a bomb had been planted on board prior to sailing, and was due to detonate at 8 pm that day. P&O acted at once and alerted the Ministry of Defence, who immediately despatched three experts from the RAOC, led by Major Ross. The army team, which had been specifically trained for ocean parachute drops, flew out in a Hercules aircraft while a Nimrod search plane went on ahead to pinpoint *Oriana*'s position. Meanwhile, even before they had taken off, Captain Philip Jackson began his own search of the ship in accordance with a well-practised emergency procedure. Every cabin and compartment in the ship was searched and the

An aerial view of Oriana *at sea* (Skyfotos Ltd).

passengers were required to identify the contents of all baggage and furniture. By the time the Hercules reached the ship the search had been completed and the bomb disposal squad were not required to 'jump', as they had done six years earlier in a similar incident involving *QE2*. Once the 8 pm deadline had passed safely the 'all clear' was given, although the RAF continued to escort *Oriana* until she had resumed her intended course and speed. It had been an elaborate hoax, but P&O's organization and liaison with the Ministry of Defence had proved them to be masters of the situation.

When *Oriana* left Southampton on September 30 1979 for a 21-night cruise to the Bahamas and Florida, she had on board six very young stowaways. It seems that the boys, who were all between seven and nine years of age, had caught the boat train at Waterloo Station in London by using platform tickets, and had managed to slip on board *Oriana* unnoticed. Unfortunately for them they were unable to reach America as they were found by crew members just after the ship sailed, when they asked the way to 'the café' on board. The master, Captain John F. Wacher, radioed for a launch to take them ashore, where they were handed over to the Social Services.

Just over 18 months later, on May 12 1981, *Oriana* arrived back in Southampton for her final UK summer cruising season. Fortunately there were no docking problems, despite an industrial dispute by the port's dock workers. Ahead of her was a programme of 12 cruises, consisting of eight to the Mediterranean, two to the Atlantic Isles and one each to the Caribbean and the northern capitals. The final cruise in the schedule was a 'Month in the Med', which took her to 11 major ports.

On her arrival at Southampton on Friday September 4 from an Atlantic Islands cruise, the liner received a visit from her sponsor, HRH Princess Alexandra, who was accompanied by her husband, the Hon Angus Ogilvy, and their two children. As *Oriana* had just over 12 hours in port before leaving on her next Mediterranean cruise, the visit had to be carefully planned beforehand. Escorted by the P&O Fleet Director, Mr Alan Langley, and by Captain D. J. Scott Masson the royal visitors were piped aboard for their tour of the liner, during which the Princess met and spoke to a number of the ship's company. Representatives of all departments were invited to a reception in the 'Lookout Bar' where the Princess insisted on speaking to everybody there. She was presented with a posy of flowers by Junior Steward Richard Wyrill, the youngest member of the crew. The royal party were then entertained to a buffet luncheon in the captain's quarters before being piped ashore at 2.15 pm. The Princess had last visited the ship in

ORIANA

ORIANA
ORIANA

Left and below left Oriana *at Cape Town* (Robert Pabst).

Above right and right Oriana *on her last day at Southampton, November 12 1981* (Author's collection).

1967 and, as it had already been announced that this was *Oriana*'s last UK season, it was clearly her way of saying farewell to 'her ship' which she had launched over 21 years previously.

Oriana arrived back in Southampton for the last time on Saturday October 24 1981, and went into Vosper's drydock that afternoon for an overhaul prior to her final departure from the port. She was due to leave at 1 pm on Thursday November 12 1981, but as that hour approached it was clear that there would be a delay as the final preparations were still under way to get her ready for sea. Finally, at 4.15 pm in the gathering dusk of what was a dull and misty day, she set sail for Sydney where she would be based permanently. It was a poignant time for all her loyal fans who had come to wave farewell as the firefloat *Gatcombe* and the tug *Romsey* led her from the port. She sailed via Bermuda, Port Everglades, Panama, the west coast of the USA and the Pacific, arriving in Sydney just in time for Christmas.

Oriana was always a very popular ship in Australia, with at least 80 per cent of her cruises fully booked. She was particularly favoured by young people during college holidays when it was estimated that 500 to 600 of her passengers were under 23 years of age. The 'Midship Bar' on 'B' deck was converted to a period 'Aussie' pub, complete with decorative mirrors, carriage-lamps and old posters. Other alterations included a hamburger bar and beer service area by the swimming pool on the 'Verandah' deck. On the 'Stadium' deck a tavern beer bar and a gymnasium were made from the former games room.

On December 1 1983, *Oriana* made her first call at Brisbane, recalling pre-war days when the port was the final stop for Orient liners on their long voyages from Tilbury. On July 1 1985 she visited Nuku' Alofa on the island of Tonga, and Captain Philip Jackson had the honour of hosting the King and Queen of Tonga on board for a banquet luncheon, to celebrate the opening of the Queen's Wharf extension at the port, and the King's 67th birthday. Other guests included the British, Australian and New Zealand High Commissioners. At the luncheon, Captain Jackson presented the Queen with a cheque for £3,650 for the Tongan Red Cross, and in a speech of thanks the King expressed his gratitude to the ship's company and spoke of the island nation's close connections with the British Crown and people. The occasion was a great success and *Oriana*, in her 25th year of service, was still an excellent ambassador for the Union Flag.

However, although at that time her future appeared reasonably secure for two more years, there were rumours circulating that she was to be withdrawn from service. There did not seem to be any cause for concern for a few months at least, for a full programme of cruises had been published in Australia which took her through to April 1986. The longest of these cruises was a 57-night voyage to Japan, Korea, China, the Philippines, Singapore, Bali and then returning to Sydney via the south coast of Australia. The season was due to end on April 30 1986 after a 34-night 'Cherry Blossom Cruise' to Guam, Japan, Korea, China, Malaya and Papua New Guinea before returning to Sydney via Brisbane. But suddenly, on July 22 1985, the chairman of P&O Cruises, Mr Christopher Steward-Smith, announced that, although a final decision on the *Oriana* had not been made, the withdrawal would take place 'sooner than we originally anticipated'. It seemed that the weak Australian dollar had badly affected P&O's earnings from Australian passengers as most of the company's expenditure was in US dollars. Another factor was that the heavily subsidized Soviet cruise ships had been allowed back into the Australian market some 18 months previously on the lifting of a political ban, and these too had taken their toll.

Then two weeks later, on August 7, came P&O's official announcement, 'that as part of a strategic review of its worldwide cruising activities, the 25-year-old, 42,000-ton *Oriana* is to be replaced in the Australian cruise market, where she has been based for the last three years. *Oriana* will be withdrawn from operational service at Sydney on March 27 1986 and no decision has yet been reached about her future.'

The 'Cherry Blossom Cruise' had been

Above Oriana *moves away from her berth in Southampton for the last time on November 12 1981* (Ray Catterrall).

Below Oriana*'s last farewell to Southampton, her home port, November 12 1981* (Author's collection).

Left Oriana*'s last farewell to Sydney as she is towed by the ocean-going tug* Lady Lorraine *past the Opera House on May 29 1986, bound for Osaka in Japan* (P&O).

cancelled, and it was a sad day for shiplovers the world over as yet another of the big liners bowed out. She left Sydney on her last cruise on March 14, with the Australian naval patrol boats *Whyalla* and *Geelong* escorting her as she sailed from Wharf 13 Pyrmont, under Sydney Bridge and out of the harbour that had been her base for five years. As she let go her last lines, 3,000 balloons in the P&O colours were released. She sailed up the harbour fully dressed with flags and pennants, including her paying-off pennant signifying her years of service. She was also accompanied by police launches, a fireboat and a flotilla of small craft. On 'A' deck, the Vanuatu Police Band, returning home to Vila, played the great ship out on her last cruise, which was a 13-night voyage to Moumea, Vila, Suva, Lautoka and Auckland.

On board *Oriana* there must have been some sadness among crew members, like Larder Cook John Dearness, who had served on the ship since she sailed on her maiden voyage. She was commanded by Captain Philip Jackson, who had been appointed to the post in 1983, having previously served on *Orsova* and *Oronsay*. All the passengers on board were given a commemorative spoon and a souvenir leaflet about the ship. On Monday March 24 she called at Auckland and a group of Maori chieftains came on board to conduct an ancient farewell ceremony.

On the completion of her last cruise early on the morning of Thursday March 27 1986, *Oriana* lay tied up 21 Pyrmont in Sydney Harbour awaiting her fate. By late April rumours of would-be purchasers abounded, with stories of intending buyers from China, Fiji, Florida, Malaysia and two from Australia, all proposing a similar use for *Oriana* as a hotel/casino ship. With port dues amounting to $1,000 (Australian) a day it was obvious that P&O would not take long to make their decision. On May 7 1986 they announced that *Oriana* had been sold to Japanese interests, but they declined to say what the vessel would be used for. However, the details soon began to filter out. *Oriana* had been bought by Daiwa House KK, a Japanese company which operates resort hotels in Japan and China. They proposed to use her as a floating hotel at Oita, near Beppu, the hot-spring resort on the southern island of Kyushu.

Oriana's last few days in Sydney were marred by a trade union dispute regarding pay rates for the crew of the ocean-going tug *Lady Lorraine*. The liner finally left Sydney on May 29 1986, towed by the *Lady Lorraine* and escorted by other small craft. She was taken as far as Sydney Heads under the command of Captain Philip Jackson who then left her. *Oriana* arrived at Hitachi Zosen ship repair works at 3 pm on Tuesday June 24 1986, and two days later delivery formalities were completed in London, a few hours after which the flag change and handover of the ship's keys took place in Sakai. After a refit she was to take up her new role in Beppu Bay, so breaking her last link with the Orient Steam Navigation Company.

Technical data

Gross tonnage: 41,923
Net tonnage: 22,373
Cargo deadweight: 1,150 tons
Length overall: 804 ft (245 m)
Length bp: 740 ft (225 m)
Breadth moulded: 97 ft (29.5 m)
Load draught: 31 ft 6 in (9.5 m)
Main engines: Twin screw, two sets Pametrada design double-reduction geared turbines; service shp 65,000 at 147 rpm; maximum shp 80,000 at 158 rpm; service speed 27.5 knots; trials speed 30.64 knots
Boilers: Four Foster Wheeler Superheat boilers, 750 psi, 950°F
Capacities: General cargo 117,500 cu ft, insulated cargo 55,000 cu ft, oil fuel 6,800 tons, fresh water 3,000 tons
Passengers: First class 688, Tourist class 1,496; 1973, One class 1,700
Ship's company: Deck dept 115, Engineers 62, Catering 722

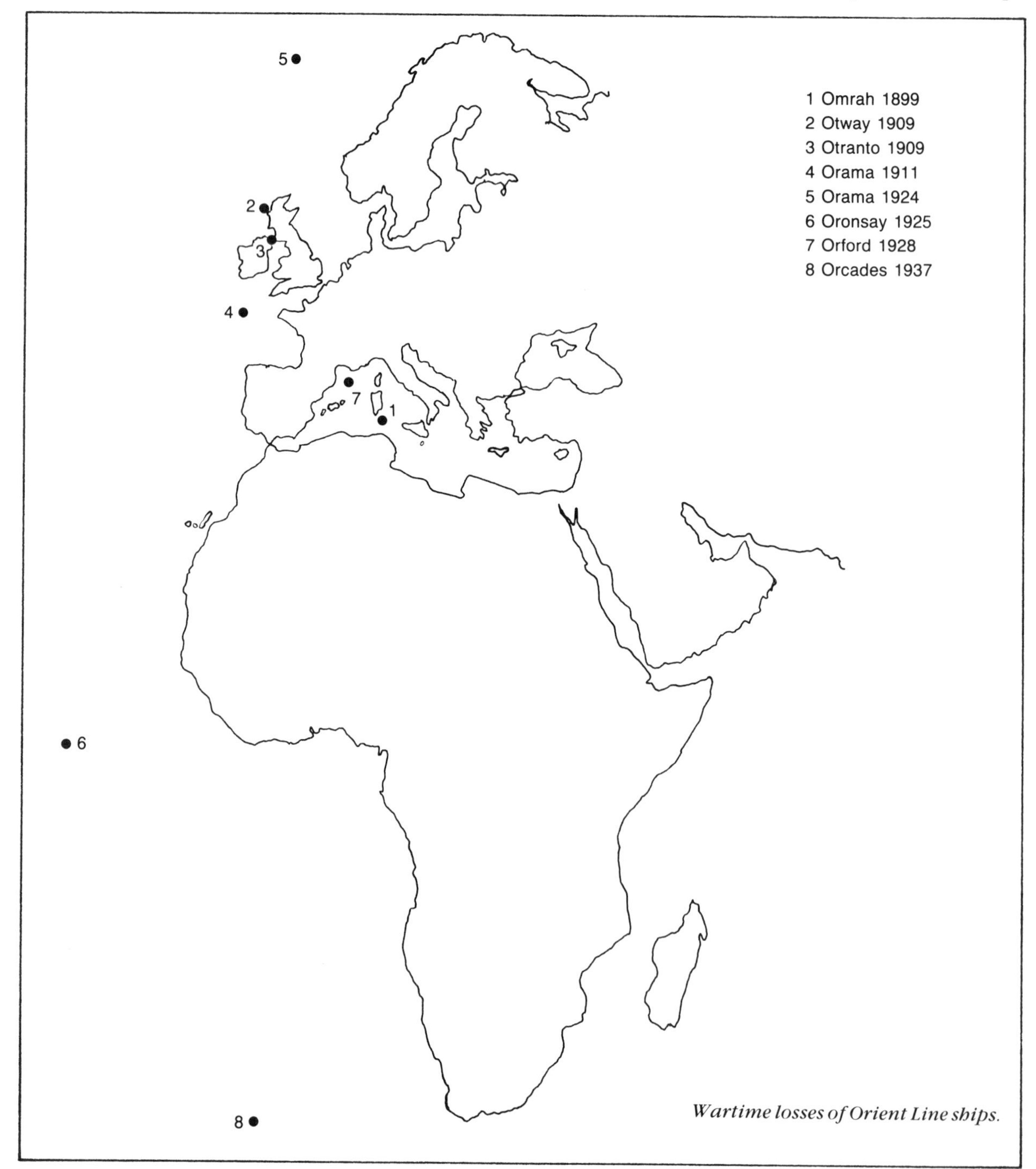

Wartime losses of Orient Line ships.

Bibliography

The Enemy Fought Splendidly, Surgeon T. B. Dixon RNVR, Blandford Press 1983.
The Blockaders, A. Cecil Hampshire, William Kimber 1980.
The Big Blockade, E. Keble Chatterton, Hurst & Blackett
British Vessels Lost at Sea 1914–1918, HMSO, Patrick Stephens Ltd 1980.
British Vessels Lost at Sea 1939–1945, HMSO, Patrick Stephens Ltd 1980.
Coronel and the Falklands, Geoffrey Bennett, B. T. Batsford Ltd 1962.
Naval Battles of the First World War, Geoffrey Bennett, Pan Books 1974.
The Last Cruise of the Emden, Edwin P. Hoyt, Andre Deutsch 1967.
Defeat at the Falklands, Edwin P. Hoyt, Robert Hale Ltd 1981.
The Royal Tour 1901, or The Cruise of HMS Ophir, Petty Officer Harry Price, Webb & Bower 1980.
Troopships and Their History, Colonel H. C. B. Rogers OBE, Seeley Service & Co 1963.
Hipper Class Heavy Cruisers, C. J. Pargeter, Ian Allan 1982.
Prologue to a War (The Navy's Part in the Narvik Campaign), Ewart Brookes, White Lion Publishers Ltd 1977.
Armed Merchant Cruisers, Kenneth Poolman, Leo Cooper/Secker & Warburg 1985.
Merchant Fleets in Profile, Volume 1: P&O Orient and Blue Anchor Lines, Duncan Haws, Patrick Stephens Ltd 1978.
Merchant Fleets, Volume 8: Pacific Steam Navigation Co, Duncan Haws, TSL Ltd 1985.
About Ourselves, The house magazine of the P&O-Orient Line.
Wavelength, the house magazine of the P&O Line.
Orient Guide, Kate Greenaway 1889.

Unpubished Sources

Orient Line records held by the National Maritime Museum.
Admiralty records held by the Ministry of Defence, Naval Historical Section.
Department of Trade records held by the General Register of Shipping and Seamen.
British Newspaper Library, Colindale, London.
Department of Trade, Ministry of Transport, and Admiralty records held by the Public Records Office, Kew, London.

Newspapers

The Times; Daily Telegraph; Daily Mirror; Southern Evening Echo; Greenock Telegraph & Clyde Shipping Gazette; Glasgow Herald; Sydney Morning Herald; Melbourne Argus; Belfast Telegraph; San Francisco Chronicle.

Acknowledgements

Thanks to the following for their kind assistance: John Newth, Editorial Director, Blandford Press Ltd, for permission to quote from *The Enemy Fought Splendidly;* Derek H. Deere, Managing Director, Marine Publications Ltd, for permission to use deck plans taken from *Shipping World* and *Shipping World & Shipbuilder;* Stephen Rabson, P&O Group Librarian; Paul J. Kemp, Imperial War Museum; Alasdair M. Aitken, Glasgow; Anthony H. S. Robinson, New Milton, Bournemouth; Susan Whitley, Haslemere, Surrey; Gilbert Clark, Port Charlotte, Islay; Patrick Holden, Hemel Hempstead, Hertfordshire; Keith Byass, Bingley, West Yorkshire; Miss H. P. White, Naval Historical Library, Ministry of Defence; Len Baynes, Great Shelford, Cambridge; Leonie Twentyman-Jones, University Library, University of Cape Town, South Africa; Robert Pabst, Camps Bay, Cape Town, South Africa; Major A. E. Vaan Jaarsveldt, Military Information Bureau, South African Defence Force; Mike Smith, Press Officer, Vickers Shipbuilding & Engineering Ltd, Barrow; Nigel Overton, Keeper of Aviation & Maritime History, City of Southampton, Tudor House Museum; Brian Wexham, Photography & AV Manager, Vickers PLC, London; James L. Shaw, Milwaukie, Oregon, USA; Theodore W. Scull, New York, USA; Andrew Kilk, Oakland, California, USA; Mrs A. Williams, General Register and Record Office of Shipping and Seamen, Cardiff; Yoshiho Ikeda, University of Osaka, Japan; Yoshiku Fukawa, Hiratsuka, Japan; J. C. Purser, Caterham, Surrey; staff of the Public Records Office, Kew, London; staff of the Reading Room, British Newspaper Library, Colindale, London; staff of the Readers' Room Services, National Maritime Museum, Greenwich, London; staff of the Reference Library, Cheltenham Public Library; and finally to my wife, Freda, and my sister, Mrs Sheila Murphy.

Index

Oriana, *in P&O's white livery, alongside Southampton's Western Docks* (F.R. Sherlock).